Gender Quality

Stefan Liston

Published by Relational Mission

Jubilee Family Centre, Norwich Road, Aylsham, Norfolk, NR11 6JG, UK

www.relationalmission.org

Cover Design by Tuuli Platner

ISBN 978-1-9162781-7-2

Acknowledgements

All Scripture quotations, unless otherwise indicated, are taken from the Holy Bible, New International Version®, NIV®. Copyright ©1973, 1978, 1984, 2011 by Biblica, Inc.™ Used by permission of Zondervan. All rights reserved worldwide. www.zondervan.com The "NIV" and "New International Version" are trademarks registered in the United States Patent and Trademark Office by Biblica, Inc.™

GOD IN THE DOCK by C.S. Lewis copyright © C.S. Lewis Pte. Ltd. 1970. Extract reprinted by permission.

A catalogue record of this book is available from the British Library

Acknowledgements

There are just a few quotes in this book, though I have drawn from lots of different authors, scholars, speakers and thinkers. There is an annotated bibliography at the end where I attempt to give credit where it's due. I doubt anything much here is original - however I do take full, personal responsibility for any bad jokes!

I'd like to acknowledge Andrew Bartlett for your work 'Men and Women in Christ' and Terran Williams for 'How God Sees Women'. I used both of your books for 'reading circles' and have been personally helped and challenged by your work. I'd also like to acknowledge John G Stackhouse Jr, Richard M Davidson, Gordon Fee, Ronald W Pierce, Rebecca Merrill Groothuis, Linda Belleville, Craig Keener and Katia Adams, who are all egalitarians and have all produced helpful and quality work on this subject. I trust your hearts, I listen to your arguments, you've really challenged and helped me. I owe y'all.

I'd like to acknowledge Michelle Lee-Barnewell. You get your own space because I'm not sure if you're egalitarian or complementarian! Nevertheless, your book (appropriately titled 'Neither complementarian nor egalitarian') is excellent. Thank you.

I'd like to acknowledge John Piper, C S Lewis, Wayne Grudem, Kevin DeYoung, Leanne Payne, Thomas Schreiner, Andreas Kostenberger, Terry Virgo and his team, Mike Winger and Andrew Wilson - complementarian scholars, theologians, authors and pastors who are faithful and courageous in an age where your perspective is becoming increasingly scrutinised. We all only know in part. Thank you for your example and clarity.

Thanks

Thanks to my Davina. I love our Fridays, our friendship and our freedom. After 25 years, you are still a glorious mystery to me and you know what - I love that. We have been kept. We are being kept. We will be kept.

Thanks to my kids - Daisy, Levi and Melody. Conversations with each of you have helped me in the writing of this book. You bring me, your mum and many others more joy and satisfaction than can be put into words.

Thanks to so many in my church community - Rev Church London. You know a Revver when you see one - quirky, kind, authentic, creative. You are my family. I love you.

Thanks to my wider family in Relational Mission. It's been a great journey so far - I'm cleaner, stronger and happier because of you. I'm amazed by your support.

Thanks to sharpening friends who have been particularly helpful on this journey - Rebecca Whittlesea (a more than able sparring partner), Phil Whittall (one of the best thinkers I know), Adam Voke (ultra resourceful - finger always on the pulse), Marcus Tutt (man of diligence, conviction and grace), Oobie and Yael (wise beyond your years), Matt Fell (sender of the longest and profoundest voice notes ever) Dan Hayter (a true gentleman, fine theologian and long-term co-labourer), Daniel and Anna Goodman and Malcolm Kyte who took the time to read the manuscript and give extensive and very helpful feedback, Jane Tompkins, Angela Kemm, Marie Revey and Annice Green for provocative and helpful conversations, David Devenish for reading the manuscript thoroughly and bringing enormously helpful feedback and to Mike Betts and Maurice Nightingale who have been immensely helpful and supportive in the whole process. Big shout out to Jon Beardon, Adam Voke (again), Martin Segal, David Bareham, Kev Reilly, Daniel Goodman (again) and Tom Scrivens for precious Wednesday mornings and those conversations in the barn!

Thanks to Kit Green who has been an enormous help on so many levels and to Sonja Stojanovic, Tuuli Platner and Simon Tarry for your great help and work.

Thanks to Goff and Angie Hope for friendship, hospitality and rich conversations!

Thanks to my parents and siblings. I've been very blessed. The laughter, the adventures, the craziness and all the care do not go unnoticed.

Thanks to the many women - my sisters in the faith - who have modelled extraordinary resilience, courage, gentleness, patience and faith for years. Respect.

Thanks to the mothers and fathers in the Lord that my own heavenly Father, in His bountiful care for me, has always abundantly supplied at just the right time. You have rescued me from a multitude of snares and made my life so much brighter.

Final thanks to our Great God, the Lover of my soul, my betrothed, my King. All to Jesus, I surrender - gladly and utterly. You are worthy of it all.

A Handful of Dedications

As one of my aims in this book is to articulate and display the high place in which God holds women, I'd like to dedicate this book to four women in my life.

Firstly, I dedicate this book to my mum, who is now with the Lord and having a great time.

Mum, no more tears, no more sighing and no more pain. You showed the most extraordinary resilience and strength over many, many years. Your deep humility and quiet confidence in God had way more impact than you will ever know. Your sausage rolls were great too. I miss you. I miss them too. And those cakes you used to make. Your brown-eyed boy.

Secondly, I'd like to dedicate this book to Davina. Early in our courtship one of your friends described you to me as 'all woman'. I couldn't agree more. You have been more forgiving and releasing than anyone deserves. Your resilience is beyond the pale. Your beauty gives me the zipperoos (I just made that word up). Never has there been someone so predictable and unpredictable exist in one human body; what a box of tricks you are.
Your Stefi.

Thirdly, I dedicate this book to Daisy Dream. I know how much this book matters to you and for you. In some strange way and to some small degree, your future is wrapped up in it. I can see that Jesus has given you to His church. It's obvious. As Mum says, you are me but in a dress! What does all this mean? What are we to make of it? We are in deep waters - let's swim and see where He takes us!
Forever your loving and proud Dad.

Fourthly I'd like to dedicate this book to Melody Love. You are a leader, like it or not! You walk with God in no-non-sense truth. You may struggle reading the Word but I have rarely come across someone so fiercely dedicated to 'doing' the Word. You are genuinely the most excellent company - life bubbles out of you. I love your name but maybe we should have called you Matilda after all!
Forever your loving and proud Dad.

Contents

Introductory Section

1. Oiling the Cogs — 1
2. Who's Saying What? — 9
3. Handling the Word — 11
4. The New 'Wild' West — 21

Main Bulk

5. Equal! Egalitarian Pillar One — 29
6. Equal and Some! Complementarian Pillar One — 37
7. Household Rep: Complementarian Pillar Two — 47
8. Bad Rule: Egalitarian Pillar Two — 53
9. Power Struggle: Complementarian Pillar Three — 57
10. Patriarchal Pollution: Egalitarian Pillar Three — 61
    THE INBETWEENERS — 79
11. Jesus Revolution I: Egalitarian Pillar Four — 83
12. Jesus Revolution II: Complementarian Pillar Four — 87
13. Pentecostal Parity: Egalitarian Pillar Five — 93
14. Headship Revisited: Complementarian Pillar Five — 113
15. Roman Numerals: Egalitarian Pillar Six — 121
16. Oversee Don't Overlook: Complementarian Pillar Six — 129
17. Contextual Competence: Egalitarian Pillar Seven — 127
18. Bigger Story: Complementarian Pillar Seven — 139
19. The $10,000 Question: What are Masculinity & Femininity? — 153
20. Getting Practical! — 163

Concluding Thoughts

21. Affirmations and Denials — 167
22. Some Short and Relevant Reflections — 171
23. FAQs — 177
24. Hearing the Woman's Voice — 195

Annotated Bibliography — 205

Chapter One
Oiling the Cogs

Reading a book is a risky thing. If you don't see it through then it could end up as another unfinished book in a pile of many. If you do see it through, then you will essentially have listened to someone else speak for hours and hours on end with no chance of getting a word in!

Subjecting yourself to another person's thoughts in that kind of way requires discernment. Especially if they are very persuasive! One of the early church fathers (I think it was Tertullian) said that "heretics convince by persuasion, whereas teachers of the truth persuade by conviction". Now I'll be honest - I can be very persuasive! Because of this, I have deliberately decided not to use persuasion in areas of this conversation that are more ambiguous. My chief aim is to aid your own thinking about this vital subject, rather than simply let you know what I think and get you to agree.

Therefore, I would ask that if you start it, you finish it. Come on the journey. See it through and follow the arguments. Don't make assumptions, but grapple with the scriptures.

Humility needed

When speaking about this age and comparing it to the next, the apostle Paul said that we "know in part", so we should approach all matters with a blend of conviction and humility: conviction that the Lord will give us the light we need to find a good way through on important matters, and humility in that none of us are seeing the whole picture. But there's more to it. One of the most challenging scriptures I know says this:

> *Anyone who chooses to do the will of God will find out whether my teaching comes from God or whether I speak on my own.*
> JOHN 7 V 17

It's challenging because it shows me that what we want is often at the root of what we see or understand. Sometimes we don't understand or notice certain things because we don't want to. When it comes to a subject as emotive (in the West) as gender, let's be honest, there are certain things we simply do or don't want to see.

All of us will bring philosophical assumptions, personal damage, un-sanctified attitudes, nagging fears and sinful blind spots to this conversation. Better to acknowledge this near the start; that way we can check ourselves as we work through the book rather than believing everything we think or feel! So before you read on, please ask yourself: what do I want this book to say? It will help you to take a moment to ponder your answer; maybe even write it down, so you can refer back to it as you read through the book.

Defining Gender

People often use the same word in different ways so it's smart to nail the definition early.

How do I differentiate 'gender' from 'sex'? I don't. When talking about gender I am simply referring to the fact that He made us male and female[1]. There is a growing message in the evangelical world that sounds a bit like this: gender, being physically determined, is essentially that, and nothing more.

It's helpful in two ways: First, it resists the ideology that encourages people to define their gender by their feelings rather than by their physicality. Second, it resists unhelpful and unbiblical gender stereotyping, e.g., real men should like cars but not flowers, and vice versa for real women.

But there's a problem also. It's too reductionist, shrinking gender from multi-dimensional to one-dimensional. Our maleness or our femaleness (our gender) involves far more than differing sexual organs; it shapes us psychologically and, I believe, that it also means something spiritually.

More on that in a bit.

What's all the fuss about?

When it comes to the matter of sexuality, those of us in the West recognise that we are in the midst of a cultural revolution. This book is an attempt to help us figure out, from the scriptures, what God thinks about it all. At the time of printing there are the very live issues of gender fluidity, gender dysphoria, gender neutrality and being transgender, and alongside these there are the more familiar issues of sexual orientation and sexual lifestyle choices.

For the most part Evangelical Christians have clear and agreed beliefs on the above matters. While these are being challenged in certain quarters, the teaching in scripture is so clear on the above that those who hold to the authority of scripture as an absolute priority can't see how we can change our stance without the whole house falling down.

As a very brief interlude the church, we are told in scripture, is:

---

1   Genesis 1 v 27.

...the pillar and foundation of the truth.
1 TIMOTHY 3 V 15

This means that part of the church's calling is to hold up the truth by faithfully championing God's revelation in scripture. If the church gives way on the truth, the truth caves in. Not in the sense that it's no longer true, but in the sense that she who was entrusted to hold it up has neglected her calling. Those who previously found shade under truth upheld by the church are now exposed to the scorching rays of multiple deadly ideologies that deceive hearts and destroy lives.

Back to the cultural revolution.

The more nuanced issues of male and female personhood, equality and differences, what it means to be a man or a woman, and what the implications are in the church and the home, well... evangelical Christians, for the most part, do not agree on these. Seemingly simple matters can be surprisingly complex, with every issue contested, but the search for clarity is surely worth it!

This book is an invitation to journey through the scriptures, searching for the meaning of male and female, and if we can find one, making sense of it together. We'll excavate down to the foundations as much as possible; the further we go down and see what's really there and what isn't, the better idea we'll have of how to 'build up' with maximum wisdom. The aim is to serve God's people well, from those in leadership who need to make decisions about these things, to those helping and supporting others, to those in the midst of their own personal struggles.

Heat or Light?

We need to proceed with care; outside the church there is far more heat being generated than there is light. Divisive arguments, acrimonious accusations, bitter mistrust and confusion - this isn't how we do things. Maintaining the unity of the Spirit is absolutely key to all we do - Jesus paid a huge price to bring us together, and so we ought to act like our togetherness matters.

It's no surprise that the outside world is confused, but we, as the church, have both the scriptures and the Holy Spirit, and so what we don't have is an excuse. We have not been left without a witness.

I hope to write in a conciliatory spirit and I'm going to assume that at the bottom of different perspectives on these matters is a desire to honour the Lord, serve people well and be faithful to scripture. Having said that, I hope it will be a searching book. I would hazard a guess that our perspectives on these matters are as much to do with the condition of our own hearts as they are to do with anything else. As I noted earlier, if there is anything in us that wants the answers to matters of gender to fall a certain way, then we are immediately vulnerable; biased hearts create dark and dangerous blind spots.

There are so many different reasons for our various preferences and prejudices. Whether it's our own sense of personal value as a man or a woman, a knee-jerk reaction rooted in our own personal pain, misunderstandings around what the different perspectives actually believe, fear of being perceived in a certain way, or loyalty to our particular tradition or tribe, the list goes on. I am convinced that if we can get to the point where we are as objective as possible, where we are deeply submitted to the revealed will of God in scripture, then this will impact our progress significantly.

It's also important to note that the Bible, while interested in our gender, by no means emphasises our differences. Our shared humanity as men and women, our shared goals of growing out of childish ways and into maturity and out of old ways into Christlike ways are its true emphasis. When the Bible writers exhort their readers to 'act like men', it's not contrasting this with acting like women, but with acting like children. As men and women, we have way more in common than what separates us.

Terminology

Although there are numbers of different perspectives on the matter of male and female, in the evangelical[2] world, those perspectives, for the most part, fall into two main 'camps'. The first is known as 'egalitarian' as its emphasis is on the equality of men and women, and the second is known as 'complementarian' as its emphasis is on the complementary differences between men and women. It's a funny old game because egalitarians believe that men and women are designed in a complementary way and complementarians believe that men and women are equal!

Egalitarians believe, if you like, in an essential symmetry between men and women, a symmetry that - other than all of us looking to be more and more like Christ - leaves no other important things to say about how a man and a woman ought to conduct themselves in the church and in the home. Complementarians want to talk about the asymmetry between men and women and the various distinctive implications involved in this. When you really zoom in to the centre, you'll find the issues of authority and responsibility are where the sparks tend to fly.

---

2   The word 'evangelical' has become a bit of a dirty word among certain sections in the UK. It conjures up images of far-right, homophobic, hysterical religious extremists. I am using the word 'evangelical' to describe Christians whose general approach to the Bible is that it is authoritative for belief and practice. I use the word as a contrast to 'liberal'.

For the sake of integrity I feel it's important to briefly share my own church background and what's going on in my own heart on these matters. The family of churches that I was born again into are more along the complementarian line, and that has been my world for the past 30 years or so; essentially it's all I've ever known. The experience of over 25 years serving as a pastor in predominantly urban settings (where the majority of 'new' and 'progressive' thinking and perspectives arise), and shepherding congregations made up of people mostly in their 18-30s (those still young and bold enough to question the status quo), has made me stop and think really hard about all of this, especially during the writing of this book over the last few years!

I have wholeheartedly sought to understand the egalitarian perspective, and it has been a real eye-opener, shaping my perspective to a significant degree. Exactly where I've landed will become apparent as the book develops.

All the Single Ladies...

And all the single men! This book will, quite often, focus particularly on marriage. The principles that we will be exploring are much wider than marriage but they come to their zenith in marriage. This doesn't mean for one moment that I believe marriage is some kind of exalted state. While I would be the first to champion godly marriage, I also have huge regard for an unmarried life in the service of Christ. Both conditions are Biblically celebrated. In light of this, I would particularly ask those who are unmarried to remain engaged (pardon the pun) in these sections for good reason. God is a God of order and consistency. While the marriage relationship is a unique one, any fundamental and timeless truths we discover concerning male and female are relevant for all of us.

We may need to carefully consider what application looks like in various differing relationships, but the principles hold true. Hope that makes sense.

Confession time

There is definitely a part of me that wants to be egalitarian. There are a few reasons.

Firstly, I think that if there is something that is theologically ambiguous, it's best to fall on the side of whatever appears kinder and I think, at first glance at least, the egalitarian perspective looks kindest, simply because it doesn't involve anything prohibitive. Secondly, I think that it's always best, if a matter is unclear, to do that which will cause least difficulty in the wider world and will have the greatest chance of commending the faith to those looking on from the outside. Currently in the West, there is no question that that would be the egalitarian perspective. Thirdly, where our church has been complementarian, we know there have been people who have made the decision either not to join us or to leave us, based on that doctrinal position - this is rarely a joy for a pastor. Finally, the complementarian position is increasingly associated with oppression and this is very hard to be associated with when we know that the Lord hates all forms of oppression.

There is also a part of me that wants to remain complementarian. Why? Again, there are a few reasons.

Firstly, it's all I've ever known and it would feel incredibly unfamiliar and disorientating to change now; I'm not sure I'd understand the implications until I was right in the thick of it. Secondly, loyalty is a big deal to me and I'm part of a 'tribe' that is complementarian; I am somewhat afraid of the response if I were to change. Thirdly, I feel indignant at the thought of the wider culture encroaching into God's Kingdom in the church, and I'm struggling to shake off the notion that the egalitarian perspective is a symptom of a church on the back foot, a church defeated by the ideas of the world, a church losing its defining markers and losing its grip on its story-telling power.

But notice that none of those reasons above (there are so many more, I just chose the first ones that came to mind) are decisive because none of them get us into the actual relevant texts. They are all about what I *want* and don't *want;* what I desire and what I fear. If I leave those desires and fears unchecked, that will be a recipe for really bad Bible study! We must all face our fears from whatever direction they come, we must fear God and not man, we must be willing to move into uncharted territory - we just need to know that in doing so, we are being faithful; that will make it worthwhile and eternally fruitful.

I will also say this. While I care that people reach the right destination on this matter, I care more that people engage the right process. I'd enjoy fellowship more with someone who saw things differently but had arrived there with theological rigour, openness of heart, reverence, the honouring of scripture, prayer and tears than someone who saw things like me but who had simply chosen the 'easier' option, or gone tribal, or ignored relevant interpretive criticism or was just lazy.

While I'm not adopting the post-modern stance of not caring about absolute truth, I am saying that you are much more likely to arrive at truth if you walk the journey in a manner worthy of the subject. And trust me, this subject matters.

Pencil, Ink and Blood

Someone once spoke to me about approaching various doctrines by asking the question, "Is this particular matter something that ought to be written in pencil, ink or blood?" What they meant was that different subjects carry different weight and we all have to decide what weight they carry, from 'pencil' being not that important, to 'blood' being something we'd go to the stake over. I think, in terms of where you land, this is an 'ink' issue; in terms of how you get there, well, I think that could be 'blood'. How so? If you arrive at your conclusion by playing fast and loose with scripture or by ignoring 'inconvenient' Biblical truths, then your whole commitment to revealed truth is obviously questionable at best.

But this issue itself is, from my perspective, not a 'gospel issue', i.e. what you believe about it will not determine whether or not you are saved. But I do think it matters. I think it matters in terms of our faithfulness to the creation narrative, the faithfulness of how we tell the story of salvation, and the quality of our relationships.

Sorry

As I said earlier, complementarianism has been my world for over 30 years. If I'm to be really honest, I've become increasingly aware that for some (many?) women in that world, there have often been glaring inconsistencies in church practice, dismissive attitudes and postures towards women, poor communication and teaching on gender, and leadership that sometimes hasn't followed through on agreed plans. As a church leader who's inhabited a complementarian world for decades, I'd like to apologise representatively to any women who have been treated in ways that do not reflect their dignity as co-heirs with Christ and gifted members of His body. Please forgive us.

Selahs and Interludes

 SELAH

INTERLUDE

Throughout the book you'll notice the occasional 'selah' or 'interlude'. The selah is taken from the Psalms, where scholars suggest that the word is used to help us to pause for a moment and consider what we've just read. That's what my selahs are there for too.

I guess the interludes are self-explanatory!

They are opportunities to either head off on a bit of a (relevant) tangent or dig deeper into something we're looking at.

Chapter Two
Who's Saying What?

Below I have attempted to outline some of the main 'pillars' that egalitarians and complementarians use to hold up their various perspectives. It's not an exhaustive list, but it will hopefully give a sense of who's saying what. I will use the pillars throughout the book as the framework for our study. I have ordered them in such a way as to help us follow things as chronologically[1] as possible.

The Egalitarian Perspective

PILLAR 1. Genesis 1 makes it explicit that men and women are created equally in the image of God, and both are destined to rule. There is nothing in Genesis 2 to undermine or significantly alter this equality.

PILLAR 2. Genesis 3 makes it clear that the dominion of a man over a woman is a result of God's judgement on their sin of disobedience, and is therefore never an expression of God's perfect will or original design, but rather the result of a fallen world.

PILLAR 3. The patriarchal backdrop of the society in which the Biblical narrative is set is a result of Genesis 3. The male/female dynamic we see is not prescriptive of how life in God's Kingdom should be, but merely descriptive of what life in a fallen world is like, with occasional redemptive rays of hope shining through.

PILLAR 4. The coming of Jesus is a second Genesis. As we observe Jesus' interactions with many different women, we see something brand new. The revolution has begun!

PILLAR 5. The outpouring of the Holy Spirit on the day of Pentecost was indiscriminate by nature; 'all flesh'. Therefore the only qualification for ministry is Spirit-giftedness. If the Spirit chooses to gift someone for a particular task, then they are good to go; gender is irrelevant. This is made abundantly clear when Paul says that in Christ there is now no longer male nor female.

PILLAR 6. Paul's list of co-workers in Romans 16 is approximately 25% female. Given the patriarchal back-drop of the wider society, this is quite extraordinary. This points to the kind of scenario, in different cultural circumstances (like ours today), where we could easily imagine a 50/50 gender split of gospel ministry.

---

1   By 'chronological' here I am referring to the order in which these things appear or are emphasised in scripture, though it's impossible to do this entirely cleanly.

PILLAR 7. Headship and submission dynamics taught in the New Testament, are no more than culturally binding. They were written in order to protect the church in that age from charges of disorder in the wider culture. They are not timeless reflections of God's Kingdom. We must read the epistles with a keener eye for context.

The Complementarian Perspective

PILLAR 1. Genesis 2 tells a story within a story. Adam and Eve are gloriously equal, but not interchangeable. Adam, alone in the garden, needs help that only Eve can bring. Before Eve is built from Adam, God entrusts Adam with a task and a command. This asymmetry speaks of his prominent responsibility and her unique contribution.

PILLAR 2. Humanity is a household. God appointed Adam as head of the house, which is why he is uniquely blamed for the human predicament. With headship comes representative responsibility. The coming of the woman's seed brings hope as a new head appears - One who will crush the enemy!

PILLAR 3. The fall introduces us to a cursed power struggle between men and women. Women will struggle with warped desires towards men and men will use their superior physical strength to dominate women. The harmony is over - blame and shame are now the name of the game.

PILLAR 4. Jesus shows us what true headship is like, specifically in the way that He treats women. He values, honours, befriends, invests in, and gladly receives from many women. Jesus' undoing of the curse didn't stop Him from appointing twelve male apostles, though the new community was anything but a male monopoly.

PILLAR 5. Headship does not disappear in the new community; Paul is clear that God is the head of Christ and husbands are the heads of their wives. It's not something to avoid but something to embrace, and something that exists, in some mysterious way, even between the Father and Jesus.

PILLAR 6. The early church was overseen by male elders. The qualifications for elders that we find in Timothy and Titus are aimed explicitly at men. These men are to copy Jesus, who sacrificed His life for the sake of the flock.

PILLAR 7. The relationship between a husband and a wife is way bigger than itself. It tells the transcendent story of Jesus and the church. Two united as one flesh has always been about the gospel! Interchangeable roles and symmetrical submission in a marriage will never tell this story faithfully.

Chapter Three
Rightly Handling the Word of God

Now, you don't need much more than a cursory look at both lists to see that neither of these perspectives is silly or thoughtless, or to be dismissed out of hand. Sure, if you're feeling defensive and under threat, you might be tempted to reject whichever one is making you feel that way, but when you simply and calmly look at the arguments, I don't think either perspective is weak or pathetic or bigoted, but both require serious reflection.

A sage once said:

> In a lawsuit the first to speak seems right, until someone comes forward and cross-examines.
> PROVERBS 18 V 17

I have at times felt like a ping-pong ball as I've read one perspective and then the other. The power of compelling arguments succinctly put (when mixed with personal fears and flaws) can at times be overwhelming!

Oil & Water?

This leads us to the key question: are these two perspectives oil and water, or is there a way of harmonising them, and actually finding a fascinating beauty together? I think it's some and some. Some of the arguments point blank contradict each other, and when it comes to those, our responsibility is to work out which arguments are most compelling, most true, most loving, and run with those, whilst rejecting the weaker perspectives that are built on weaker arguments. But it could be that there is a way of 'layering' some of these perspectives in order to keep the best and lose the worst of both. By 'layering' I'm suggesting that life in the world is essentially a fairly complex and multi-layered thing.

Best not to ignore that.

Sometimes I think that Christians deny the complexity of reality when it comes to scripture and walking with God. While the faith is simple enough for a child to embrace, there is plenty of mystery and complexity involved. This means that we have to learn how to carry ourselves with poise, think things through, and handle a bit of nuance here and there. I'm not saying that we have to let go of our convictions - far from it, but we mustn't try to make things simpler than they actually are. Let me give you an example. The gospel comes to us as a message of great joy - that our sins can be forgiven and we can be reconciled to God, through Christ, as a free gift; it really is magnificent. The most common word used to describe this is grace. Grace carries with it the idea of a gift given freely and happily. We are very blessed.

And yet frequently throughout scripture we are motivated by this idea of reward, a word which actually translates to mean 'wages'! But, we ask, how can these two things co-exist? Doesn't the one exclude the other - gift and wages? When I'm teaching on this subject and I see people's quizzical looks, I will draw the listeners' attention to a relationship that is fundamental to the vast majority of us - that of being brought up as a child within a family. How did we get there? Freely - we just arrived. We were created out of love and were welcomed in love - we did nothing to earn it, but found ourselves fully part of this family we were born into. We have enjoyed our parents' unmerited love songs and bedtime stories from day one. Grace!

But our parents wanted us to grow and to mature and as the years went on, they motivated us through the mechanism of reward and loss. It's very effective. It doesn't impact upon our identity as loved children, but our response over the years to our parents' requirements of us to tidy our room, help with chores and generally pull our weight, will, as we grow up, most definitely impact upon our identity as friends of our parents and trusted family members. There you go - gift and wages in the same context - it's a simple analogy but it helps us to layer one truth upon another in a way that doesn't damage or detract from either. My hope is to help us see the various and relevant layers involved in gender and understand how we might rightly interpret the various, relevant scriptures.

Reading in the Fear of God

If we are going to get this right, we need to take a moment to consider what the major dos and don'ts are when it comes to approaching the Bible. If I can be very candid for a moment. As a pastor I have at times been aghast when talking to church members particularly about marriage, family life or parenting. The approach has at times been far from biblical. When I've raised what the Bible teaches, it's been very discouraging at times to discover that they either don't know, or don't seem to care, or have been looking elsewhere - blogs or chat rooms or the opinions of others, to provide their main ideas.

Now I realise that we won't all be theologians, and yet the Bible we have in our hands cost people dearly; there was a time where no one had their own copy in their native tongue, but had to rely on what others said. Those who led the way in fighting for the Bible to be translated and printed into the common language often did so at the loss of either their physical liberty, or even their life.

We are so deeply privileged, and one of the ways we can respond appropriately to that privilege is by giving time consistently to the study and understanding of God's word. We have so many excellent tools at our disposal now, that there is really no reason why the vast majority of us can't engage with serious and profitable Bible study.

Let's not approach the most extraordinary body of literature the world has ever known with less rigour and respect than we would a newspaper. It's not just historical, rich and hugely interesting…it's inspired! This is the word of God. This means that though we look to do our best to understand it properly, we don't do so in a way that places ourselves over it, but in a way whereby we are submitted to it; we want to understand it in order to obey it, not in order to cast judgement or espouse opinions!

Heading in the Right Direction?

It's also important, in fact very important, for us to reject the idea that the Bible only gives us hints, or a starting point on God's thoughts that sends us in 'the right direction', without being the final say on the matter, almost as if the Bible gave us the right trajectory and nothing more. This is an idea that is proposed by I. Howard Marshall, a contributor to a book called 'Discovering Biblical Equality'. He says, when referring to marriage in the Bible, "The concept of marriage between equal partners is just beginning to be perceived in the New Testament, and Paul should not be expected to step outside his time and see the consequences of his teaching any more than he is to be faulted for not commanding the abolition of slavery or the development of universal suffrage."[2]

It's clear that the saving purposes of God outlined in the Bible happen within a historical narrative and unfold bit by bit. This means that as we read the Bible chronologically, certain things that were to some degree 'hidden' in the earlier epochs are revealed more fully later on. All well and good. However, this doesn't mean that the fundamental revelation of God's purposes is still being unfolded. God's final word is Jesus, and the apostle's doctrine (commonly known as the New Testament) is the final record of God's saving purposes in Christ - we're not waiting for any new revelation in that sense; we have it. The work has been done on the cross: "It is finished". The record of what has been, what is and what will be has been completed by those authorised to do so in the writings of the Bible, which is a closed canon, meaning that it's the rule by which we measure all other ideas and beliefs, and that it won't be added to any further.

When we say that we believe in the inspiration of scripture, we mean that while we acknowledge the reality of a cultural backdrop (the Bible writers were not writing in a vacuum but they were like us, both imperfect and to a certain degree products of their environment), none of this would have adversely affected or limited their ability to articulate scripture in the way that the Lord wanted them to. Because of their being

---

2   Page 195, Discovering Biblical Equality.

'carried along by the Holy Spirit',[3] He saw to it that their written words were, while human, of a transcendent nature. Peter is clear that no prophecy of scripture comes from someone's own interpretation.[4] The idea that the teaching of the Bible is somehow insufficient or incomplete must be rejected.

Now within the canon of scripture itself, I acknowledge that there is something of a 'trajectory' in certain matters - here are a couple of examples. Firstly, Jesus' teaching on marriage, divorce and remarriage makes it clear that the commands of God in the Mosaic Law concerning the same were not a revelation of God's perfect will, but instead, knowing just how hard their hearts were, the Lord permitted an arrangement of comparatively easy divorce, that, while it was much kinder and more protective than the surrounding culture, it still fell short of His ideal.[5] Jesus brings the focus back to the creation narrative, in order to show how it was to truly be in God's Kingdom.[6] So the creation narrative shows us the ideal. Under the Mosaic Covenant we find a solution to marital difficulty that is pragmatic but not ideal. And then in the New Covenant, we find a return to what was originally intended. Not exactly a trajectory - more of a full circle! But we still have a sense of movement within the canon of scripture.

Secondly, I agree that with the role of 'deacon' in the early church there seems to have been a development of thought over a number of decades concerning whether or not it was an appropriate role for a woman. The first deacons appointed in Jerusalem had to be men; this is explicitly stated just prior to their appointment.[7] Later, in Romans 16 we read about Phoebe, a deacon of the church in Cenchreae. Why was this? Was it to do with context? Maybe Cenchreae, just south of Corinth, was more liberal than Jerusalem? How much should our context impact upon our practice? Or maybe, it being some years later that Romans was written, as thought developed on the role of a deacon and how it worked, it came to be considered appropriate.[8] We don't know, but I'm happy to accept that *within* the canon of scripture we do see development of thought from one place or time to another.

---

3   2 Peter 1 v 21.

4   2 Peter 1 v 20.

5   Matthew 19 v 8.

6   Matthew 19 v 1-12.

7   Acts 6 v 1-7.

8   The church in the early chapters of Acts was clearly embryonic. At that point, what we might call 'offices' in the church don't seem to be clearly established - the apostles were serving as much as local elders as they were apostles. In light of this, it's not a stretch to consider that the Seven - for whom the verb to serve and not the noun (deacon) was used - while not explicitly 'deacons', give us the prototype for what deacons look like.

Seeds or Flowers?

As in the quote above, perhaps one of the most persuasive arguments for the validity of this 'trajectory' approach to scripture is the argument concerning slavery. Here's how the argument goes: while slavery is not roundly condemned in the Bible, the seeds of the ideas that fuelled the likes of William Wilberforce, Frederick Douglass et al. to fight for the abolition of trans-Atlantic slavery are there in the Bible. In light of this, there are most likely other matters, particularly around gender and sexuality, where we don't see the full flower in the Bible, but we do undoubtedly see the seeds sown for a more 'progressive' perspective.

William Webb uses the topic of slavery as a pillar for his argument for what he calls a "redemptive movement hermeneutic".[9] He argues persuasively that if the Old Testament is 'God's revelation to His covenant people within the constraints of a curse-laden and culturally shaped world' and the New Testament is 'still revelation from God within a curse-laden and culturally distinct world' then surely, as we happily receive the Old Testament as revelation with an incremental, developmental edge, we can do the same with the New Testament. He uses the subject of slavery to demonstrate clearly that there is significant movement from Old Testament to New Testament and also that 'we can scarcely argue cogently for a proactive abolitionist position in today's world based on a words-on-the-page understanding of the New Testament texts on slaves.'[10]

Webb also helpfully shows how Jesus adjusts some of the emphasis around male/female relationships, using the examples of His teaching on marriage and divorce, as well as His targeting of men in the matter of lust instead of blaming women for all sexual indiscretion (common in the day).[11] If the argument concerning a more liberated and modern perspective on gender and sexuality being present in seed form in the Bible stands on the shoulders of the slavery argument, then the slavery argument has to stand up. But I don't think it does.

Slavery in Bible times could be forced or it could be voluntary. It could be the result of poverty, war or kidnap. But here is the clincher: whether it's the horrors of centuries-long African kidnap by European and Arab slavers or the disgusting practice of human trafficking today, the Bible roundly and explicitly condemns all forms of 'man-stealing', whether in the Old Testament or the New. It's not just the 'seeds' that are present in the Bible - the whole flower is. See below:

---

9   Chapter 22, Discovering Biblical Equality.

10   Page 394, Discovering Biblical Equality.

11   See Matthew 5 v 27-30.

Anyone who kidnaps someone is to be put to death, whether the victim has been sold or is still in the kidnapper's possession.
EXODUS 21 V 16

We know that the law is good if one uses it properly. We also know that the law is made not for the righteous but for lawbreakers and rebels, the ungodly and sinful, the unholy and irreligious, for those who kill their fathers or mothers, for murderers, for the sexually immoral, for those practicing homosexuality, for <u>slave traders</u> and liars and perjurers—and for whatever else is contrary to the sound doctrine that conforms to the gospel concerning the glory of the blessed God, which he entrusted to me.
1 TIMOTHY 1 V 8-11 (EMPHASIS MINE)

So there it is, that's the first point. In both Old Testament and New Testament, both to steal someone and enslave them, or to buy a stolen person in order to possess them is a sin worthy of death. How certain European enslavers ever got away with instigating such crime across Africa in the name of Christ beggars belief, but hear this: the fault was with them, not with the Bible. They were roundly condemned by scripture the whole time they were doing that; the Bible is explicit.

But as I said above, not all slavery in Bible times was the result of kidnap. While slavery will not be part of the new creation, Paul didn't see it as a 'must' to liberate oneself from slavery, though he encouraged it where possible.[12] But it could be that for a season it would serve you much more beneficially than being out on a limb in a cruel world if you had no family, social security or benefits. If the argument for a more 'progressive' view on matters of gender and sexuality stands on the idea that kidnapping and enslavement are not explicitly condemned in scripture, well, the argument doesn't stand.

The vulnerability is that if we embrace this 'redemptive movement hermeneutic' wholesale, we become the final arbiter of what is final revelation and what isn't; we determine God's *final* thoughts. Webb does recognise the inherent dangers here,[13] and looks to protect the idea of the final revelation of the New Testament by pressing for what he calls an ongoing 'realisation' of that revelation. He points to examples like head coverings, silenced women and wives calling their husbands 'Lord' - practices very few contemporary evangelicals encourage, in order to make the point that all of us are already involved in and employing this 'redemptive movement hermeneutic'. I believe that in those areas where we do adjust the realisation of the revelation (head coverings etc.), we do so for good reasons that can be justifiably

---

12   1 Corinthians 7 v 20-24.

13   Pages 392-393, Discovering Biblical Equality.

explained. I appreciate the tightrope he is walking, but I would encourage more caution than he seems to. We never want to find ourselves, even accidentally, asserting our own will over the Lord's.

Summing up, I believe the jump from slavery to male/female dynamics is not straightforward and needs much closer inspection.

One final thought. If we can demonstrate that the reasons the New Testament writers give for the submission of wives to husbands is the same as they give for the submission of slaves to masters, then we can treat these two relationships similarly. We will work through the household codes in the epistles throughout the book and see if that's the case.

Eavesdropping Carefully

The final thing to think about - and it's a big one - is how to read all of scripture with a keen eye for context. This is especially important with the epistles. Why? Because an epistle, being a letter written from one party to another, means that it can be a bit like listening to one side of a phone call - you have to pick up the clues and read between the lines in order to understand why certain things are being emphasised, or why certain subjects seem to have elicited such a strong response.

A silly example. You might hear me on the phone say "When you go outside make sure you wear a hat". It's obvious what I'm saying, the content is clear. But what about the context? The time of year it is will make a difference to how you interpret it. If I said it in December, you'd know that it's a good idea to wear a hat in order to keep your head warm! Not so in August, when it's more to do with avoiding sunstroke! I could say certain words at any given moment, but if you read or hear them six months later, you could misunderstand my motives, what I actually *mean.* The words themselves may mean the same thing, but it's about more than words; the context also impacts on the meaning.

Taking a biblical example, why does Paul suggest that rejecting certain foods is a doctrine of demons in his first letter to Timothy, and then to the Romans seemingly 'soft pedal' and speak about dietary choices as a matter of individual conscience? Context is all. Why does he open fire on the Galatians for embracing circumcision and then circumcise Timothy himself? Again, context. It's a vital matter for the subject of this book, because some of the most controversial or emphasised scriptures on male and female in the New Testament are in the epistles. Paul talks about man being the head of woman. What does that mean? He also states that there is no male or female in Christ. How do we reconcile that? Paul seemingly charges women not to teach or exercise authority over men. Really? Peter believes women are the weaker vessel.

How so? This sampling alone ought to help us realise how important it is to understand the context of certain epistles.[14]

So what are the principles for reading the Bible in context? We've already laid down the first principle, which is that our default position is to yield and not resist - we're not to go looking for ways of getting out of teaching we find difficult; if that's in our hearts then our approach is all wrong.

Next, we're to do all we can to try to discover the context from the actual text itself. We sometimes don't have to look far! As mentioned above, why does Paul roundly condemn not eating certain foods in some letters and then seem pretty relaxed about such things in others? It's clear if you read a few sentences before and after, that his stance is impacted by the particular issues he is facing in that particular church or group of churches. For example, in Rome he's really trying to get the Jews and the Gentiles to make room for one another so that they can grow together in harmony, expressing loving patience for those with weaker consciences. In Ephesus he's confronting false teachers who want to drag the predominantly Gentile church into spiritual slavery through adherence to either Jewish or novel food laws - as a result his posture is very different.

Then, once we've done this, we would want to search a bit wider in scripture for other references that might be particularly relevant. For example, if you're in 1 Corinthians, have a read about Paul's visit to Corinth in Acts and have a read of 2 Corinthians so that you are gathering all the relevant data.

Next, is there anything in the whole of scripture that can help? It's always best to weigh scripture with scripture. What else has God revealed about Himself and His purposes that might help us to fill out the picture?

Finally, what do we know about a given location or moment in history that might help us? This has to be last in terms of importance because our sources here will not be inspired, and new discoveries mean that our understanding of history is always under review, but this can provide something of a help nevertheless.

Right Answers, Wrong Questions

I also think it's important to say that the Bible doesn't necessarily give us the answers to the questions we are asking! I'm not saying that there is not sufficient spiritual content in the Bible. I'm simply saying that we may find ourselves asking certain questions that the Bible doesn't directly answer. When we do this, we must make sure that we don't take certain answers we find in the Bible and make them the answers to our particular questions.

---

14   1 Corinthians 11 v 2-16, Galatians 3 v 28, 1 Timothy 2 v 11-15, 1 Peter 3 v 7.

The debate over male and female equality is not actually a matter that comes up a lot in the Bible.

Male and female unity is.

Male and female equality is not making the headlines; it's a foundational truth but it's not considered to be either controversial or the goal of our togetherness. I'm not saying the Bible has nothing to say about it, but we mustn't make it a central biblical debate as if the Bible was written in London last week. If we understand this, it will keep us from airlifting scriptures out of their context in order to make them serve as answers to our own particular concerns.

If we are fixated on what the gender question means in terms of who can do what in church, we mustn't immediately expect to find huge amounts of content in the Bible on this. There will be some, but we mustn't decide that this is the heart of what God thinks being male and female is about and therefore demand that the Bible will centre in on this. This will lead to either disappointment or misuse of scripture - or both.

Chapter Four
The New 'Wild' West

It's one thing to try to understand and grapple with the context of different passages of the Bible, but it's another thing to understand our own context.

I'm writing from the West and as I consider this subject, I have the West in mind. Not because the West is best, but because I know the West and I live and work in the West. As we look together for timeless and transcendent truths, I will automatically apply them in a 'Western' way; I do it without thinking. While this is not wrong (we all need to apply truth in our various settings), it's a fine line to tread. Having said that, the West, due to its riches, is currently disproportionately culturally influential across the globe, and the reality of globalisation means that many of these perspectives and arguments will be both familiar and hopefully useful in many contexts.

There's a book in the Bible called Judges, and it's a book that has a lot of similarities to the modern Western world. It's also a very depressing book. It is essentially a cycle of disasters and deliverances. Terrible things happen at an alarming rate in the book of Judges. The whole book is summed up in the final two sentences:

In those days Israel had no king; everyone did as they saw fit.
JUDGES 21 V 25

I think we're heading into what can only be described as wild and lawless times. There may not be gunfights and shootouts, but instead, trolling, ghosting, cancelling and cyberbullying are the order of the day. Any who disagree with the core tenets of secular individualism are shot down. Below are some observations about our own context in the West that I believe, when taken together, form something of a perfect storm for the sincere believer. Most of these observations have a particularly timely edge to them - they are, in a sense, part of our cultural moment but they are also rooted in timeless truths about fallen humanity.

#1 Thought

The first observation, and I'll phrase it as a question, is, "Have we stopped thinking?" Nearly. Have you noticed this? We've become very bullying; we're neither encouraged to think, nor are we allowed to say what we really think, even as part of a discussion, and even if it would help us to learn and re-evaluate what we ought to think! A vicious circle.

As with all bullying, it plays on fear and can only really succeed if those on the receiving end give way to intimidation. The threatened punishments of ostracism and slander are sufficiently undesirable for most people to toe the line. This could lead to a generation that not only won't know what they think but also won't know *how* to think - imagine that. If a society removes the freedom to think as individuals, then we all inch closer to crossing the threshold into a kind of cultural totalitarianism.

We are being programmed and pressured to say 'the right thing', not from a place of conviction but from a place of fear; fear of saying 'the wrong thing'. And all of this in what is supposedly the 'free' West. Sounds like the very intolerance our culture is supposed to defeat…! Crazy times.

It has been said that many Christians nowadays process their opinions via outrage rather than genuine argument; that's scary. Now it's obviously very important to bear in mind that we don't live in a spiritually neutral environment. Just as swimmers can find themselves swept away by invisible currents, there is a strong undertow in the world moving us away from the Father's perfect and loving truth. If we don't consider that and take it seriously, the undertow remains but we simply miss it. The Bible says that the whole world is under the power of the evil one.[1] Switching metaphors for a moment, this passage is saying that the 'strings' behind the age we live in, with its values and narratives, are being pulled by the great deceiver. And so, unfortunately, unless we learn to think critically and scripturally, with a humble and courageous heart, I think we will most certainly drift and maybe even get washed away.

Let me just say that critical thinking and a critical spirit are two very different things. Critical thinking is a vital part of the discernment process, whereas a critical spirit is simply looking for the negative in everything for the purpose of tearing down; we reject that wholeheartedly. I'd love for this book to aid deep and critical thought, meaningful reflection and healthy conversations.

#2 Authority

The second observation is that, in the West, we really, really don't like authority. We don't get authority. We think the world would be better off without authority. We don't want to exercise authority for fear of being misunderstood or criticised, and we don't want to submit to authority for fear of being mistreated or abused. This has been toxically blended with, and exacerbated by, the exposé of all kinds of brutal abuses that have been perpetuated by vast numbers of 'authority figures'. Those in positions of influence in seemingly every walk of life, from parents to teachers to care home workers to celebrities to industry bosses and fat-cats to sports coaches to the super-rich to religious ministers to the police, have been found out.

---

1   1 John 5 v 19.

It's been utterly devastating. Reports of paedophile rings operating in the care system, the abuses that catalysed the 'Me too' and the 'Black Lives Matter' movements, the cover-ups by senior church ministers who knew about sexual abuses that were going on in the life of the church: is it any wonder that we've had enough of authority?

We all feel much safer with a system where no one carries authority, and where there is no one and nothing to submit to. And I get it. I see the logic and actually feel an enormous amount of sympathy towards this outlook. But we also have to consider that the Bible likens us to sheep, meaning that we are made for a shepherd - we want to be led and led well. It's only when we're led badly that we decide we don't want to be led at all because it feels much safer, but actually, if that pain were to be healed, we'd love a good leader. Not one that will take away our freedoms or take advantage of us or use and abuse us, but one that will take an interest in us, invest in us, believe in us, and call us into something amazing and exciting! It makes doing your own thing look a bit sad.

Perhaps we've lost the precious truth that authority is given primarily to protect and not to punish. It's supposed to create the kind of safety that leads to immense and joy-filled flourishing. Perhaps if we were to dig to the roots of our culture and find what motivates many of the values, choices and priorities we hold so dear, we would find a whole lot of pain, disillusionment and cynicism, which really says, "If we're honest; we've lost hope". So we do what we default to when we lose hope - we find safety in ourselves, and we create our own systems that will protect us, or at least keep us from too much danger. Not the best foundation.

#3 Trust

A third observation is that a lot of women don't trust men. In some ways, guys and gals can't get enough of one another, but we also frequently drive each other crazy, hurt each other badly and misunderstand each other! Truth be told, for the vast majority of history and in the vast majority of cultures, women have, to varying degrees, ended up being treated in ways that have very often left them damaged, degraded and disenfranchised. And it's men who have done this and perpetuated it. Therefore, any idea of some kind of innate male 'headship' whatever that might mean, is often immediately met with deep fear, understandable suspicion and a fierce kind of rejection. Entirely understandable.

Let me explain with some of my own story. Growing up, aged seven to thirteen I lived with my mum and siblings in a number of refuges for victims of domestic abuse - it was a female-only environment unless you were under sixteen. There were a lot of good memories and a lot of great people that we lived with; it was a safe place. There was also - understandably - a lot of pain and a lot of mistrust towards men. Now that I'm older, I get it. Back then, as a young man, even though no one was ever hostile to me personally, I felt it in the atmosphere and didn't really know what to do with it. The point is, the personal histories that converged in those places affected their culture; the bad things that had gone on helped to create the air we all breathed there. What a shame that the negative experiences of our lives seem to wield so much more power over us than the positive ones!

#4 Freedom

A fourth observation is around the subject of freedom. Whether you're in church or in the wider culture, 'freedom' and 'liberation' are themes that everyone loves, and why not? I love them too. But like anything precious, we need to understand where it fits in the bigger picture, just to make sure we don't abuse it or misapply it. The Bible talks about freedom in two ways: freedom *from* sin, the devil and legalism, and freedom *to* love God and serve others. So it works in two directions - freedom *from* the bad stuff sets us free *to do* the good stuff. But. The Bible never encourages unregulated freedom. The Bible actually calls that slavery. When we throw off restraint in the name of freedom because we can't resist certain impulses it's because we are enslaved to them. I guess that calling it 'freedom' just makes us feel better about it! That's certainly how I lived for a number of years, totally 'free' and yet utterly enslaved.

There are very clear things written about God's design and plan so that we use our God-given freedom for His glory and our good.[2] So, the freedom that Jesus brings comes with instructions.[3] These instructions make sure that freedom serves the higher purpose of love. Yes, there is a higher purpose than freedom. It's called love. This is frequently misunderstood, even in Christian circles. There is a misunderstanding that freedom is the end goal, whereas actually, love is. Without love, freedom doesn't know where to go and so normally ends up taking us back into simply another kind of bondage. This is ever so important when it comes to relational dynamics and male/female relationships, as we can be tempted to try to break

---

2   Just to say, those two things always go together; His glory and our good. It's neat.

3   While we're on the subject of 'freedom' it's also vital to observe how the issues of race, gender, disability and sexuality are often lumped together under the freedom/oppression narrative. It's clear why - non-whites, women, the disabled and LGBT folk have all been persecuted as minorities in many contexts - but it's also important to inspect each one of these matters in their own right and there's reason why. Let me illustrate. Imagine a frozen pond; at first glance the whole surface looks the same. With that in mind you strap your skates on and away you go, not realising that certain icy points in the pond are much thinner than others; appearances can be deceiving - it looks uniform, but when you inspect it more closely you realise that it presents a diverse reality. Treating each part of the pond as if it were the same puts you in harm's way. Such is the case with the above four issues; the Bible will have different things to say about each one - just because sinful humanity has responded in similar ways to all four, it doesn't mean they're the same. All four of those culturally hot topics have their own unique theological contours - they are not the same. There may be both theological and contextual overlap with some, but trust me, they are all different matters and need to be approached as such. If you approach them all through the same lens you could find yourself - and forgive my mixing of metaphors - in really hot water!

free from all restraint or guiding principles and simply let things happen. But that's not the goal; Christian love is.

#5 Exception

The fifth observation is what I will call 'the rule of one'. In bygone days we were told that every rule has an exception but that the exception itself proves the rule! In the West, we seem to have altered our perspective on this. We now build whole arguments and create entire policies based on the experiences and feelings of a few vocal minorities or individuals, regardless of the experience of most people. Don't get me wrong - individuals matter and the Bible reveals that God Himself has a special eye on those who are outnumbered or stranded on the edges or disadvantaged, and I actually believe that one of the great things about current Western culture is that it's very compassionate.

But, unfortunately, we feel so good about letting a lone voice win the day that the majority perspectives are silenced and presumed foolish. If you begin to let the experience of an individual shape thought and policy for the whole, it becomes a kind of madness. Why? Because when the common experience of humanity is overlooked and overshadowed by the experience of any number of lone voices or individual perspectives, you create a scenario where, simply put, the individual is king. And this is the darker side of it. This attempt at compassion can easily go wrong and begin to feed a beast that all of us are susceptible to, the beast of 'me'. It's something I call the Sovereign-self; where self becomes the final word on a matter and the ultimate source of wisdom. It works a bit like a cult, because here my opinion becomes the only opinion that can't be criticised or disagreed with, and if you try all hell breaks loose.

In this scenario the Bible is no longer the word of God, a disclosure from a higher place. It becomes something that we criticise and scrutinise and chop away at until what's left feels comfortable to 'me'. Then it's no longer God's word, but rather it has been so edited by 'me' that it's now my word.

May I be bold enough to say that this is simply self-worship. If we continue on this track, the idea of an agreed truth that we are all under no longer exists. All that will exist is you and me simply doing what's right in our own eyes.

#6 Story

My sixth observation is what we might call 'the small story'. Closely linked to the above point, over the last few decades we've been told repeatedly from the get-go that life is all about 'me', that 'I'm' the main character in the story, that it's 'my' story. And I wonder if it's killing me (and you). Surely this cultural air produces an atmosphere starved of all spiritual oxygen, creating tiny people that have nothing worth dying for, and so nothing really worth living for.[4] If the statistics are true, maybe it's to blame for forming the kind of people who have no great cause to lay their lives down for, and who take their own lives at a more alarming rate than any generation before it. What's going on? What if the plug has been pulled on the big story - and this grand narrative that we all desperately need in order to understand ourselves is being systematically and powerfully untold, leaving us whirling in the waters of hopelessness. The only way is down in this scenario.

When we are told that we are the ultimate goal and so we ought to indulge ourselves and consume all we possibly can even though none of it satisfies, it actually leaves us feeling emptier and emptier. It's what I call the L'Oréal gospel: "Because you're worth it". It starts and finishes with me. And it is utterly uninspiring. It must soon be time to wake up from this nightmare. There's a higher goal than you. There's a worthier hero than you. These words may cut, but as the wise man said: faithful are the wounds of a friend.[5] There's a reason why the end goal of God's outrageous blessings outlined in the first chapter of the book of Ephesians is "to the praise of His glory". It's because all things are from Him, all things are through Him and all things are to Him. It's all about Him.

#7 Meaning

The final observation is concerning how secularism, being built on atheistic materialism, has meaninglessness as its foundation. There can be no ultimate meaning in an atheistic universe; everything that is here is here accidentally. There is no ultimate personality or design behind nature. This leads to a flattening out of our understanding of life. Symbols become increasingly unnecessary because symbols rely on meaning and story. We find ourselves floating in a vast, cold and one-dimensional reality. Sex is simply sex; it's about genetic survival or animal pleasure and nothing more. Male and female become simply functional, like everything else in life. There is nothing transcendent, and therefore what we see in front of our eyes simply is; it doesn't point to anything bigger or greater. There is nothing bigger or greater.

This ideology, if followed to its logical conclusion, leads to terrible things. Very few atheists live like atheists; if they did there would be hell to pay. Love, loyalty, courage, or any other virtue you might name have no place in this kind of universe. As believers we do, of course, reject such a worldview. Nevertheless, it can seep into our thinking and we can lose that sense of multi-layered meaning that is packed into symbols as metaphorical signposts to greater things. In a nutshell, we can become pragmatists. This is tragic for

---

4   Martin Luther King Jr made this powerful point.

5   Proverbs 27 v 6.

the believer. All that God made points to Him and tells the story of His mighty purpose in Jesus Christ. We must not give this away.

I hope these observations have been helpful - I'm trying to help us to have a good and sober sense of ourselves, not just as spiritual beings but cultural beings. We bring innumerable preconceptions, preferences and prejudices to every matter with which we engage. If we can remember this, I think we will do better. As an aside, and if you are reading this from a non-Western perspective, it might be a good exercise to reflect upon the impact of your own culture on your thinking.

Buttons and Triggers

What we have experienced in terms of male and female relationships is a storehouse of information we carry around within ourselves that informs everything we hear and see, and if we are not aware of that then - again - we impair ourselves further. We all have buttons that get pressed, which may not be logical but are certainly powerful! I remember watching a fairly harmless and light-hearted film with my wife, when I found myself on the brink of walking out. At a certain point, the dynamics at play between two of the characters were so reminiscent of certain dysfunctional and traumatic events in my own life that I literally found it almost unbearable to remain. If I had to explain it to someone it would sound pathetic, but it was actually incredibly powerful. The point is this: we all carry certain sensitivities that can impair our judgement, and we must do our best not to allow ourselves to become victims of certain traumatic events in our lives. The Lord knows we carry these vulnerabilities, but He doesn't want our lives to be dictated to by them; He wants us to be healed of them.

Finally, just as we are about to get into the meat of things, let me say that the only noble and worthy goal of this book can be that we all grow in true, Christian love. What we experience in terms of loving relationships in life carries huge power in forming beliefs that are helpful and true. Whether you are a man or woman, if you can feel genuinely loved and honoured through the experience of reading this book, that will be a huge win as far as I am concerned.

How we're going to do this...

I will take the seven pillars (see chapter two) of each argument and respond to them as best I can. My aim will be to weave together the strongest arguments of each of the points. I hope we end up with something that will be stunningly beautiful. As I said earlier, the aim is to work through the topic chronologically, and by that I mean from Genesis through to the end. The more I have read on this subject, the more I have realised just how vital it is to have a sound grasp of the creation narrative because, obviously, it is the starting point, and so it gives us a plumb line by which to measure everything else.

As mentioned earlier, the way Jesus dealt with the subject of marriage, divorce and remarriage was by rewinding the conversation right back to the start and using what Moses wrote as a foundation for everything else. The creation account may not give us the perfect destination because we are all now dealing with the realities of the new creation, but it will give us the perfect foundation. A firm grip on both the original creation narrative and the new creation realities spelt out in the New Testament should help us to 'walk the line' as we look to be as fruitful as possible living 'between the ages'!

Chapter Five
Equal!
Egalitarian Pillar One

Genesis 1 makes it explicit that men and women are created equally in the image of God and both are destined to rule. There is nothing in Genesis 2 to undermine or alter this equality.

> *Then God said, "Let us make mankind in our image, in our likeness, so that they may rule over the fish in the sea and the birds in the sky, over the livestock and all the wild animals, and over all the creatures that move along the ground." So God created mankind in his own image, in the image of God he created them; male and female he created them. God blessed them and said to them, "Be fruitful and increase in number; fill the earth and subdue it. Rule over the fish in the sea and the birds in the sky and over every living creature that moves on the ground."*
> GENESIS 1 V 26-28

Foundations always go in first, and so this first account of creation is a vital foundation for us. We see that God both created mankind in His image and created them male and female. This seems to suggest that our distinctions as men and women, when brought together, fill out our imaging of God in ways we could never do alone. This is borne out in the Bible, where, although God has revealed Himself as our heavenly Father (not our heavenly Mother), and Jesus is a man (not a woman), it's also true that God uses maternal imagery concerning Himself in the Old Testament,[6] and Jesus does likewise in the New Testament.[7] Here we see that where God has revealed Himself to us in a way that we associate with maleness, He, at the same time, manifests female characteristics. The point is simple but profound. Only together as male and female can humanity most fully reflect the Divine Image. This means that we need one another in order to fulfil our purpose - that neither of us can do without the other.

A deep and honest felt need for one another will go a long way to healing a lot of wounds that exist between men and women. I'm thinking beyond marriage here, and touching on things more generally. Imagine for a moment an environment where both men and women lived with a genuine sense of need for the other.

---

6   Isaiah 66 v 13.

7   Matthew 23 v 37.

That's powerful. This means that we can and must do away with any attitudes that exist around superiority or inferiority of any one of the sexes. Sounds obvious, right? You'd be surprised. Everyone approaches this subject from slightly different starting points, and for any readers who come with an assumed sense of superiority or inferiority with regards to their gender, you'll need to 'put off' such attitudes as they are part of the old order that is wasting away. This means also that, for the purpose of showing creation what God is like, we can only be the image-bearers we were made to be when we are together. Simply put, without one another we don't tell the full story. God's plan, therefore, is that our appreciation for one another runs both mutual and deep.

Speaking as a man, God's design in creation ought to leave me feeling that without meaningful and healthy female relationships in my life, I'm experiencing an incomplete sense of humanity, and with that, missing a vital part of God's image! As well as brothers and fathers, I need sisters and mothers in the Lord. I need them personally to help me grow and understand and appreciate the full image of God, and I need them standing shoulder to shoulder with me facing outwards as we engage with the mission of God to serve the rest of creation. Vice versa for women.

Focussing on marriage for a moment, please note also that God calls on the man and the woman to multiply. This union of male and female is both sacred and life-giving as man and woman in sweet intimacy fill creation with the divine image!

SELAH

Let's get physical

Perhaps the church hasn't always done well in this area of sex and the unavoidable physicality of it. The posture that casts a suspicious eye on the material realm is not a biblical one at all - God saw all that He had made and pronounced it to be good.

Perhaps the church has promoted a sense of guilt around our physicality and around the enjoyment of sexual intimacy, and in doing so, has de-spiritualised who we are as sexual beings. Now is an important time to reassert the truth of the divine ordering and design of our sexuality, and to celebrate that. This truth, of course, extends a lot further than the act of sex itself because healthy sexuality is not dependent on our being sexually active (see Jesus, Paul and countless other men and women down the ages), but the multiplication of the divine image, as the unique fruit of sexual intimacy, is a powerful and vivid demonstration that the union of male and female leads to life. In a culture that has divorced sex from procreation and sees it as nothing more than a means of personal pleasure, this is a rich and profound corrective.

Authority, Gender and the Divine Image

Please also see that authority and dominion over creation have been entrusted to mankind, that is, to men and women - not just to the men! Together we are to take responsibility for the well-being of the whole of creation, from the rich array of creatures, to the planet itself and all its phenomenal resources. We do this together as men and women, and if we stop doing this together, our rule will bear strange fruit. The end result will either be too masculine or too feminine, instead of the rich blend that God has ordained.

God has ordained us to care for the sacred creation. God has blessed us in it, and so we ought to expect to be fruitful. We have authority to do this, which means we have divine permission or 'freedom' to exercise spiritual power in it. There it is.

Mankind is male and female, together we image God, together we create more images of God, and together we are to rule over creation. Genesis 1 gives us the backdrop, the foundation, the initial idea. It's like the wash on a painter's canvas that goes on before everything else, and which everything else is then built upon, layer by layer. It's perhaps also worth noting, and it will come out more clearly as we move through the book, that within the being of God there are three distinct persons. We come across this mysterious plurality in Genesis 1 as God talks about creating mankind in 'Our' image. 'Our' is a plural word and yet God is one. Reflective of this, in the creation of humanity we see two distinct persons that make up this one category of mankind. Just as the persons of the Godhead, Father, Son and Spirit, are essentially equal, of the same substance, distinct and yet one, so the man and woman are essentially equal, of the same substance, distinct and yet, in their coming together, one. The word for their oneness, *echad,* is the same word used in the Shema[8] where it says the LORD your God is 'one'; it carries a sense of plurality within it.

I'm making this point now because we see it in Genesis 1, and also because analogous ideas are brought into the conversation about the Father, the Son and men and women as we go through the scriptures.[9] It has been suggested that because the other creatures (who aren't made in God's image) are also formed male and female, our sexuality is not essential to our imaging of God. While it's true that the other creatures

---

8   The Shema is a Jewish prayer comprising Deuteronomy 6:4-5 and 11:13-21, and Numbers 15:37-41. The first part encapsulates the monatheistic essence of God: "Hear, O Israel, the Lord is our God, the Lord is One".

9   It is currently a very live topic among theologians and scholars as to how appropriate or not it is to take the trinitarian nature of God and make parallels into the gender conversation. I am aware of this and will look to tread a careful path through, doing my best to avoid the pitfalls.

are also sexed, surely the fact that our gendered nature is explicitly mentioned at the creation of humanity in God's image, is significant. In fact, I would argue that the fact we are made in His image means that everything about us carries extra significance!

Agreed, we are part of the animal kingdom, we are fellow 'Day Sixers' along with the buffalo and the spiders, but there is a dimension to us that makes every part of us unique and special. All other creatures verbally communicate but the noises that come from our mouths are in a different class. They reflect God's own words, having the very power of life and death.[10] All creatures have minds, but the way we can reason and reflect and make sense of life is of a very different order to those not human. So, yes, we are also 'animals', but being made in His image adorns all of our faculties with unique divine meaning.

INTERLUDE

As we consider our mandate to rule creation, let's pause for a moment...

There are three different ways that people tend to approach creation. The first is when creation is treated as *divine*, where it's seen as some kind of god and is, therefore, in a sense, worshipped. The Mother Earth idea and many pagan practices come out of this belief as well as, to some extent, some of the major ancient Eastern religions. This is also becoming quite a common idea in the West - that God is everything and in everything; it's at the heart of what we tend to call 'New Age' spirituality. By deifying creation we end up worshipping and serving created things instead of the Creator. Not good.

The second is when creation is treated as *utilitarian*, where it's seen as simply here for our selfish purposes and personal pleasure. This belief leads us to do whatever we like with creation: whatever we like environmentally, whatever we like sexually, and whatever we like to those weaker than us. At the bottom of it is this idea that everything has been put here for our own priorities and purposes instead of His. In a sense, it's just another manifestation of worshipping and serving created things instead of the Creator, only this time that created thing is no longer 'Mother Earth' or dolphins or the ozone layer but 'me'. Not good.

The third is when creation is treated not as divine or utilitarian but as *sacred*. In this line of thinking, all things were made by God and ultimately for God, and therefore all things belong to God; humanity, as both part of God's creation and as ruling stewards of His creation, ought to treat everything, from the planet to

---

10   Proverbs 18 v 21.

other people, with a sense of awe, wonder and deep care. This approach puts us 'over' creation but only so far as we are 'under' the Creator, recognising that none of it is ultimately ours, but His. Good.

Furthermore

The second half of this first pillar is that Genesis chapter 2 does not carry sufficient weight to undermine or alter this equality. Let's look at this carefully.

This is the account of the heavens and the earth when they were created, when the LORD God made the earth and the heavens. Now no shrub had yet appeared on the earth and no plant had yet sprung up, for the LORD God had not sent rain on the earth and there was no one to work the ground, but streams came up from the earth and watered the whole surface of the ground. Then the LORD God formed a man from the dust of the ground and breathed into his nostrils the breath of life, and the man became a living being. Now the LORD God had planted a garden in the east, in Eden; and there he put the man he had formed. The LORD God made all kinds of trees grow out of the ground—trees that were pleasing to the eye and good for food. In the middle of the garden were the tree of life and the tree of the knowledge of good and evil. A river watering the garden flowed from Eden; from there it was separated into four headwaters. The name of the first is the Pishon; it winds through the entire land of Havilah, where there is gold. (The gold of that land is good; aromatic resin and onyx are also there.) The name of the second river is the Gihon; it winds through the entire land of Cush. The name of the third river is the Tigris; it runs along the east side of Ashur. And the fourth river is the Euphrates. The LORD God took the man and put him in the Garden of Eden to work it and take care of it. And the LORD God commanded the man, "You are free to eat from any tree in the garden; but you must not eat from the tree of the knowledge of good and evil, for when you eat from it you will certainly die." The LORD God said, "It is not good for the man to be alone. I will make a helper suitable for him." Now the LORD God had formed out of the ground all the wild animals and all the birds in the sky. He brought them to the man to see what he would name them; and whatever the man called each living creature, that was its name. So the man gave names to all the livestock, the birds in the sky and all the wild animals. But for Adam no suitable helper was found. So the LORD God caused the man to fall into a deep sleep; and while he was sleeping, he took one of the man's ribs and then closed up the place with flesh. Then the LORD God made a woman from the rib he had taken out of the man, and he brought her to the man. The man said, "This is now bone of my bones and flesh of

my flesh; she shall be called 'woman,' for she was taken out of man." That is why a man leaves his father and mother and is united to his wife, and they become one flesh. Adam and his wife were both naked, and they felt no shame.
GENESIS 2 V 4-25

Certainly, the equality we find in Genesis 1 is not undermined in Genesis 2. In fact, it's further underpinned. Adam's first statement on seeing Eve is not that she is from Venus and he is from Mars, that is to say, "Wow, aren't we really different?!"

No.

Rather, his first statement is "Bone of my bones and flesh of my flesh!" It's their similarity that strikes him.

The 17/18th century commentator Matthew Henry made the beautiful point that God did not take the woman from his head that she might be above him or from his feet that she might be beneath him, but from his rib that she might be alongside him. Amen to that. That she's taken out of him and then brought back to him by God means their coming together as one flesh is more than just a union - it's a reunion! The nakedness of their bodies, accompanied by a profound lack of shame, paints a picture of ease and confidence in one another's presence, the kind of unity and ease you find in a fellowship of equals.

As is made clear in Genesis 1, both are involved in the work of guarding and ruling creation, and as becomes clear in Genesis 3, both are held to account for the sin of disobedience against God's only prohibition. The picture that is being painted is one of partnership, interdependence and mutual accountability. That he needs a helper for the task that God charges him with seems to be speaking of his need, and certainly not her subservience. She is created to fill a gap that exists in his life without her. Whenever the word 'helper' (ezer) is used in the Old Testament, it's used to describe a role that brings assistance and aid to a situation of need - 15 out of 19 of those times that helper is God Himself! To describe this helper as a 'powerful ally', a term used by a number of egalitarian authors, is, it seems to me, completely appropriate.

This scenario doesn't just point to his need but also points to her sufficiency as a helper, messaging that this woman brings gifts and perspectives into the mix that are absolutely vital for what they are called to do together. He was mysteriously 'alone' without her, even though he had God!

SELAH

The situation is so serious that in the midst of God's good and sinless creation, him without her is described by God Himself as 'not good'. That she is targeted by the serpent in Genesis 3 can be taken in as many ways as we choose. For example, was she targeted because she was weaker and so the serpent went for the 'weakest link'? Or was she targeted because she carried the most influence and so if she was to fall then she'd most likely take him with her, which is essentially what happened? Or something else? We can only speculate but there are elements of the story that we can read either way.

Similarly with Adam naming Eve; some complementarians see this as a sure sign of his authoritative role in their relationship, but I'm not so sure. The fact that it happens directly after he has named the animals (surely an act of authority, given the charge in Genesis 1), hints that maybe it is. But, consider also: when Hagar ascribes to God the name 'The God Who sees', this by no means places her in an authoritative role over Him, so naming doesn't necessarily denote authority. I'm happy to sit on the fence on that one.

Up to this point, as we have in a sense focused the zoom lens onto the creation narrative in Genesis 2 (and a brief excursus in Genesis 3), nothing as yet seems to have suggested a clear complementarian pattern. Let's now move to the first argument of the complementarian side of things in order to dig further into Genesis 2.

Chapter Six
Equal and Some!
Complementarian Pillar One

Genesis 2 tells a story within a story. Adam and Eve are gloriously equal, but not interchangeable. Adam, alone in the garden, needs help that only Eve can bring. Before Eve is built from Adam, God entrusts Adam with a task and a command. This asymmetry speaks of his prominent responsibility and her unique contribution.

Some people have raised concerns that Genesis 1 and Genesis 2, on a number of levels, are contradictory. Really? The ancients may not have known all that we do, but that certainly didn't make them any less intelligent. If these accounts that exist side by side are contradictory, wouldn't this have been immediately apparent, and wouldn't it have been either erased or adjusted by the writer or later editors? If it's not contradictory then what is it? It's essentially just a more detailed account, an account that draws out different learning points. Below is a modern day example.

I could describe how Liverpool Football Club won the Premier League in the year 2019-2020 and how their passionately devoted fans cheered them on to the title, creating that unique atmosphere that only Anfield can. That's a true statement, but I may have to lay something else alongside it, something like this: during the latter half of the season there were no fans present due to the Coronavirus pandemic, and they played many games with virtual silence from the stands and no fans present. That's also true. The first statement is the big picture - by the time football resumed in the empty stadiums the league was as good as won, with Liverpool approximately 20 points ahead of everyone else, so the fans deserve their part of the credit. The second statement involves me zooming in and filling out some detail.

These first two chapters enrich and inform one another. Genesis 1 gives us the main idea and Genesis 2 adds layers of detail, both about the relationship between mankind and the rest of creation and the relationship between the man and the woman. As I mentioned earlier, the idea of layers can be very helpful. In our various fears and struggles, we sometimes over-simplify or flatten out certain revealed truths and at great cost. Genesis 1 is the foundation, the bottom line, the heart of the matter. Genesis 2 introduces another layer; add it in and we end up richer. Genesis 1 is particularly focused on the relationship the man and the woman have with the rest of creation - they are to subdue it, look after it and fill it.

But it says very little about the relationship *between* them. This is different in Genesis 2 - here, while the other animals and the garden remain in view, their relationship with each other is filled out.

Recap

Let's round up chapter two. The man (Adam) is created first, a mixture of dust and breath, and put into the garden in order to guard and keep it. He is told the rule about the tree - eat from whatever one you like except *that* one. Then God assesses that someone is missing. Adam, although he knows God, is considered by God to be 'alone'. It's not good for him to be alone. He needs a helpful companion and co-worker. Adam names all the animals as part of the searching-for-a-helper-exercise. None of the animals are appropriately fitting. God puts the man to sleep, removes part of him, and builds a woman from what's been removed. God brings her to him like a father walking his daughter down the aisle. Adam's very excited by what he sees and writes the world's first love song (the words in Hebrew rhyme). Theirs is the first marriage, naked and unashamed together.

Let's dig in again to Genesis 2, but this time we are looking for the strength of the complementarian argument above.

Narrative Theology

Firstly, remember that Genesis is a narrative, which means that we read it differently from how we read, say, the Psalms, or the ten commandments or the epistles. Of course a narrative, at its most basic level, simply describes what happened. However, we all realise that one of the main purposes of story-telling is to teach the listener. Whether it's to avoid the vanity of Snow White's stepmother or to stand up to bullies like the third billy goat gruff, we all remember the power of stories in our early years. And so there is what we might call 'narrative theology', where we might not find reams of explicit comments about what is right and wrong, but there are clear clues in the narrative to guide us. We need to keep a good eye out for that throughout much of the Old Testament.

Please note also, what we see here was pre-sin. There are only four chapters in the whole Bible that are outside the influence of sin - the first two and the last two, meaning that what we see here has not been influenced by the fall or the devil or any kind of darkness.

 SELAH

This means that, even though it's a narrative and therefore primarily descriptive, it's describing something entirely untainted. Egalitarians and complementarians both agree with this. Perhaps most pertinently of all, as mentioned above, the New Testament authors *do* point back to this narrative, and use what we find here to make what seem like spiritual points that are presented in a *binding* way upon believers. If we are to approach the narrative in the same way as the apostles did, we'll take note of what they infer from the narrative of Genesis 1 and 2, because both Jesus and the apostle Paul point back to the creation narrative and draw out deep spiritual meaning.

Not only must we be careful *not* to see things that aren't there, but we must also try to see things that *are* there, even if they're in symbols and suggestions - this takes sensitivity and discernment. When people say that the plain reading of a particular text doesn't yield certain truths or ideas and so those truths or ideas are therefore not in there, they perhaps have not quite understood how the scriptures work. For example, at first glance, without the New Testament, would we know that the speaking serpent is Satan himself? No, we wouldn't. We only know because other parts of the Bible tell us this is so.[1] Or, when we read about Noah's ark, do we see baptism? No. So how do we know it gives us a picture of baptism? Because Peter, in his first epistle, lets us know that this story corresponds to baptism.[2] Would we have known that the rock that Moses struck with his staff was representative of Christ?[3] Nope.

Therefore we ought not to be surprised if the creation and fall story is both a historical narrative and a theological gold mine of symbolic signposts. We obviously can't make up hidden meanings in the text, but where the rest of scripture reveals layers of meaning in other parts, then we, of course, accept it as true. Let's look at some of those layers.

Order!

Notice the asymmetry in Genesis 2 that we don't see in Genesis 1. Genesis 1 is full of pairings - day and night, earth and sky, male and female. It's a deliberate device and the rhythm is very symmetrical. As we zoom into the creation of Adam and Eve in Genesis 2, we come across a different rhythm, moving from straight rock to a jazz fusion! The man and the woman are not made at the same time or in the same way. Their interactions with God and the serpent also differ.

---

1   See 2 Corinthians 11 v 3, Romans 16 v 20 and Revelation 12 v 9.

2   1 Peter 3 v 20-21.

3   1 Corinthians 10 v 4.

A complementarian reading of Genesis 2 would say that the big deal is that whereas in chapter 1 there is no distinction concerning the *order* of the creation of the man and the woman, in chapter 2 there is.

This leads to the next question: Does that *mean* anything or is it simply incidental? 'Firstness' (for want of a better word) can be very meaningful; if you were the firstborn son in ancient cultures that would mean a lot; it would impact your life hugely. You would receive a double portion of the inheritance and would assume a unique kind of responsibility in the family. There are times when this order is deliberately over-turned,[4] so it's not 100% universal, but when this happens it's remarked upon because it is, for the most part, a recognised principle. Adam is God's firstborn son in the created order.[5] In 'Bible speak' this means something that becomes clear as the salvation story unfolds. The firstborn son motif is a signpost to Christ the true 'Firstborn Son' and heir of all things.[6]

Also, in the much disputed second chapter of Paul's first epistle to Timothy, Paul refers to Adam being formed first as significant in some way, and so we would do well to mark it and not overlook it.[7] At this stage of our study, we won't go much further on this, but it seems to mean *something*.

From and For...

Next, Eve is created *from* Adam - 1 Corinthians 11 v 8 is interested in this and considers it meaningful. As stated earlier, they are made of the same stuff - but there is more to it than that - God didn't just form them both directly out of the earth.

It's fascinating that when God says "Let us make man..." that word for 'man' is both the word for 'mankind' and 'Adam' and so some complementarians argue that it's because he, in some way, represents both of them as humanity; he has a 'representative role'. If this is so, this would potentially be a key concept that we need to become familiar with and take seriously.

Eve is also created *for* Adam, for his sake. Again, 1 Corinthians 11 v 8 is interested in this and considers it meaningful. As stated earlier, this points to his need for her, not her subservience. He has been given a job to do, but he can't do it alone.

---

4   For example Ishmael and Isaac, Jacob and Esau, Ephraim and Manasseh.

5   Luke 3 v 38.

6   Colossians 1 v 15.

7   1 Timothy 2 v 13.

But there is more to it. She is brought to him to help him with a job that he had previously been given to do. Sure, she is a powerful ally, but she is also to assist him in a job he was entrusted with before her creation. While the 'helper' motif in scripture never suggests the inferiority of the one bringing the aid, it almost always suggests that the one needing the help carries primary responsibility for the thing that requires assistance. This could be a very important point. To sum up: he was made first. She was made from him. She was made for him.

As we consider these points, it's important to remember that egalitarians are not against the idea that men and women complement one another; their only problem is with the idea of some sort of authority imbalance in the relationship. Do any or all of the above three points suggest an authority imbalance?

His 'firstness' could do. In many ancient societies, if you were the firstborn son, it would fall upon you to take responsibility for the family if and when the father died. This kind of responsibility would be akin to a seniority within the household that people would be encouraged to respect for the sake of orderliness. This was called 'primogeniture'. This doesn't determine the answer finally, and is overturned by God's elective choice numbers of times so we must be careful we don't place too much onto it, but it's an idea that is worth bearing in mind.[8]

Her being created *from* him doesn't obviously point to authority dynamics, but as we go through the study, we'll see that it might speak into something around showing honour to him as the one from whom she came. We can explore that as we go through and see if that's the case or not.

Her being created for him as a helper, while it doesn't denote subservience, it does denote assistance. Quite what this means in terms of an authority/power dynamic is hard to say, given that God is a helper to His people, suggesting, if anything, that the helper is the one who brings the powerful stuff! Assessing authority dynamics between the helper and the helped depends entirely on context, meaning that the idea of 'helper' isn't, by itself, determinative.

---

8   Some egalitarians have alternatively suggested that since humans, the pinnacle of God's creation, were created *last,* this could cast the idea of being created first in either a more *negative* or *ambivalent* light; that is to say, if God created humans last of all as the pinnacle, why should Adam's being created first represent anything significant? Complementarians respond that firstness only denotes prominent responsibility within the same category of being - to compare the order of creation between cows and humans and then between humans and humans is a classic case of what we, in England, call 'apples and oranges', which is a saying that means you're comparing things that are of different categories and therefore ought not to be compared.

In light of this, I think it's fair to say, at this stage of the study, that his firstness could be pointing to some kind of asymmetrical authority dynamic, but we must probe further. Perhaps the best way of doing this is by exploring, as best we can, *why* he was created first.

Entrustment

Scholars seem to agree that the garden of Eden was the first representation on Earth of God's temple.[9] We see the ultimate fulfilment of this in the new Jerusalem of Revelation 22, with vivid and unmistakable similarities between the two. There is also the fascinating parallel whereby in ancient times when people built a temple, the finishing touch was that an image of the temple's god would be placed inside. It's no coincidence, therefore, that as the image of God, Adam and Eve, are created climatically and placed in the garden at the end of God's creative work. After day six, the temple is ready!

Adam is given the command from God about the trees and he is commissioned with the work of the garden-temple, both before Eve is created. Why? If we don't ask that question or simply assume it's meaningless, it could be because we are avoiding something. We know once the serpent comes along that Eve has some kind of knowledge about the command, but we don't know from whom. (My tongue-in-cheek response is, from Adam, because she recalls it imperfectly, and husbands are infamously bad at communicating any details of previous conversations and interactions… maybe he only gave her the headlines and left her to fill in the gaps!)

In all seriousness, we know for sure that God explicitly entrusted the command to Adam, and I think that it stacks up that he, therefore, had a peculiar and unique level of stewardship and thus accountability in this matter - I think this becomes clearer as the story unfolds in both the next chapter of Genesis and the next chapter of this book. If this is the case, we could say that one of the reasons God created him first was in order to lay this responsibility on him; it was a deliberate and not an incidental act. We are also asking the question: why was he commissioned with the role of serving and protecting the garden before she was made? In order to answer this, we may have to delve even deeper.

Secret Garden?

I want to ask…is the woman, in some mysterious way, a garden within the garden that he is also called to serve and protect? Does this explain why he is charged with looking after the garden before Eve is created, because his service and protection of the garden operated on two different levels? Let's move for a moment to a book in the Bible that most likely gets the closest to Adam and Eve's existence before that

---

9   See the work of John Walton and Greg Beale as examples of this.

serpent came along. In the Song of Songs we have two lovers who spend a lot of time out in the garden naked together, like our original lovers.

But there's more...

> _You are a garden_ locked up, my sister, my bride; you are a spring enclosed, a sealed fountain. Your plants are an orchard of pomegranates with choice fruits, with henna and nard, nard and saffron, calamus and cinnamon, with every kind of incense tree, with myrrh and aloes and all the finest spices. _You are a garden fountain,_ a well of flowing water streaming down from Lebanon.
>
> SHE
>
> Awake, north wind, and come, south wind! _Blow on my garden,_ that its fragrance may spread everywhere. _Let my beloved come into his garden_ and taste its choice fruits.
>
> SONG OF SONGS 4 V 12-16 (EMPHASIS MINE)

Notice how the garden imagery is suddenly talking about something very different from literal fruit trees and other things previously enjoyed. She is the garden. In the space of five verses, this sensuous poetry takes us from garden locked (she has kept herself for him), to garden fountain flowing (she gives herself to him).[10] She is explicit that she herself is his garden. It was Rabbi Akiva (50-135CE) who described the Song of Songs as "the holiest of holies". No surprise. Its vivid depiction of intimate love takes us to new heights in understanding both the Creator's love for His people and His affirmation of marital intimacy.

Back to Eden. We have a garden that is a temple. The man, this son of God, is put in the garden to serve and protect it. It becomes apparent that he needs help. She is then given to him to help him. How will she help him? Well, God entrusts this precious beauty that He has personally built, to Adam. She's not just going to help him in the garden, perhaps she is also going to help him _as_ his garden. In light of the Genesis 1 mandate to multiply, he is all seed and no garden - he needs her help! God builds Eve with the extraordinary capacity to literally incubate the divine image within her very body. Is that all she can do? Of course not. Is it what she can uniquely do? Yes.

Now we see that Eve is not just a garden. Like Eden, she also is a garden-temple.

---

10   See Proverbs 5 v 15-19 as explicit confirmation of this meaning.

Imagine if men understood that the heart of God's creative plan placed them as servants (not masters), and protectors (not predators), of the women in their lives.

Summing up

A closer look at the creation story leads me to think that it's not appropriate to simply say the same for the man as you would for the woman. Genesis 1 gives us equality as a foundation; everything that is said of one is said of the other. Genesis 2 underpins that equality, or sameness, with phrases like "bone of my bones and flesh of my flesh".[11] But other nuances are added, and if we are going to be true to the text regarding men and women, we must make room for this. I believe that his being created first, and being entrusted with the command about the tree, and the guarding and keeping of the garden-temple, was a deliberate act on the Lord's part for him to feel a unique responsibility as both servant and protector of Eve and doctrinal steward.

Concerning authority, if God set him apart in these matters then he is of course authorised to do them. Having said that, as far as I am concerned, this is a world away from him having authority over her - I can't see that in the text.

INTERLUDE

As you've probably realised, the title of this book is a deliberate play on words. Gender equality is one of the big talking points in the world right now, and rightly so. But. I don't think the equality of the genders is the *main* message of the Bible. The reason I bring this up is that we can sometimes find ourselves on a bit of a wild goose chase when we end up trying to get the Bible to talk about things that we are particularly focused on, but that *it* isn't. Scripture is more interested in *unity* between men and women. As the story of salvation develops, the twinned themes of unity and diversity become very apparent as key markers for life in the Kingdom. Whether it's to do with Jews and Gentiles, or slaves and freedmen, or men and women, or varying giftedness, there is this repeated emphasis of one body (unity) and many members (diversity). The Bible never dissolves unity into uniformity and never confuses diversity with division.

---

11   Genesis 2 v 23.

God, in His unsearchable wisdom, can do things that people, in their own wisdom, can't. He can bring different people together and make them one, while maintaining their distinctives. It's this coming together of those who are the same but different, different but the same, imaging the One who created them. Gender quality.

———————————————

Chapter Seven
Household Rep: Complementarian Pillar Two

Humanity is a household. God appointed Adam as head of the house, which is why he is uniquely blamed for the human predicament. With headship comes representative responsibility. The coming of the woman's seed brings hope as a new head appears - One who will crush the enemy!

To put the egalitarian and complementarian conversation to one side for a moment, it's important to draw attention to the fact that the Bible presents to us a particular worldview that is quite different from the Western worldview. This idea of households as the fundamental societal building block is quite foreign to Western ears - we think primarily in terms of the individual, and then in terms of the nuclear family, and then in terms of macro structures like government, etc.

Let's try to get to grips with the household idea. Back in the day, a household would consist not just of parents and children but any number of servants and relatives. Ever wondered how Abraham had 318 trained men in his house when he went to rescue his cousin Lot who had been kidnapped? In order to understand the concept of households as a spiritual reality, it's important to say that being a member of a household does not negate your own individual status. Both are actually tied together and though what household you are part of will very much impact upon your experience as an individual, it won't nullify or overrule it.

The first household to consider is that of humanity as a whole. We are God's earthly family - we all trace our lineage from Him. The idea of the whole of humanity being 'in Adam' and therefore 'fallen' and 'in sin', is based on humanity being considered before God as a household, with Adam as the head or representative of us all. Now, just as Adam is considered the 'head' of fallen humanity, so Christ is most certainly the head of redeemed humanity.[12] From that perspective we see that through Christ, the household of humanity has been made into two households, with Adam as head of the first and fallen humanity and Jesus as head of the second and redeemed humanity. So...more profound than the colour of your skin or your age or gender is whether or not you are 'in Adam' or 'in Christ', as this determines your standing before God. True, this is

---

12   Romans 5 v 12-21, 1 Corinthians 15 v 45, 47, Ephesians 5 v 23.

something of a foreign idea to a culture that is increasingly built upon and only concerned with individual identity and rights, but it's most certainly a very real 'thing' biblically.

Considering that humanity in Christ (also known as the church or the body of Christ) is called the household of God more than once in the New Testament,[13] the picture becomes clearer and clearer.

Where is Adam representing?

Let me try to show you where I think perhaps we can see the concept of this 'headship', or 'household representation' in the second and third chapters of Genesis.

God, when walking in the garden in the cool of the day, explicitly asks where *he* is; He knows what's happened and could it be that He is looking for the person primarily responsible? This would make sense of that.

Adam is rebuked for listening to the voice of his wife, not because husbands shouldn't listen to their wives (most should a lot more than they do!), but could it be because he had been entrusted with the commandment directly from God and instead of listening to His voice, he yielded to her voice which was, in this instant, a contrary voice? This would make sense of that.

Adam's judgement from God impacts upon the actual planet (contrasting with Eve's more local judgement). Could it be that the commission to tend the garden sat with him in a unique way? This would make sense of that.

Fast forward a few thousand years and Paul says that sin came into the world through one *man;* could it be that he uniquely represented *us!* This would make sense of that.

The complementarian proposal is that he was created first and given the job and command first, because God chose him to carry a unique stewardship for those things. He is therefore primarily accountable. Not exclusively accountable. But primarily and representatively so. That is the complementarian perspective. I think it's important that we don't dismiss it. Firstly because it holds together like a cord with a number of continuous threads. Secondly, because it carries within it a pretty huge gospel point, and here it is...

The Bible teaches that in the same way that Adam blew it for humanity, that somehow we were all *in* him, as he sinned, and in doing so we all wound up charged as guilty and corrupted through that act.[14] In the

---

13   Ephesians 2 v 19, 1 Timothy 3 v 15, 1 Peter 4 v 17, Hebrews 3 v 6.

14   Romans 5 v 12.

same way, Jesus has rescued humanity, and for all of us that are *in* Him through faith, we are counted as righteous and made brand new through *His* one act of obedience.[15] It's a like-for-like comparison and you find it in Romans 5 v 12-21. The point is that if you don't like the idea of what the theologians call 'federal headship', then you potentially end up removing a pretty hefty plank of the gospel.

It's a funny idea for Westerners - this idea that we don't all simply stand alone. Yes we are known by name and adopted through Christ as beloved and chosen individuals. Yes we will be individually held to account. But the idea of households and headship does NOT negate this. It *adds* to this by revealing that God *also* considers us to be under a head, either Adam or Jesus.

These two historical figures represent one theological truth, that our standing with God and our spiritual condition is determined ultimately by which one of these men we are united with. The Bible teaches that we are born in Adam, and so by nature we are all united with him and thus fallen in sin. The Bible also teaches that, through faith, we can move out from our union with Adam and into union with Jesus Christ. In that moment we move out of Adam's disobedience and into Christ's obedience, thus moving out of Adam's guilt and into Christ's righteousness, and consequently out of Adam's death and into Christ's life!

Perhaps one key phrase, when trying to understand the context of headship, is 'representative responsibility'. This means that God has established an order in relationships whereby in any given household, someone will be entrusted with a unique measure of responsibility for the condition of that household. They will carry that household representatively before God, and will have a unique responsibility of ensuring the maximum flourishing of all those involved.

Same Piece of Fruit, Different Sin

I have not found an egalitarian argument that comes close to making sense of why Adam was held primarily responsible. Twice the New Testament talks about Eve's deception.[16] But when referring to Adam, it talks about transgression and trespass.[17] Why? The nature of their sin was different. He gets primary blame because he transgressed a command he was explicitly given by God. It seems hard to escape the fact that 'something is going on here'.

In conclusion, I'm saying that while I agree that Genesis 2 in no way undermines the equality in worth and value of both the personhood and contribution of man and woman (a foundation firmly laid in Genesis 1 and

---

15 Romans 5 v 18-19.

16 1 Timothy 2 v 14, 2 Corinthians 11 v 3.

17 Romans 5 v 14-15.

re-affirmed in Genesis 2), it does seem that the asymmetry of the creation and fall narrative adds a layer onto that.

Perhaps it's a good moment to highlight that the equality of any two objects does not denote their being identical. Things can be equal and yet different. Two people can contribute differently to the same cause in ways that carry equal value.

Egalitarians and complementarians alike agree on this.

The key question, at the end of this section, is to ask whether or not I see a unilateral authority in the relationship between Adam and Eve.

I think that his being created first, and the commandment and commission coming before Eve's creation, along with the manner in which he is held to account by God, all taken together, suggests to me that he carries a unique representative responsibility on behalf of them as a married unit. What that means in terms of the authority dynamic between them, at this point in the story, I'm not sure I could say.

This is because, while it is clear that the sun was to rule over the day and the moon was to rule over the night, and that Adam and Eve were to rule over the rest of creation in Genesis 1, it is *not* stated at any point in chapters 1 and 2 that he was to rule over her.

The only time it is said that he will rule over her (same Hebrew word) is in Genesis 3, which is essentially linked to sin and judgement, not original design (we'll go there in a minute). Because of this, we must tread very carefully in how we speak about these matters. Maybe a word on authority...

INTERLUDE

Let me start with an illustration. When I was 16 years old I learnt how to touch type. I'm so glad I did, as it's made at least one thing about writing this book easy! But the key is this - you have to start with your hands in the right place, it all hangs on that. Let me show you what happens if you start with your hands in the wrong place:

ura BUXW St qw;ew gCUBF UR=AB;R UR,

That was me literally typing 'It's a nice day we're having, isn't it?' The problem was that even though my fingers worked (almost) perfectly, because the starting position was wrong, the end result was utter nonsense.

I think that many people have completely the wrong idea when it comes to authority. The Greek lexicons define the word 'authority' as 'liberty'. It means that if you have authority to do a particular thing, you have the freedom to do it, the jurisdiction, the permission. It means that you are not restrained or held back but that you have a 'green light'.

Genuine spiritual authority is, for a large part, to do with spiritual permission to exert power over demons.[18] In the Kingdom, rather than ruling over people, it is better to think of serving people and ruling over demonic enemy intruders.

When thinking of human household relationships, we might prefer the phrase 'authority on behalf of' rather than 'authority over'.

While the word 'over' is used in the New Testament to describe the relationship between leaders and members of the church,[19] and the term 'overseer' is a frequent term used to describe church leaders, I think the idea of having an overview, looking over the flock protectively and having a good sense of what is going on is very appropriate. Having authority over church members in a way that moves into 'lording it over' is not at all appropriate.

Therefore, if someone is leading a household, what does godly or spiritual authority look like? We might suggest that it's the liberty from God to deal with demonic intrusions and attacks upon that household. It has nothing to do with lording it over people; that's a worldly idea; and the whole world is under the power of the devil.[20]

You won't find a situation where God gives believers authority to simply impose their will on others.

Healthy spiritual authority never impinges upon issues of equality, but does require the person entrusted to step into the role faithfully, and the person/people on the receiving end to willingly receive what's being given. Without this, everything grinds to a halt.

All believers have authority from Christ over the enemy, but the issue and question in this book revolves around these two matters:

---

18 See Luke 9 v 1 where the ESV and KJV make it clear that the word 'epi' in Greek, which means 'over' is used with regards to the apostles' power dynamics towards demons but in the same sentence makes it clear that they have power to cure diseases. Power over demons and power to cure diseases. Fascinating. Authority is the permission, the liberty to exercise God's power in these various ways.

19 1 Thessalonians 5 v 12 refers in the ESV and KJV as those 'over you in the Lord' when talking about leaders.

20 1 John 5 v 19.

- Does the husband have a particular liberty from God to do this in marriage?

- Should the elders, who do have a particular liberty from God to do this in church, only be men?

We have a lot of ground to cover yet, but on this point I think it's most honest to concede that something meaningful, along the lines of unique male responsibility on a household level, is going on in the created order we find in Genesis 2. What that means for the fall, what that means for the new creation, what that means for us who live 'in between the ages', well, we'll see.

Let's move together on to the second egalitarian pillar.

Chapter Eight
Bad Rule:
Egalitarian Pillar Two

Genesis 3 makes it clear that the dominion of a man over a woman, is a result of God's judgement on their sin of disobedience and is therefore never an expression of God's perfect will or original design but rather the result of a fallen world.

Genesis 3 is a chapter full of tragedy and pain.

> Now the serpent was more crafty than any of the wild animals the LORD God had made. He said to the woman, "Did God really say, 'You must not eat from any tree in the garden'?" The woman said to the serpent, "We may eat fruit from the trees in the garden, but God did say, 'You must not eat fruit from the tree that is in the middle of the garden, and you must not touch it, or you will die.'" "You will not certainly die," the serpent said to the woman. "For God knows that when you eat from it your eyes will be opened, and you will be like God, knowing good and evil." When the woman saw that the fruit of the tree was good for food and pleasing to the eye, and also desirable for gaining wisdom, she took some and ate it. She also gave some to her husband, who was with her, and he ate it. Then the eyes of both of them were opened, and they realised they were naked; so they sewed fig leaves together and made coverings for themselves. Then the man and his wife heard the sound of the LORD God as he was walking in the garden in the cool of the day, and they hid from the LORD God among the trees of the garden. But the LORD God called to the man, "Where are you?" He answered, "I heard you in the garden, and I was afraid because I was naked; so I hid." And he said, "Who told you that you were naked? Have you eaten from the tree that I commanded you not to eat from?" The man said, "The woman you put here with me—she gave me some fruit from the tree, and I ate it." Then the LORD God said to the woman, "What is this you have done?" The woman said, "The serpent deceived me, and I ate." So the LORD God said to the serpent, "Because you have done this, "Cursed are you above all livestock and all wild animals! You will crawl on your belly and you will eat dust all the days of your life. And I will put enmity between you and the woman, and between your offspring and hers; he will crush your head, and you will strike his heel." To the woman he said, "I will make your pains in childbearing very severe; with painful labour you will give birth to children. Your desire will be for your husband, and he will rule over you." To Adam he said, "Because you listened to your wife and ate fruit from the tree about which I commanded you, 'You must not eat from it,' "Cursed is the

ground because of you; through painful toil you will eat food from it all the days of your life. It will produce thorns and thistles for you, and you will eat the plants of the field. By the sweat of your brow you will eat your food until you return to the ground, since from it you were taken; for dust you are and to dust you will return."
GENESIS 3 V 1-19 (EMPHASIS MINE)

This second key egalitarian argument rests on the interpretation of this phrase that the Lord says to Eve:

"Your desire will be for your husband, and he will rule over you."
GENESIS 3 V 16

Whereas before, it was all naked and unashamed and eating passion fruit in their lunch breaks, from now on things are going to change.

What Women Want

We are told that going forward, her desire would be for him or contrary towards him (due to the nuances in the wording, different translations take different approaches), but that he would rule over her. What does this phrase mean? There is difficulty with the two key words, 'desire' and 'rule'.

Let's start with desire. Is her desire for or against him? It's not clear, though most of what I've read seems to suggest that 'for' is more likely. In what sense her desire will be for him is not easy to discern. It could simply be a part of the statement that isn't inherently negative, but then coupled with his rule over her becomes so. Let me explain. In Song of Songs the woman says:

I belong to my beloved, and his desire is for me.
SONG OF SONGS 7 V 10

This is clearly a positive idea and the word used is the same as in Genesis 3. So, it could be saying that while her desire for her husband remains, rather than him reciprocating in a healthy way, he moves towards her with an inappropriate rule or dominance. It could mean that. Alternatively it could mean that her desire for him is somehow distorted to the point where it is no longer healthy. It could mean that she needs him a bit too much and yet he will take advantage of her by dominating her. All of us can probably think of people or relationships where this seems to be the reality.

It could be pointing to the idea that certain realities that existed between them, before the fall, are mutually skewed in this moment. Let me explain. She was made for him and so longed to be with him, but in the fall begins to overly need him in a dysfunctional and unhealthy way. He was made first and had some kind of leadership role, but through the fall this distorts to become dominating and ruling. This works because we know that sin, rather than creating new realities, essentially just distorts already existing realities. But an egalitarian wouldn't appreciate this theory, because they simply cannot entertain the idea that before the fall Adam had some kind of leadership responsibility.

There's one further option to consider and it's a bit of an outlier. It could mean that, while her desire remains for him, he now rules over her, not necessarily in a negative way, but in a way that will actually afford her some measure of protection in a fallen world. This interpretation affirms male rule, not as God's original design, but more as a kindness from God in what is now a dangerous world. This is neither a typical complementarian or egalitarian perspective. I found it thought-provoking when I first came across it,[1] but I don't find this option particularly convincing; to have her desire as a negative and his protective rule as a positive confuses more than it clarifies. It seems to make much more sense for the pairing to contain two positives or two negatives and seeing as it's judgement I think it's clear that it will be negative.

INTERLUDE

It's so important that we bear in mind that Genesis 3 isn't God introducing malicious dynamics from a place of spite; instead it's God essentially acknowledging that the man and woman have chosen to go their own way, and so He is giving them over to what they have chosen. It's a bit like God saying: "This is what you want? OK, what you have chosen looks like this." Simply put, from now on this is how it is going to be.

Something that Christians often don't realise, and I think it's very pertinent to this story, is that the most common way the judgement of God is expressed, in this age at least, is that He gives us over to the things that we, in our sinfulness, choose to do. Let me show you what I mean from the infamous passage on human sinfulness that we find in Romans 1 v 18-32. The section begins with saying that the wrath of God is being revealed from heaven on all ungodliness and unrighteousness. To set the context for that, he talks about the way humanity deliberately and wilfully suppresses the truth of His existence, and instead goes after created things and worships and serves them.

Then come three hammer blows when we find the repeated phrase, "God gave them up..." in verses 24, 26 and 28. He gave them up in the lusts of their heart to impurity (v 24), He gave them up to dishonourable passions (v 26), and He gave them up to a debased mind (v 28). This is the way Paul understands the wrath

---

1   Richard M Davidson - Flame of Yahweh; an egalitarian scholar.

of God: that when you see someone abandoned to those things, you are witnessing a manifestation of the wrath of God.

The day will come when God will more proactively execute judgement, but in this age, God's disapproval is most often manifest by His _lack_ of intervention; the things that humanity in general chooses, from a place of sin, He simply lets us do. That's how we know He's angry about it. Sobering.

Some Sad Realities

Now let's think about his 'rule' over her. Again, the word itself isn't necessarily negative. The first chapter of Genesis speaks of the rule of the sun over the day, the rule of the moon over the night, and the rule of Adam and Eve over creation - all designed and declared by God to be good.

But context matters. And the context here is judgement. There will be a shift in the way they relate. He will now rule over her. It was never God's original design for things to be this way, but this is now how it will be. They are being given over to disorder. We must clearly see the truth that God did not create things in such a way that a man should rule over a woman. Wherever we land on our understanding of godly and renewed gender relations, we mustn't land there.

While the various ruling dynamics in the original creation were ordered and fruitful, this ruling dynamic that appears between Adam and Eve after the fall, is the opposite. This is why a man's involvement in a woman's life is often either restrictive or oppressive or controlling or patronising or domineering or threatening or dictatorial. In case you were in any doubt, this is all wrong and where it is taking place, deep repentance is needed. It is not in the created design of God for men to rule over women; they are created to rule creation together. In light of this, I agree wholeheartedly with this second egalitarian pillar.

Genesis 3 is the epicentre of an earthquake whose tremors we see in every news report of rape, injustice, adultery, divorce, murder, oppression and violence; that's where it started, and we must give it the weight it deserves, shaping our worldview sufficiently. We ignore it at our peril.

Chapter Nine
Power Struggle: Complementarian Pillar Three

The fall introduces us to a cursed power struggle between men and women. Women will struggle with warped desires towards men and men will use their superior physical strength to dominate women. The harmony is over - blame and shame are now the name of the game.

The traditional complementarian perspective is that men carry representative responsibility for their households from the beginning, but now Eve fights against Adam in this role. This is how she falls. Adam, rather than manifesting gentleness and humility, will instead use his superior physical strength to dominate or rule over her. This is how he falls.

I tried to demonstrate earlier that I think there is enough asymmetry and meaningful nuance in the creation account of Genesis 2, the fall in Genesis 3, and then the commentary on how sin entered the world later in Romans 5, to suggest that Adam, as representative head, has been layered onto the foundation of equality that we find in Genesis 1. This is something that I believe existed prior to the fall as part of God's good creation.

If this scenario is true, then our focus on understanding the curse in Genesis 3 shifts from some kind of inherent problem with men as heads of households to a more mutual problem of tension between men and women - essentially a power struggle. Let's look at how a complementarian would understand the Genesis 3 passage, where it says her desire would be for him and he would rule over her.

Parallel Passages?

Maybe it's no coincidence that in Genesis 4 we find exactly the same phrase used in a very different context. Adam and Eve's firstborn, Cain, is planning on murdering his younger brother, Abel. God warns him against it and uses this exact same phrase, telling him that sin's desire is for/against him, but that he must rule over it.

"If you do what is right, will you not be accepted? But if you do not do what is right, sin is crouching at your door; <u>it desires to have you, but you must rule over it</u>."
GENESIS 4 V 7 (EMPHASIS MINE)

Identical words used in Hebrew. And the meaning here is clear. War. Sin wants to wield the influence over Cain, have the sway, determine his actions, gain mastery. Cain is to tread sin down - he is to rule over it. If this phrase is being used in the same way to describe what happens to Adam and Eve as a result of the fall, then this seems to be suggesting that her desire will be for him in terms of wanting some kind of mastery over him, and he will tread her down and rule over her.

If you have a complementarian understanding of creation then this makes sense - the harmony is over and now we have a power struggle. The man's unique responsibility is being challenged by her and he turns to domineering oppression.

The fact that it's the only place where you'll find the identical phrase, and it appears so close to the passage in question, may well give us reason to believe that the passage in Genesis 4 indeed sheds much light on the meaning of our passage in Genesis 3.

A complementarian would want to highlight the text of Genesis 3 v 16, and draw our attention to the fact that God brings judgement on both of them as they both sinned, and that this will eat away at the previously healthy dynamic they enjoyed. They will now be dysfunctional. It will involve a man using his strength inappropriately. But it will also involve something dark in the heart of a woman.

A man may shout, a woman may manipulate. A man may strike, a woman may humiliate.

A man may threaten, a woman may tease. A man may use, a woman may be overly needy. Both are against God's original design. Both have at their root either desires to get one over on the other, or desires ultimately centred on one another rather than on God - this is all wrong.

The complementarian says that, as in Genesis 4, where sin's 'desire' for Cain aims at influencing and swaying him to its own plans and purposes, similar will be Eve's 'desire' for Adam. She will not move in unison with him, but will want to strike out by herself.

There is a kind of 'rule' a man has over a woman that is a part of the fall, and that is to be absolutely done away with when we come into relationship with Christ. There is a kind of 'desire' a woman has towards a man that is a part of the fall, and that is to be absolutely done away with when we come into relationship with Christ.

Let each of us search our hearts.

What's vital to note is that for the most part throughout human history, men have won in the power struggle, and therefore women have often been disenfranchised and marginalised when it comes to power and influence in the church, as well as in the world.

He will Wipe Away every Tear

I was in conversation with a woman recently about this book and about the subject of gender in general. This was a very God-fearing, humble, academically minded woman who is committed to scripture. During our conversation about gender, I was making the point that if I could find sufficient scriptural content on the matter, I would happily be egalitarian. At that point she burst out crying. We were both surprised. After she composed herself, she confessed that she had been surprised at her own emotional response to my words, and her reflection was simply this: "When you said that, it felt really kind." Deep waters.

When complementarians see that the issue of men and women is not simply a theological one but also a matter of justice and kindness, at that point something significant has happened. We ignore this at the peril of God's glory in the church, the church's witness to the world, and the experience of countless women.[1] If women feel disempowered, marginalised, overlooked or dismissed in the church, something is seriously wrong and we must look into it. Where fallenness is at work in the church unchecked, we must undo it decisively.

While societal structures that are systemically oppressive or even questionable ought to be challenged, complementarians insist male headship is *not* an inherently oppressive structure. Hidden heart attitudes however, can definitely lead to oppressive behaviour regardless of structures. We are the community that is supposed to be marked by redemption and restoration - in Christ the old has gone and the new has come! Make way for the new. Anything less is simply not Christian.

Regarding this pillar, I can see how it holds together from the biblical text and how it helpfully shines the spotlight on both men and women. The argument doesn't work if there is no such thing as headship before the fall, but if there is, and I think there is, then it works very naturally.

---

1   Many complementarians will say they believe that God calls women to leadership as well as men. And yet there is often this carelessness with language when the default term in complementarian churches is 'leaders and wives'. This sort of language disenfranchises both women and the unmarried in one fell swoop. This isn't about treading on eggshells with our language; it's about having our minds renewed, about thinking more Biblically. Our words are the overflow of our heart. Let's do the work of allowing the scriptures to wash us repeatedly so that better words come out of our mouths.

Chapter Ten
Patriarchal Pollution: Egalitarian Pillar Three

The patriarchal backdrop of the society in which the biblical narrative is set, is a result of Genesis 3. The male/female dynamic we see is not prescriptive of how life in God's Kingdom should be, but merely descriptive of what life in a fallen world is like, with occasional redemptive rays of hope shining through.

This will be the only point in the book where I focus on the bulk of the Old Testament. In this debate, because complementarians don't seem to focus as much on this part of the Bible as egalitarians, I've not included a complementarian pillar that focuses here. As a result, there will inevitably, in this chapter, be a bit of back and forth between the views, rather than a straightforward presentation of the egalitarian perspective above. My main aim in this chapter, however, is still to assess the above argument.

What exactly is patriarchy? Defined simply, it's a blend of two Greek words. The first is 'father' (patria) and the second is 'rule' (arche). So essentially, it means that a household is ruled by the father. If only it were that simple! There is no denying that the word now is immediately associated with male oppression of women. As I said in the last chapter, if that's what we mean by patriarchy, we must reject it outright.

Considering that one definition of patriarchy is, in at least a linguistic sense, how the church operates as a household under the rule of Father God, it's a concept that needs careful handling.

When considering Israel in the Old Testament, how we read the text is, again, determined by our understanding of creation. If you read with complementarian lenses, you may see the emphasis on the men as simply reflecting their representative roles in households. If you read with egalitarian lenses, you may see more of a manifestation of a fallen backdrop that needs a revolution. I wonder if there may be some truth in both.

As we explore this pillar, may I be a little cheeky and ask if egalitarians are perhaps guilty of wanting to have their cake and eat it. In what sense? It's common in their writings to denounce the Old Testament patriarchy of Israel as oppressive for women, and then insist on demonstrating how women in the Old Testament carried positions of significant leadership and ministry. Which one is it? Surely either it's oppressive and *therefore* there are no significant women leaders, or it isn't oppressive and *therefore* there are.

Not that complementarians are innocent! It's common to detect a seeming lack of concern from them when it comes to passages in the Old Testament that *could* signal the comparative devaluing of the woman. This can be confusing and painful for women.

We'll have to do our best to pick through what's what, avoiding unhelpful extremes.

INTERLUDE

Over the few years that I've been writing this book, and as I've been in conversation with different people, at times I've heard, and have myself also thought, that it would be much easier to move to a more extreme position. What I mean is that sometimes it seems a bit more straightforward to either be patriarchal or feminist; at least that way the lines are clearer and there's way less nuance.

Increasingly, the world of complementarianism feels like a highly complex dance in which none of those involved have the same version of the steps.

But of late, I've found a deeper and deeper desire to see if we can 'thread the needle'. If we stop to think about Christian doctrine, so much of it involves doing exactly this. Whether it's about God's sovereignty and our free will, or whether it's about the possibility of losing our salvation, or whether it's about the place of ethnic Israel in the purposes of God - you may disagree, but I find all three of those major subjects only remain simple if I refuse to engage with those outside my tribe; when I do engage, I find myself deeply challenged.

I remain a convinced 'baptist' by conviction but I still remember the disorientation I felt when I read my first decent defence of paedo-baptism!

I don't know if there is a name for where I will land in this book, but I remain gripped and fascinated by the possibility that the truth might be richer and deeper than simply this or that.

Let's look at the Old Testament together. It's a large part of our Bible, and it would be unrealistic to think we might survey the whole thing, but we will try to spot some trends as well as some of the more outstanding examples.

The early chapters of Genesis directly after the fall are pretty grim and conclude with the flood as a judgement on corrupt mankind. In these chapters we see murder, polygamy, violence, revenge and, depending on how you read it, either certain men or fallen angels, intoxicated by female beauty, taking women for themselves. It becomes clear, through the flood, that God hates the violence and the wickedness that is now firmly embedded in the human heart. There is no tolerance in God's character for such conduct, and it grieves Him to the point of some mysterious kind of regret at ever creating us![1] This gives us a firm foundation that vengeful violence will not be tolerated among the people of God. The Bible recognises that not all violence is physical, and that our words can be just as damaging as a literal sword swipe.[2] Whether verbal or physical, it is condemned.

This is relevant for our point around patriarchy because, unfortunately, in many of the ancient and contemporary patriarchal cultures of the world, violence against the women of one's own household is often culturally tolerated, legally permitted, or overlooked by the authorities.

I think this happens because in some patriarchal cultures there is an underlying belief that women are inferior in some way, whether intellectually, socially or morally. With that ideology comes a kind of dismissive posture on the part of men, and it creates room for certain vile and wholly unjustified attitudes to grow around what is and isn't OK in the treatment of women.[3]

Let me say once and for all that there is no teaching in scripture either explicit or implicit that men are superior. It is sadly true that many Christian theologians down the ages seem to have taught this, but it's not true and cannot be found in the Bible. We must deal with erroneous ideologies if we are going to deal with erroneous behaviour. All churches, whether complementarian or egalitarian, must be as far removed from any kind of oppression or violence as night is from day. The Old Testament affirms this.

---

1   Genesis 6 v 6.

2   Proverbs 18 v 21.

3   We must never overestimate the power of ideology. The horrors of Hitler's Germany and ISIS serve as potent reminders that the deep narratives and truths to which we hold provide the seedbed for our attitudes and behaviour. We must allow God to get deeply into us with the beauty of the creation and salvation story if we are to see fullness of life between the sexes.

One Plus One Makes One

Let's keep going.

In the creation narrative we are told that one man is to marry one woman, and that the man is to leave his parents and be fully joined to his wife. We know that this is God's ideal for marriage, as re-affirmed by Jesus himself. This tells us that although God tolerated polygamy under the Old Testament, He never designed us for it. It becomes clear as we move through the story of salvation and into the New Testament that it's not part of His original plan. A husband is to be fully committed to his wife, heart, mind, body and soul. Remember what we looked at earlier, what I called 'narrative theology', where we might not always get explicit condemnation of certain actions, but there are enough clues in the text to serve as a 'Don't go there!' sign? Here are a couple of examples…

In Genesis 4 v 23-24 we read of Lamech, who is seventh from Adam through the line of Cain, and in Genesis 5 we read of Enoch, who is seventh from Adam through the line of Seth. The number seven in the Bible represents completion. The line of Seth is the godly line, and Enoch, as seventh, represents the ultimate heights of godly humanity - a man who walked so closely with God that he actually cheated death as God simply *took* him!

The line of Cain is the ungodly line, and Lamech, as seventh, represents the ultimate lows of ungodly humanity, and look at what marks him out - polygamy and violence.

In Genesis 26 Esau marries two Hittite women, and we are told that they make life bitter for his parents, Isaac and Rebekah. In Genesis 28 Isaac makes clear that Jacob mustn't follow suit. The messaging is obvious - polygamy and marrying foreign women are not good things (on the matter of marrying foreign women, it's not to do with ethnicity but to do with religion - a foreign woman would bring her foreign gods with her into the home, because only Israel worshipped Yahweh; that was the problem).

Other examples are Jacob's polygamy with Rachel and Leah (what a mess), Hannah's rivalry with Peninnah (full of pain), Solomon's 700 wives (just wow).

God, in His redemptive sovereignty, brings good out of a lot of these situations, but we are not protected from the mess and the pain involved in these stories, and this gives us a clear message about polygamy - don't go there. It is hard to know precisely why God's response to polygamy is less harsh than to other expressions of marital sin. Perhaps it was part of what theologians call 'divine accommodation'. This is the idea that God will accommodate certain non-ideal scenarios with a degree of pragmatism, not as a stamp of His approval, but in order to make the best of a bad situation.[4]

In the Footsteps of Giants

Let's keep walking through the Old Testament.

Let's consider Sarah and Abraham. God called Abram and spoke to him and made him promises. By virtue of Sarai being his wife, she was caught up on this faith journey with him in a way that was manifestly uncomfortable at times. Bear in mind the promise was a child. Bear in mind that she was his wife. Bear in mind that she couldn't have children.

You might think that God would have spoken to her directly at the start of the journey…why didn't He? Well, a complementarian would suggest that He did. How so? In promising Abraham, God promised her. If the New Testament went quiet on this, then we might be left to speculate that maybe God speaking directly to Abraham in this way was simply an example of God ordering His ways in light of the patriarchal backdrop. But the apostle Peter, in his first letter, makes it abundantly clear that Sarah's fearlessness in submitting to Abraham was to be a model to the women in the early church (more on that later). I'm not saying for one minute that God wouldn't have promised Sarah directly - later in the story He does. I'm simply saying that if headship is true, then in the same way that the Father's promises to Christ are ours because we are wrapped up in Him as our representative Head, the promises made to the head of the household extend to all those in the household.

This can be a bit difficult when we think about everything from an individualistic perspective, but it is surely clear that - however it works itself out - the idea of corporate identity is as much of a reality as individual identity in the Bible.

To clarify, this idea of representative responsibility does not negate the personal responsibility of both parties: the call to courageous faith was also on Sarah (who is both personally challenged by the Lord in Genesis 18 and personally commended for her faith in Hebrews 11), and we can see the trouble that started when she wavered in unbelief and called on Abraham to have intercourse with Hagar.

---

4   I have neither the experience or expertise to comment in detail here on how the issue of polygamy needs to be handled sensitively in cultural contexts where it is still an established and common practice. This is not to say that I endorse it, but to say that in situations where it is embedded, great pastoral care is required to bring about godly and righteous practices with as little damage as possible.

Regarding the Hagar incident, Abraham's response is identical to Adam's in the garden - he "listened to the voice' of his wife".[5] Again, for a husband to listen to his wife is, as a rule, an excellent thing; but, if a man does this when his wife is speaking out of unbelief, a complementarian would say that he is abdicating his role of headship, and trouble will soon follow, as it did with the birth of Ishmael.

Am I saying that, in a marriage, if a husband speaks out of unbelief and a wife listens to him, that's OK? No. I'm simply saying that a complementarian view would see an added layer to it, that it represents something *on top of* a straightforward, usual dysfunction!

So where are we up to through our study of the Old Testament? We see that polygamy, violence and oppression are clearly wrong. We also see that a husband who believes the promises of God and follows the Lord, and a wife who willingly and courageously walks with him on that path, are a model that is held up and commended in the New Testament.

Call Her Either Pearl or Ruby

It may be a good time to take a moment to look at the praiseworthy wife of Proverbs 31.

It's been a bit of a sad story of late to hear her spoken about very often in quite negative terms in the church by some women. Thus, the narrative can go, "All of us feel completely intimidated by this woman and of course none of us could ever live up to this ideal etc., etc…" Might I suggest that this is not the right response to this passage. Let's take a look at it together. Right bang in the middle of the Old Testament, we find this extraordinary description of the 'excellent wife'. It's a fascinating read, and it really helps us to get a sense of the attributes that are admired in a godly woman.

> *A wife of noble character who can find? She is worth far more than rubies.*
> PROVERBS 31 V 10

Talk about honour! The writer is saying that there are women who are so magnificent, such high quality, that they make a chest full of treasure seem cheap and tardy!

> *Her husband has full confidence in her and lacks nothing of value.*
> PROVERBS 31 V 11

There is something about this woman whereby her husband just feels relaxed and deeply confident in her - she's not going to embarrass him, she's not going to ruin him, she's not going to do him down - her

---

5   Genesis 16 v 2.

character will simply open up all manner of blessings and goodness in his life. There is such a depth of appreciation for her and confidence in her that it almost jumps off the page.

> *She brings him good, not harm, all the days of her life.*
> PROVERBS 31 V 12

She is utterly committed to his good - until the day she dies. She doesn't blow hot and cold, she doesn't play with his heart, she is fixed and firm in her agape love for him.

> *She selects wool and flax, and works with eager hands. She is like the merchant ships, bringing her food from afar. She gets up while it is still night; she provides food for her family and portions for her female servants. She considers a field and buys it; out of her earnings she plants a vineyard.*
> PROVERBS 31 V 13-16

She is entrepreneurial, she is resourceful and she is hard-working. She is what we might describe as a 360 leader who seems to miss nothing. She is on the front foot, and notice that here she is described as one who provides - this poses an interesting challenge to the traditional role models of 'man as provider'.

> *She gets about her work vigorously; her arms are strong for her tasks. She sees that her trading is profitable, and her lamp does not go out at night. In her hand she holds the distaff, and grasps the spindle with her fingers.*
> PROVERBS 31 V 17-19

There is nothing weak about this woman! She carries herself with immense dignity and might, and is full of skill. She is also incredibly perceptive when it comes to business, and is able to spot how to make a good return on her investments.

> *She opens her arms to the poor and extends her hands to the needy.*
> PROVERBS 31 V 20

She is both merciful and generous, and her concern extends beyond the realm of her household; she is concerned with wider needs and wants to make a contribution towards those who are really struggling.

When it snows, she has no fear for her household, for all of them are clothed in scarlet. She makes coverings for her bed; she is clothed in fine linen and purple.
PROVERBS 31 V 21-22

She makes sure that everyone in the home is well looked after and provided for. She is skilful and well presented. You don't get the impression that this woman views looking after her children as a nuisance or as something that she can't wait to move on from.

Her husband is respected at the city gate, where he takes his seat among the elders of the land.
PROVERBS 31 V 23

Some people misinterpret this as a situation where the man is a lazy good-for-nothing, sitting in the gate drinking coffee and she's running here, there and everywhere making it all happen! Not so. The man is one of the elders sitting in the gate, meaning that he is one of the community leaders and is busy judging, giving advice and making decisions that will impact the whole community; in short, it would seem that he is in a governmental position.

She makes linen garments and sells them, and supplies the merchants with sashes. She is clothed with strength and dignity; she can laugh at the days to come.
PROVERBS 31 V 24-25

She is confident, not crippled with anxiety. What is her secret? We'll find out in a minute.

She speaks with wisdom, and faithful instruction is on her tongue.
PROVERBS 31 V 26

She is well able to instruct and teach, and does so with kindness and wisdom.

She watches over the affairs of her household and does not eat the bread of idleness. Her children arise and call her blessed; her husband also, and he praises her: "Many women do noble things, but you surpass them all."
PROVERBS 31 V 27-29

She is incredibly honoured and esteemed by her husband and children; they live in the richness of her happy and competent sacrificial service.

Charm is deceptive, and beauty is fleeting; but a woman who fears the LORD is to be praised.
PROVERBS 31 V 30

This is her secret! She fears the Lord. She's not self-made. She's not doing her own thing. She is a woman of awe, a woman of wonder, a worshipper; she knows and trusts and fears the LORD, and as a result she is not enslaved to 101 other fears.

Honour her for all that her hands have done, and let her works bring her praise at the city gate.
PROVERBS 31 V 31

She will be duly acknowledged - she's done too well to be overlooked. Here we have a striking account of an immensely impressive woman. She is devoted, first and foremost, to her immediate family, which would be seen by many as an immensely feminine attribute; the woman, Eve, can nurture like no other. She teaches and instructs, demonstrates leadership and business savvy. These are qualities to be championed, and they deal decisively with unhelpful caricatures of women chained to the kitchen sink. There is nothing passive or weak about her. She is proactive and yet content, busy and yet peaceful, both caring and confident. If there was ever an argument that the Bible is neither aware of or keen to promote such strength, dignity and resourcefulness in women, I think we can confidently say that this passage puts pay to it.

Here we see this woman operating in what we know is a patriarchal context. For the purpose of this book, and this particular moment of this book, a very fascinating find!

This is not an incidental narrative (is any part of the Bible?), but rather we are told with certainty that this woman is to be praised and is being held up as exemplary. It may be that not every woman is as gifted as this woman, but that's not really the point. We have instead been asking the question of ancient Israel: is it a place that is oppressive to women? Is the general dynamic one that holds women back? This example would seem to suggest not.

The main point for now: Godly confidence and the maximum employment of what this woman has been given by God is clearly championed in a context that is patriarchal; there is no sense of oppression or disqualification.

A Mother in Israel

Perhaps now is a good time to consider the story of Deborah in the book of Judges. Not only was she a prophetess, but she was also a judge - the only female judge recorded, as well as the only major[6] judge who also finishes her race well!

Now Deborah, a prophet, the wife of Lappidoth, was leading Israel at that time.

She held court under the Palm of Deborah between Ramah and Bethel in the hill country of Ephraim, and the Israelites went up to her to have their disputes decided.

She sent for Barak son of Abinoam from Kedesh in Naphtali and said to him, "The LORD, the God of Israel, commands you: 'Go, take with you ten thousand men of Naphtali and Zebulun and lead them up to Mount Tabor. I will lead Sisera, the commander of Jabin's army, with his chariots and his troops to the Kishon River and give him into your hands.'" Barak said to her, "If you go with me, I will go; but if you don't go with me, I won't go." "Certainly I will go with you," said Deborah. "But because of the course you are taking, the honour will not be yours, for the LORD will deliver Sisera into the hands of a woman." So Deborah went with Barak to Kedesh.

JUDGES 4 V 4-9 (EMPHASIS MINE)

Here we have a woman serving in what was the highest leadership office in Israel. It really is quite extraordinary and proves a fascinating study for a number of reasons. It shows that in this particular patriarchal society a woman reached the highest echelon of leadership. We observe that this is exceptional because she is the only instance we have of a female judge in scripture. So it gives egalitarians food for thought about how this could happen in a patriarchal society.

But it gives complementarians more food for thought and good reason for pause. In a society where senior men are heads of their household, it seems clear from the story of Deborah that here we have a situation where a woman is called by God to carry the most senior level of authority and responsibility. I can't see any other way of interpreting the data.

Complementarians would have some comments, and it's only fair to put forward what some of their arguments might be...

------

6   By 'major' I mean a judge who gets significant attention in the book. Some get a line or two, some get a chapter or two.

Firstly, the whole purpose of the book of Judges is to introduce us to the chaos that happens when a nation like Israel repetitively backslides. The final line of the book, referred to earlier, that there was no king in those days and that everyone did as they saw fit, is clue enough, that as a whole, the book of Judges is most certainly not a 'How to...' book. This is a contextual insight on the book of Judges as a whole, and probably a fair one. An egalitarian response to this would be that she is the only judge who both gets a lot of airtime and who doesn't one way or the other end up going sideways! What is narrative theology telling us here? At the very least, comparatively speaking women in senior leadership are no worse, and often better at handling themselves, than male leaders.

Secondly, we know for sure that the people of Israel during the time of the judges were disobedient and rebellious and frequently under the judgement of God. In fact, the reason they are constantly defeated and conquered is explicitly referred to, repeatedly, as the disciplining judgement of God. In Isaiah 3 v 12, it says that one of the marks of judgement upon the people of God is that "women rule over them". The backdrop of the story is not a straightforward one, but is part of the story of God's judgement on the nation. A complementarian would want to ask if, in Deborah's appointment as a judge, God is both judging and saving Israel at the same time. An egalitarian would want to point out the complete lack of content in this story to suggest anything as negative as this. Judges 2 v 16 makes it clear that "the LORD raised up judges, who saved them out of the hand of those who plundered them". The bottom line surely is that God raised Deborah up, even though the phrase 'God raised her up' isn't used explicitly about her (as it is with the other major judges).

Thirdly, unlike all the other judges, Deborah did not lead the people of Israel into battle. As a prophetess she seemed convinced that it was Barak that was to do that, and she encouraged him to do so. We see an implied rebuke of Barak when he refuses to go up to battle without her. She rebukes him by pointing out that as a result of his attitude, the end result will be that the glory of the victory will go to a woman instead of to him (to Jael, who killed Sisera with the tent peg). Why does she say this? What is happening? Is it that she is expecting more of Barak than he is ready to give? Does she think that the one who leads the people into battle is the one who should receive the glory? Contrary to the pattern of all the other judges, she looked to hand over the moment of key military leadership to another person, and that person was a man. Some might argue here that Deborah respected, dignified and even promoted the role of male leadership of some kind. I haven't heard a strong egalitarian response to this.

What we know for sure is that she understood herself as a "mother in Israel".[7] She wasn't trying to be a 'father in Israel' but was comfortable in her womanhood. There is no sense of strife or competitiveness with men, rather we see her encouraging Barak to step up; her conduct was exemplary.

Fourthly, why is it that, when Samuel is rehearsing the faithfulness of God to the people of Israel, he gives the credit to Barak for delivering them?[8] And why, again, does the writer to the Hebrews do this?[9] Why do we never hear of Deborah again? I have no answer.

I think perhaps an egalitarian would want to point out that the backdrop to every Bible story is imperfect, and we wouldn't have to look too hard to find similar discrepancies in any other story. To make those complementarian comments work against the appointment of Deborah as an example of a woman in a senior leadership/headship role is simply not fair.

For the complementarian, these anomalies provide potential insights into a scenario that is undoubtedly exceptional in Old Testament terms, and one that seems to cut across the grain.

Either way, the story of Deborah didn't just happen in a patriarchal backdrop, but is recorded in holy scripture and she is presented very favourably. What is at least clear is that the backdrop of ancient Israel did not seem to hold her back.

She's Calling Out!

While we consider Deborah, both a judge and prophetess, we are perhaps reminded of the mysterious 'Lady Wisdom' that we find throughout the book of Proverbs.

As we see Deborah sitting under the tree, judging and prophesying with great wisdom we perhaps are transported to the Proverbs where we read of wisdom that:

> She is a tree of life to those who take hold of her.
> PROVERBS 3 V 18

How dignifying it is to have wisdom, that which is more precious than rubies, personified in the feminine. Surely this undermines any notion that in Israel women were viewed as foolish or simple. As Lady Wisdom

---

7   Judges 5 v 7.

8   1 Samuel 12 v 11.

9   Hebrews 11 v 32.

says, "Whoever listens to me will dwell secure and will be at ease, without dread of disaster".[10] We see that she holds incredible promise for all who will listen to her. Again, subtly the messaging is coming through that to listen to a woman is not something to be despised.

Also in the book of Proverbs we find instruction being given to a young man. This young man is old enough to be warned about the dangers of adultery. He is therefore no longer a boy but a man. He is exhorted to keep his father's command and not forsake his mother's teaching. They are both teaching him, mother and father. He is being encouraged to value both of their voices.

Please note: the woman's voice in the sacred scriptures of Israel is again valued and esteemed.

Super Sisters

There are so many excellent women in the Old Testament who held incredibly influential roles as wives, mothers, queens, leaders, intercessors, prophetesses, hosts and rescuers.

They committed great acts of faith and showed immense courage and purity. Like the men, their flaws and failings are also recorded, and through them we are given an honest and very helpful window into the struggle of the life of faith.

As noted above, we see Sarah trying to make sense of a promise given to her husband about multiple descendants, when her own body can't conceive even one. Not one. For years. And years. It's brutal. But she is commended for following this man courageously - imperfectly and very humanly - and yet with endurance and, finally, an immense reward.

We see Hannah mocked and cruelly treated by her rival Peninnah. We see her praying. We see her weeping. We see her coming into a season of deeper and deeper consecration to the Lord through the trial. We see her honouring her promise to God and bringing Samuel, this gift, to the Lord for His service. This man becomes the voice of God to the nation at a very precarious time.

We see Abigail displaying immense discretion and influence towards King David, her words keeping her foolish husband's blood from being spilt violently. The king was so impressed by her, that when her husband died of (un)natural causes shortly afterwards, he immediately relieved her of her widowhood!

We see Huldah the prophetess sought out and called upon to speak God's word to the king.

---

10   Proverbs 1 v 33.

We see Ruth's incredible loyalty to both her mother-in-law and her mother-in-law's God, Yahweh. We see her willingness to walk faithfully through thick and thin. We see her trust in God, as well as her trust in her godly mother-in-law, who had lost almost everything.

We see Rahab's surprising and risky faith in the LORD when, if discovered, it would most certainly have cost her her life. We see her mighty confession of faith and confidence in the true God, pulling her out of a lifestyle of sin and idolatry. We see her name and her family line rescued out of indignity and shame and placed beautifully into spiritual prosperity and honour.

We see Queen Esther putting her own life on the line for the sake of her people, God's people, and winning their rescue from a Satanic plan of total extermination. We see her courageously submissive heart towards her uncle Mordecai. We see her sacrificial bravery and the extraordinary favour offered to her from the most powerful man on the planet, as God raises her up for such a time as this.

These are incredibly inspiring women - women we can and do learn so much from - and there are plenty of others: Rebekah being willing to leave her home and family under God's leading to be with Isaac, Miriam serving faithfully alongside Aaron and Moses, the widow of Zarephath hosting Elijah with incredible faith, the Shunammite woman opening her home to Elisha and laying hold of the prophet to bring her son back from the dead!

The Bible certainly isn't backward about praising and lifting up great female role models that knew God deeply and saw Him move in power. We ought to do the same. These women and their faith are not just to be role models for other women, but for all of us.

Whatever conclusion we come to in this study, it is clear that a spiritual community that doesn't invest in, encourage, release and hold up godly women as examples of faith and godliness, is a community that has lost its way.

Given that the Old Testament backdrop is a patriarchy, the influence of godly women and the expression of their spiritual gifts is still plentiful. Magnificent women shine through again and again as we follow the story of God's salvation plan.

Back to the Garden

It wouldn't do in this section to *not* look at the Song of Songs. As I said earlier, while set in a fallen backdrop, it looks and sounds and smells so close to the garden of Eden with this man and woman, naked and unashamed in the garden of delightful rest and intimacy, that we seem, for a moment, to be lifted to another time and place.

There are some fascinating and heart-warming dynamics that we see in this relationship that will really give us a window into the plan of God for man and woman.

We find extraordinary mutuality between them. The emphasis that comes through time and time again is this beautiful back and forth. But I also think there is more - an added textural layer. I particularly want you to hear the woman's voice as we stop here for a while. My voice is male, most Bible voices are male, but here we have a woman's voice.

Firstly note that she begins, and she begins boldly.

> SHE
> *Let him kiss me with the kisses of his mouth.*
> SONG OF SONGS 1 V 2A

Please note very carefully: She initiates, but her initiation is an invitation for him to initiate.

Her posture welcomes his movement. There is no passivity on her part but she wants to be the one kissed first, not the one who kisses first. It's a subtle but powerful picture of femininity. Not a note of passivity but a strong note of receptivity. He is to move towards her, but she encourages him to do so.

> SHE
> *Take me away with you—let us hurry!*
> SONG OF SONGS 1 V 4A

Again she articulates her heart - she wants to run with him (not behind him). She can run with him, she is well able. But she wants to be drawn up into the race by him, drawn up and drawn in by him. She expects much of him and is confident in him.

> SHE
> *I delight to sit in his shade, and his fruit was sweet to my taste.*
> *Let him lead me to the banquet hall, and let his banner over me be love.*
> SONG OF SONGS 2 V 3B-4

Here, she delights in the shade that he provides for her, and gladly sits under his 'banner of love'. A banner would often denote leadership and protection. If this is about authority, it's not about authority over her, it's about authority for her sake; it's about a God-given liberty to provide a sense of rest, where she knows she is safe, and knows that this is a relationship where she doesn't need to prove herself - she is simply delighted in and known and loved.

Listen! My beloved! Look! Here he comes, leaping across the mountains, bounding over the hills. My beloved is like a gazelle or a young stag. Look! There he stands behind our wall, gazing through the windows, peering through the lattice. My beloved spoke and said to me, "Arise, my darling, my beautiful one, come with me. See! The winter is past; the rains are over and gone. Flowers appear on the earth; the season of singing has come, the cooing of doves is heard in our land. The fig tree forms its early fruit; the blossoming vines spread their fragrance. Arise, come, my darling; my beautiful one, come with me."
SONG OF SONGS 2 V 8-15

Here she delights in his vigour and energy as he bounds towards her. He calls her away into a new season of life and fruitfulness; he is going somewhere and wants her to come with him. She delights in this - she's in! We don't find her competing against him, but we find her delighting in him.

At the end of this section, he needs her help to catch those things that will potentially spoil their fruitfulness, the 'little foxes'. He recognises in her the ability to spot and deal with those little things that bring harm. She will see and catch these things before he has ever noticed them, because she is Eve and she intuitively understands relationships, because she is the mother of all living.

There is so much more we could draw out, but more than anything I want you to see the freedom and mutual delight between Solomon and the Shulammite, coupled with the asymmetry of their relationship. As I noted earlier, most of the book has a very symmetrical and mutual feel to it as they admire one another's faces and bodies and invite each other here and there, but there are also these notes of asymmetry as highlighted above. Layers.

See his vigour and energy and her delight and desire to run alongside him. See his invitation for her to come away with him and run together. See his shade and banner that provide rest and joy for her as she knows deeply that she is delighted in and protected. See her desire to be kissed by him and her bold invitation to him to do so.

It's subtle and nuanced but...there's something going on! There's a direction of travel, a dynamic, a flow to it, birthed in desire and attraction. Whatever label we give this, I think it's magnificent.

Summing up

I acknowledge I have been very selective in this study. In some ways, the body of literature is simply too big to treat comprehensively in this kind of book, but I also recognise there are incidents, principles and even teachings in the Old Testament that raise significant questions about the place of women in Israel as equals.

We have to recognise a few key things. In the Old Testament, we have a nation that is being formed within a wider patriarchal backdrop and before the age of Pentecost where the Spirit is poured out on all members. There is, undoubtedly, divine accommodation present, but there is, alongside that, no shortage of female leadership role models. Israel, in its day, was undoubtedly revolutionary.

But we know that what we see in Israel is a long way off what the Lord perfectly wants. We know this because there are some core elements to the Jewish faith that are transformed as Jesus the Messiah steps into the world.

In Judaism the priesthood was exclusively male.[11] The priesthood was the ministry that focused primarily on the teaching and instruction of God's word,[12] as well as all of the representative temple duties. The priesthood opens up in the New Covenant, as we are introduced to what we call 'the priesthood of all believers'.[13] The implications for this are potentially revolutionary, particularly for the role of women in the church.

Next, in Judaism the covenant sign was circumcision - male circumcision. There was no way that a woman could bear on her body the marks of covenant with Yahweh. The covenant sign becomes baptism in the New Covenant.[14] This is, again, a hugely significant marker, and one that we mustn't ignore. The New Testament is full of men *and* women getting baptised.

Thirdly, in Judaism the Jewish men were allowed into a part of the temple where women weren't allowed. I'm not sure at what point this was introduced, whether in Solomon's temple, or the second temple. It

---

11   Why was this? It could be down to representation as I stated earlier. This, and the fact that the teaching was entrusted to the priests, would be the complementarian's perspective on the matter. Some egalitarians say it's because women were considered ritually unclean for a week every month and so they would have been unable to serve as priests 25% of the time. The problem with this argument is that the Levites, at times, were also ritually unclean themselves (see Leviticus 15 v 15-32, Leviticus 22 v 4-6, Deuteronomy 23 v 10-11). Plus there would always have been a rota of sorts, so no one was expected to be continuously on duty. Some say that because the surrounding nations had cults that employed priestesses, which was in some way linked to goddess worship, having a male priesthood was one way of preserving the purity and holiness of Yahweh worship and keeping it from corruption.

12   Leviticus 10 v 11, Malachi 2 v 7.

13   1 Peter 2 v 5, Revelation 5 v 10. It's true that in Exodus 19 v 6 God expresses His desire that the nation of Israel would be a kingdom of priests, but we also know that, for the most part, Israel turned away from God's plan leaving only a believing remnant.

14   Paul, in Colossians 2 v 11-12, draws a parallel between circumcision and baptism, intimating the equivalence of one to the other.

certainly gives the impression of a kind of spiritual 'tiering'. However, we all, men *and* women, become both temples and living stones in the New Covenant temple.

Fourthly, in the Old Testament, it was typical for the sons to be the heirs. Now we find, in the New Testament, all believers, whether male or female, are sometimes referred to as 'sons' because through Christ we are all now co-heirs!

So yes, Israel was revolutionary in its time. But in the coming of their Messiah, the Israelite faith itself is revolutionised.

The Inbetweeners

This short section sitting close to the middle of the book is concerned with a beautiful season sandwiched between the two covenants and was brought to my attention by my wife after she started to read Luke's Gospel in her own devotional times. It is short and sweet; more of a reflection than a chapter.

It's worth noting that in his Gospel account Luke is particularly concerned with putting both the poor and women front and centre; if you read through with a keen eye you will see it clearly. It's not that he is adding material of his own making; he is simply putting the magnifying glass on these two often overlooked groups of people.

I wanted to create this small centre slot as readers themselves may feel somewhat expectant concerning the pages that follow. We are awaiting Jesus. We're looking forward to seeing how he ministered to, and with the help of, various women.

As we wait for him it's good to consider that Elizabeth and Mary inhabited a space between covenants. The proclaimed message was about to change from the law and the prophets to the coming Kingdom. The cross was yet to come, but loomed large from John and Jesus' earliest days. For now, the focus was still on the Jews - but this Gospel account was written by a Gentile. Much had taken place but more was still to come. In this 'hinge' moment I'd like you to notice the centrality of these two women.

Luke paints a deliberately contrasting picture between Zechariah's response to Gabriel's message to him and Mary's response to what the angel declares to her: Zechariah is struck dumb for questioning the reliability of Gabriel's account of what is to come - "How can I be sure of this?"[1] - whereas Mary simply asks a reasonable question - "How will this be, since I am a virgin?"[2] As soon as God lets her know that it will happen supernaturally she yields wholeheartedly.

Mary is to be highly recommended for asking this question, because the people of Israel had been instructed to weigh supernatural encounters with the written scriptures in order to verify that it was truly God. Had this angel told her to commit sexual immorality in order for it to be fulfilled, she would have rejected it. In these two instances we see that, as far as the Bible is concerned, men are by no means necessarily considered to be more spiritual or obedient than women.

At the beginning of what we call the 'New Testament' we find the two greatest men in history meeting each other while they are both still in the womb![3] Elizabeth is six months pregnant with John the Baptist when a newly pregnant Mary arrives at her house in the hill country of Judah. As soon as Elizabeth hears Mary's greeting, the baby leaps for joy in her womb![4] The rapport between this older lady, who never thought she would conceive, and her younger cousin who, by all accounts, shouldn't yet have, is humbling and inspiring. They are both as amazed as each other with how God has dealt with them and they spend three precious months in sweet and expectant fellowship. The older woman had known shame and the younger one was about to. In the midst of this, both retained pure hearts before God, which speaks to me of dazzling humility.

---

1   Luke 1 v 18.

2   Luke 1 v 24.

3   I'm sure you don't need convincing that Jesus is in the top two, but Jesus is clear that John the Baptist, the other man I'm referring to, is greater than all who came before him - see Matthew 11 v 11.

4   See Luke 1 v 24-56.

During the Old Covenant one of the ways that blessing was seen was in having children; the inability to conceive was part of the curse.[5] It's clear from the text that Zechariah and Elizabeth were both righteous and blameless,[6] but rest assured people would have wondered and questions would have been asked: why couldn't they have children? Was there some sort of secret sin? Should Zechariah *really* be a priest?

As for Mary - well, we are spared much of the detail of the scrutiny that would have surrounded the birth of Jesus, but her willingness to submit herself entirely to the will of God is breathtaking. We know for sure that she was a hair's breadth away from losing her fiancé, and we know that even Jesus' siblings didn't believe who He was until the resurrection. Mary's character and purity would have been in question for much of her life. She is phenomenal.

Please also note what strength there was in both women: they were both able to walk through years of difficulty. For Elizabeth it was the years before her baby was born, and for Mary it was the years after. To walk for years in holiness with God, when others are either out loud or in their hearts asking questions of you, takes supernatural strength. We draw so much strength from one another - and that's not a bad thing; it's part of God's provision for us - but we can easily begin to rely on that too much. We can forget the secret place, the refuge of God Himself, and can become enslaved to the opinions of others.

This has a severely weakening effect on our souls. Throughout the early chapters of Luke, we twice find the phrase that 'Mary treasured up all that was going on in her heart'.[7] She took it all in. She imbibed the awe and mystery around her son's birth and development, and carried it inside her through the difficult years, even when her own soul was pierced.

The God-centred and deeply spiritual qualities of these two women also jump off the page. Elizabeth was righteous and blameless and she fully embraced the vision and calling that God, through Gabriel, had given her son, submitting to the name John as given by the angel, and knowing in her heart that Mary's own pregnancy story was true. Mary, in what we know as 'The Magnificat',[8] made it clear that she had seen the bigger picture, gladly embracing inconvenience and suffering in order to play her part in God's story. She also recognised God's blessing in her somewhat controversial personal circumstances, as well as God's intergenerational plan and covenantal faithfulness. What exemplary women they are.

---

5   Exodus 23 v 26, Deuteronomy 7 v 14.

6   Luke 1 v 6.

7   Luke 2 v 19 and 2 v 51.

8   See Luke 1 v 46-55.

I also want to draw your attention to the wider context once again: *pregnancy.* There is a common thread in the Bible and it's important that we take notice of it when we consider many (though not all) of the most prominent women in scripture up to this point - Eve, Sarah, Rebekah, Rachel, Hannah, and now Elizabeth and Mary - we see that child-bearing is a central theme in their stories. Then as we move from the Old Covenant to the new, we notice something of a shift: where multiplying and filling the earth, naturally speaking, was the original commission, now filling all nations with disciples becomes the Kingdom emphasis. It's not that the first is done away with, but because 'the end of the ages' is upon us[9] there is now an urgency that, among other things, builds a strong case for remaining unmarried.[10]

I'd like to put these two things together so that we might consider and esteem afresh the incredible capacity of women to nurture life physically, and also to ask whether this might point us symbolically to particular and unique contributions that women bring to life and ministry. More on that later.

---

9   See 1 Corinthians 10 v 11 and Hebrews 9 v 26.

10   See 1 Corinthians 7 v 29-40 and Matthew 19 v 12.

Chapter Eleven
Jesus Revolution I: Egalitarian Pillar Four

The coming of Jesus is a second Genesis. As we observe Jesus' interactions with many different women, we see something brand new. The revolution has begun!

History can be confusing at times. And unless you're a *proper* historian, it's sometimes really hard to know who or what to believe! History is written by people, and people are rarely objective. Sometimes isolated facts and incidents that happened many centuries ago are highlighted as the norm, in order to bolster up a certain opinion or perspective.

It's not to say those facts are not true, but it is to say that there are other facts and incidents that could very easily bolster up the opposite opinion or perspective. As a history buff, this is highly frustrating.

For example, some historians say that life for women in the ancient near east was very limited. The perception is of them being hugely undervalued by men, drawing on facts like the testimony of women not being received in a court of law. Others will then talk about how a growing number of wealthy women ran their own businesses and enjoyed significant autonomy. Both of those, it seems, are true. It means that we mustn't over-categorise, or even caricature, the place of women in the ancient near east. Not only is this so, but we also recognise historically that the conservative Jewish culture was significantly different from Greco-Roman culture, and that both of these collided in first-century Palestine. The early church was made up, within a couple of decades, of both Jews and Gentiles. This raises all kinds of complexities for us as well, as we consider how to assess the material of the New Testament in its wider context! All this to say that what can sound like quite a straightforward exercise, isn't always. This is why, when studying the interactions of Jesus and women, we will try to focus on the things that are most obvious rather than on conjecture and speculation.

This is it

Let's start by recognising that this is the moment where all that had gone before comes to its goal. The rituals of Israel up to this point are compared to a shadow as Jesus, the substance, the actual body of all that God intended, arrives on the scene. So what we see in the arrival of Jesus is the beginning of the climax of the story of God, literally the beginning of the end. What comes through Him is not preparatory but climactic. We are not looking at the beginnings of some kind of trajectory, but we are looking at God's final word.[1]

There can be no doubt that Jesus was happy to break social convention in order to serve the purpose of His Father. We can see this principle worked out as He related to particular women: Jesus' interaction with the woman at the well,[2] is the perfect example. She's not just a Samaritan (they were regarded with disdain by Jews for their ethnic impurity and hybrid religion), but a woman. It was not considered appropriate for men and women unknown to one another to relate in ways that we are very used to in the West.

And so we see that as far as social conventions go, a Jewish man would not be seen dead talking to an unknown Samaritan woman, and yet Jesus, in the burning light of the midday sun, did exactly that. He spoke into her life prophetically, He taught her about true worship, He offered her the gift of the Holy Spirit, and He chose her to be the evangelistic catalyst to bring the whole town to Him. Maybe she even did the groundwork for Philip's evangelistic success in Samaria years later![3]

Or take the woman with the issue of blood.[4] While Jesus is on His way to heal a twelve year old daughter, He's touched by a woman with a twelve year old disease who had spent all she had on physicians to no avail. He senses her touch and healing power leaving His body. He determines to find out exactly who touched Him, and when He does so, He brings comfort and reassurance to this precious woman.

Then there is the lady bent double by a disabling spirit whom He heals. He calls her a daughter of Abraham, the only time you will hear this term in the Bible! Next we have Mary Magdalene whom He delivers from seven evil spirits, and who becomes a devoted disciple. There is Peter's mother-in-law whom He heals, and let's not forget the daughter of the Syro-Phoenician woman whose daughter He sets free from a demon. We have Mary the sister of Martha, whom He welcomes at His feet and teaches as a disciple. Then the same Mary and her sister Martha, along with their brother Lazarus, are His beloved friends.[5] And let's not forget Joanna and Susanna and other rich women who provided for Him out of their means. Then there is the woman caught in adultery, who Jesus protects from murderous hypocrisy and sets on a new path.

---

1   Hebrews 11 v 1-2.

2   John 4 v 1-26.

3   Acts 8 v 4-8.

4   Mark 5 v 24-34.

5   John 11 v 5.

Jesus clearly loves women, ministers to women, trusts women, teaches and trains women, befriends women and is ministered to and provided for by women. Jesus is happy for women to have land and money and be resourceful. Jesus is happy for women to learn theology in order to be able to pass on spiritual truth. Jesus is happy for women to form a vital part of the priesthood of believers. Jesus is intent on drawing women into the thick of the action. Then we get to the resurrection morning. The first person Jesus reveals Himself to, the first person to see the resurrected Christ in His glory, is… a woman. Mary is the one who first bears witness of the resurrection to those that Jesus goes on to appoint as His eyewitnesses!

A Breaking with Tradition?

There can be no doubt that with Jesus, we are seeing a clear view of God's original intent.

Some significant things are happening. Perhaps we do see something quite intriguing manifested in the scripture below:

> After this, Jesus travelled about from one town and village to another, proclaiming the good news of the kingdom of God. The Twelve were with him, and also some women who had been cured of evil spirits and diseases: Mary (called Magdalene) from whom seven demons had come out; Joanna the wife of Chuza, the manager of Herod's household; Susanna; and many others. These women were helping to support them out of their own means.
> LUKE 8 V 1-3

We read here of some women who are named and 'many others', accompanying and providing for Jesus. They had obviously experienced incredible freedom and new life through His ministry of compassion and power, and they were now devoted to Him. The thing I'd like to draw your attention to is that apart from Joanna, none of the others are married, or if they are, their husbands are not mentioned. This is unusual. I can't think of one woman in the Old Testament who is mentioned, without reference - sooner or later - to their husband or father. I may be wrong, but I can't think of one; if they exist, they are in the vast minority.

Perhaps what we are seeing here is an example of excellent women, utterly devoted to Christ as their lover in a spiritual sense. Perhaps there is something here in this passage that dignifies women, enabling them to walk free from the effects of the fall and an inordinate need for a husband, finding in Jesus the strength they need to stand tall in Him and not fall into unhelpful relationships with men in the search for fulfilment or validation.

The fact that these ladies were providing from their means for Jesus and the twelve is also significant, is it not? Ministry requires time and resources, and therefore it requires money. These women were enabling the ministry of Christ. Jesus here is embodying the Genesis 2 principle; the men can't do this alone. In this instance it was financial support, but the principle is wider and we would do well to take it very seriously.

Maybe it's a good moment to consider how the complementarians view Jesus and His ministry to women.

Chapter Twelve

Jesus Revolution II: Complementarian Pillar Four

Jesus shows us what true headship is like, specifically in the way that He treats women. He values, honours, befriends, invests in and gladly receives from many women. Jesus' undoing of the curse didn't stop Him from appointing twelve male apostles, though the new community was anything but a male monopoly.

I'll start by giving specific emphasis to Jesus' circles of relationships.

Moving Out

There are the three: Peter, James and John, who seem to form something of an inner circle. They alone accompany Jesus to the top of the mountain when He is transfigured, they alone accompany Him to the bedroom of Jairus's daughter before He raises her from the dead, and He calls the three of them to Himself when He is struggling in Gethsemane.

Then there are the 12 (who include the three previously mentioned): Peter and Andrew, James and John, Philip and Bartholomew, Thomas and Levi, James and Thaddeus, Simon and Judas (replaced by Matthias after his suicide). Here and there they go by different names, but there are no real disputes about who the 12 were. They form the governmental core of the new community, the counterpart of the 12 tribes of Israel, whose names are written on each of the 12 foundation stones of the New Jerusalem.[1] Their place and ministry in the church is unique; they were with Jesus from the beginning of His ministry and were also witnesses of His resurrection and ascension.

Then there are the 70 whom Jesus sent out on mission (see Luke 10). But then there are other friends and supporters, those we read about in Luke 8 v 1-3 and John 11 v 1-5, some of whom may have been a part of the 70. Then by the time Jesus ascends to the Father's throne, there are somewhere between 120-500 committed disciples. Then of course there are 'the crowds' - the multitudes that He ministers to.

---

1   Revelation 21 v 14.

Moving Back in

For the purpose of this book, what can we deduce from the above? Let's work from the multitudes backwards with our gender lens on. Of all the crowds that Jesus ministers to, there are a great variety of men and women: Jesus came to serve men and women, and He relates beautifully to both.

Of the 120-500 committed disciples that Jesus has at His point of departure, we know there are numbers of women right at the centre of the action. At the cross, certain women do a much better job of staying close to Jesus than most of the 12. On resurrection morning, it's devoted women who make their way to His tomb before anyone else does, and the fact that Jesus appears to a woman first of all is very remarkable. Mary Magdalene becomes the connecting point between Jesus and those apostles who were designated specifically to be witnesses of the resurrection. In 2016, Pope Francis called for Mary to be referred to as "Mary the Apostle of the apostles"! We also know that Mary the mother of Jesus and 'the women' were praying in the upper room over that ten day period before Pentecost.

Then we have other friends and supporters. The traditional idea of the man needing to provide financially for the woman is overturned with the rich women of Luke 8. The idea of a woman's place being in the kitchen and not the theological library is likewise overturned in the famous story of Mary and stressed out Martha![2] Jesus, it might be argued, is also ministered to by a woman in a priestly kind of way as she anoints His body for burial.[3]

When it comes to the 70, they are not named so we cannot say. The two by two pairings may have been married couples or siblings. Two women wouldn't be sent out alone and neither would an unmarried man and an unmarried woman together, but we can't be 100% sure how these pairings were made up.

A Carpenter's Dozen

When it comes to the Twelve and the Three, we know that they are men. This is potentially very significant, because it means that we have no evidence that Jesus bestows governmental office (headship responsibility) on women.

Let's stop and think for a moment about Mary Magdalene. That Jesus appeared to her first, but that she was not numbered among the original apostles who were specifically designated as 'eye-witnesses of the resurrection' is striking. The fact that Paul, when defending his apostleship and talking about those who

---

2   Luke 10 v 38-42.

3   Matthew 26 v 6-13.

witnessed Christ's resurrection (1 Corinthians 15) doesn't even mention her in that context, should make us pause for thought. Either Paul's a misogynist[4] or, simply put, Jesus Himself didn't appoint her as an apostle.

Also for our consideration, it's been said that because the 12 were all *Jewish* men, to say that Jesus doesn't appoint women to governmental positions is the same as saying that He doesn't appoint *Gentiles* to governmental positions, something that no complementarian would ever argue for; does this argument hold any water? At first appearance it can look quite strong. But I think as we look closely at the chronology of the Gospel accounts, some leaks appear.

Firstly, we know that Jesus made it plain that His ministry during those three years in the public eye was focused on "the lost sheep of Israel" (Matthew 15 v 24).

Every now and then He reached further afield, or further afield reached him, but Jesus was very clear what He was about during that period. Would Jesus really have appointed Gentile men into His inner circle when His own earthly ministry was to the Jews? No. Why? Simply put, it was not the time for that. The gospel had not yet gone out to all nations. That time was coming, but it wasn't yet. He explicitly restricted Himself to the Jewish people but He never made such comments about gender. Jewish/Gentile matters and male/female matters are theologically separate, and for the most part are thus handled separately throughout scripture.[5]

When we get close to the time of the crucifixion, we begin to see the focus widening to the nations.[6] This is then made very explicit after the passion and resurrection, when in the Great Commission Jesus expressly commands His followers to go to the ends of the earth, making disciples of *all* nations and preaching to *all* creation.[7] That is a theologically powerful hinge moment. Once He had been essentially rejected by the nation of Israel as a whole (there was obviously a believing remnant - all of the early disciples!), and the mission had developed to encompass the ends of the earth, then the Gentiles got involved in governmental leadership in the predominantly Gentile churches. We know this is true by the non-Jewish names that are recorded in church leadership roles.[8]

---

4   Whether or not Paul is a misogynist will be looked at in our FAQ section at the end.

5   The exception that comes to mind is Galatians 3 v 28, which we will look at separately.

6   John 12 v 20-32.

7   Matthew 28 v 18-20, Mark 16 v 15 and Luke 24 v 47.

8   Acts 13 v 1, Romans 16 v 1-16.

The second leak is that the Bible likens the opening up of the Kingdom of God to Gentiles to a branch from a wild tree being grafted into a home-grown tree. We've been brought into an economy that is Jewish in root and led by a Jewish man. In a historical/chronological sense, Christianity is, in the first place, Jewish, which is why Paul in Romans talks about 'first the Jew and then the Greek [Gentile]'. This doesn't mean that Gentile believers have to convert to being a Jew before we can be accepted; our faith in Christ is what makes us children of Abraham. But it does make sense that the founding fathers of this New Covenant were Jewish, and that as part of God's multi-layered story, a believing remnant of Israel would be a blessing to the nations. And this is what happened in church history as the gospel moved out from Jerusalem to the ends of the earth.

So the above reasons why women weren't among the apostles don't seem clear to me, because if there is leadership symmetry between men and women, and if Jesus was wanting to straighten out 'dysfunctional asymmetry', to have appointed at least one Jewish woman as part of the Twelve does not seem to me to be problematic.

Egalitarians say that the symbolism of a woman or women being among the core of this newly constituted Israel wouldn't work alongside the Twelve patriarchs, but that would be a small price to pay in order to undo a symbol that apparently reflects the fall. It seems a stronger argument to say that the symbolism *wasn't* dysfunctional, and thus holds true as Jesus appoints twelve men.

Jesus as Peacekeeper?

Some egalitarians say the reason Jesus didn't appoint women as apostles is that it would have been controversial, a sort of stumbling block to those He was reaching. Jesus was happy to call certain Jews 'sons of the devil', a Gentile woman a 'dog', and the Pharisees 'snakes' and 'hypocrites'! He was happy to declare Himself one with God, and to tell the Jewish leaders of His day that the Kingdom was being taken from them and given to a people who would appreciate it. He healed on the Sabbath at the expense of His life. He broke ritual washing traditions. He turned over the tables in the temple. He reached out to a Samaritan woman in broad daylight for all to see. But He wouldn't incorporate a woman into the 12 in case someone got upset? Really?

A complementarian would want to ask the question that if He had wanted women to govern this new movement, wouldn't He have made that clear? Wouldn't He have redrawn the lines in this way? Would He have left it to the others to make that step after His departure, without even any instruction to do so? Also, in the same way that Jesus, before ascending to the Father, made it very clear that His disciples were now to go *to all nations* with the message, wouldn't it also have made sense for Him to say, at that point, that women should be in governmental leadership positions? Surely He would have foreseen the difficulties caused by this and would have left instructions? To say that it would have been controversial and so Jesus wouldn't have done it seems to show little appreciation for the historical Jesus and the nature of His ministry.

It seems clear that the Jew/Gentile matter was not about culture or controversy - it was about the appointed times and seasons for the purposes of God. So what was Jesus doing in not appointing women to be part of the governmental leadership of this new community? The complementarian would argue that, as with all things Jesus, it's a case of back to Eden. They would point out that God entrusted Adam with a job, but that he was not equipped to do the job alone. He needed a helper. So God personally built and provided him with exactly the kind of helper that he needed. He was to honour, value, and delight in her, relying on her bringing her gifts to bear in order to get the job done, because without her, it simply couldn't and wouldn't get done. She was to respect that God had entrusted the man with a representative role in getting the job done, and she was to serve God by helping him with it. This is how they express rule together. And so there are some contours, some lines that move subtly in unique directions, but there is parity, there is teamwork, there is partnership. The complementarian would say that through this model we have equality of essence, interdependence, but difference in role.

When laying these two arguments against one another, my honest assessment is that the complementarian one is the stronger. I'm not saying at this stage that it's a done deal, but it seems to reflect a stronger line of reasoning, and seems to denote more of a united voice across the scriptures; Adam is doctrinal steward in Eden, the Levites were in Israel, and the apostles are in the church - the New Testament being the record of what we call 'the apostle's doctrine'.[9]

It also seems to honour the courage, clarity and foresight of Christ.

INTERLUDE

Do you remember that awkward moment where the twelve were arguing about which one of them was going to be the greatest? Jesus, knowing that something is going on, asks them what they were talking about. Once they confess, Jesus does something utterly profound; he completely undoes their thinking about greatness. He says that to be great in the Kingdom is to be the least, and that it involves becoming like a child. He takes their wrong understanding that leadership is to do with a higher status, and turns it on its head!

---

9   Acts 2 v 42.

It's really sad that, as Christians 2,000 years on, we still haven't grasped this. Carrying responsibility in the Kingdom, while an honour, is not to be equated with 'moving up the ladder'. It's not the spiritual version of social mobility! Paul describes himself and Apollos as 'last of all…the scum of the world, the refuse of all things'![10] Wherever we get to in this study, we must remember that, in the Kingdom, first means last.

———————————

We're not done yet. There is a lot more to look at. And I think the next egalitarian argument packs a real punch.

———

10   1 Corinthians 4 v 9, 13.

Chapter Thirteen
Pentecostal Parity: Egalitarian Pillar Five

The outpouring of the Holy Spirit on the day of Pentecost was indiscriminate by nature, 'all flesh'. Therefore, the only qualification for ministry is Spirit-giftedness. If the Spirit chooses to gift someone for a particular task, then they are good to go; gender is irrelevant. This is made abundantly clear when Paul says that in Christ, there is now no longer male nor female.

The moment of Pentecost was huge. The floodgates of heaven were opened and the age of the Spirit broke in on a troubled and lost world. From a soteriological[1] perspective, the outpouring of the Holy Spirit spoke primarily of the victorious ascension of Christ. From an ecclesiological[2] perspective, the outpouring of the Holy Spirit spoke of an empowered people. From an eschatological[3] perspective, the outpouring of the Holy Spirit spoke of the beginning of the end, the ushering in of the last days.

We must see afresh what a huge deal Pentecost was and is.

God's plan and desire for a people saturated with His presence is detected all through the Old Testament. We see it from the cry of Moses in the book of Numbers, "Would that all of God's people were prophets!",[4] to the utterance of Joel, "In the last days, declares the Lord, I will pour out My Spirit on all flesh…".[5]

Big Moment, Huge Reach

The big story of the New Covenant is a people filled with the presence of God, the fulfilment of all tabernacle and temple 'types', from Eden to Jerusalem. We see the evidence that God will, by no means,

---

1   This word means to do with salvation.

2   This word means to do with the church.

3   This word means to do with the end times.

4   Numbers 11 v 29.

5   Joel 2 v 28-29.

ever truly dwell in a temple made with human hands, but will only ever truly dwell in a temple made by *His* hands - us!

It's a fascinating observation that this outpouring of the Spirit has something of an indiscriminate nature about it. All of the 120 in the upper room are filled, all of those that Cornelius gathered to his household are filled, all the disciples that Paul meets on the way to Ephesus are filled, and all those the apostles lay their hands on in Samaria are filled! Why? Because the outpouring of the Spirit is the promise of the Father, based on the finished work of the Son. Our own maturity, life experience (or lack of it), social standing or gender play no part in whether or not we are invited to the party - this promise is for all those who put their trust in Christ crucified and risen. Christ has done it, He has beaten all the powers of darkness through His sacrifice; the days of sin, Satan and death are now all inevitably numbered! His victory was demonstrated in His resurrection and ascension - Christ went up. And the Spirit comes down. The victorious Christ enters into the presence of the Father and receives from the Father the gift of the Holy Spirit, whom He pours out on His people. It's all about Him - we must never separate the outpouring of the Spirit from the precious gospel.

Because of the indiscriminate nature of the gift, when we read about the tongues of fire resting on the disciples at Pentecost it's not just on the 12 but on the 120, on all those gathered, and we know for sure that there were women present.[6] We also know that the result of the outpoured Spirit is, for a large part, both witness[7] and prophecy,[8] both of which involve divinely inspired and empowered speech. So we see clearly that women were anointed with the Spirit, and that this would issue forth in anointed speech that both brings people to Christ and builds them up in their faith.

In Ephesians 2 and 1 Corinthians 12, we also see that prophecy was considered a foundational gift in the early church, along with the gift of the apostle. This shows us that there would be women who would be helping to lay foundations in the lives of churches, working alongside apostles. The Corinthians passage says that prophets are second in the church and teachers third; this doesn't mean in terms of importance,

---

6   Acts 1 v 14.

7   Acts 1 v 8.

8   Acts 2 v 17.

but in terms of order. Because the foundation is laid by apostles and prophets,[9] they are first and second, which means that any work a teacher does is built on the foundation laid by them.

Wherever you land in terms of women apostles and women teachers (and we will go there later on), it's important to realise that, according to the New Testament, women prophets will be at work laying foundations in churches.[10]

Who are we to Hinder?

Pentecostal scholar Gordon Fee wants to make the point that if God has gifted someone by His Spirit, then that is the only qualification needed - someone's gender does not come into it.

The Bible is certainly clear that it's the Holy Spirit who determines who receives what gifts from Him,[11] and therefore it's quite a compelling argument. Also, I wouldn't want to go up against Gordon Fee without good reason. To put it in its starkest terms: how can we, in God's name, justify disqualifying someone from using a spiritual gift that God Himself has given them for the good of His church?! This line of reasoning should most certainly cause us to tremble in the fear of God and make sure that we are never found doing this.

---

9   Some theologians understand the foundation of apostles and prophets to refer to the written record of the prophets of the Old Testament and the written record of the apostles in the New Testament. While Paul *may* have had this in mind, I'm not convinced that this is *necessarily* what he had in mind, or *only* what he had in mind when he refers to the church as "...built on the foundation of the apostles and prophets, Christ Jesus himself being the cornerstone..." (Ephesians 2 v 20) because of the way he proceeds, in the same epistle, to refer to the contemporary ministry of apostles and prophets in and for the church, until the church reaches Christ's stature. So while I agree that scripture is foundational to all we do, I'm arguing that Paul had a dynamic in mind that was more to do with planting and establishing churches until maturity comes and Christ returns. Following on from that, I would also contend that apostles and prophets do the same things today in the planting and establishing of churches, but again, with all the safeguards in place of total submission to the revelation of scripture, with no fresh additions to,or subtractions from, that. While I happily concede that there are important differences to what happened in Bible times and what happens today through apostles and prophets, I would also support their ongoing ministry today in church life. It can be done well, safely and fruitfully, as the five-fold ministries are given by the ascended Christ to the church *until* the church reaches maturity. Maturity is described by Paul as the full stature of Christ; I think we'd all agree that we are not there yet!

10   At this point, some will want to make the distinction between prophets and those who prophesy, and within that some complementarian charismatics (they do exist!) might want to say that women can prophesy but can't be prophets, because of the foundation laying dynamic involved. While I agree that the two are not always the same thing, I think it's pertinent to note that in the letter of 1 Corinthians, where it talks about prophets being second in the church, it seems like Paul uses the noun prophet and the verb to prophesy as interchangeable ideas (see 1 Corinthians 12 v 10, 29 and 1 Corinthians 14 v 29-33). Maybe sometimes the lines we draw are a little bit too clean! Because I don't see New Testament prophets as primarily concerned with church oversight, I cannot see a tension around women being prophets.

11   1 Corinthians 12 v 11.

Perhaps it would be helpful to articulate how the complementarian would resolve this dilemma in order to weigh the strength of their argument. They would say that it's not the use of anyone's spiritual gift per se that they would ever question. Instead, it is the setting in which that gift is used or the way it is expressed. Let me explain using the gift of teaching, as this is a gift that both charismatic and non-charismatic believers alike still believe continues today, so we can avoid as much controversy and as many huge footnotes as possible!

In most cases, a complementarian leader would want to see a woman with a teaching gift using that gift in the life of the church for the building up of the church. What they would take issue with is a woman using that gift in the office of, or as if she were, an elder/pastor/shepherd[12] and/or a woman using that gift to teach men, as they would see that as a headship function.[13] So, to make it clear, they wouldn't be objecting to the use of the gift but the particular way the gift was being used. Some would want to see her using that gift with children, youth, and other women, and others would also want to see her using that gift in any other setting in church life that wasn't clearly an 'elders only' teaching setting. Still others would have a woman teaching in any setting provided she wasn't herself in the office of 'elder'.[14]

In light of this, a complementarian would object to the idea that they were out to hinder the use of anyone's spiritual gift, but simply out to see that the gifts are used in a way that reflects God's created order. Regardless of your stance on men and women, all of us would agree that the above principle is appropriate; we want to see the gifts used in orderly ways. For example, the Corinthians were using the gift of tongues in a disorderly way, they were all going at it at the same time with no thought of interpreting! Paul lets them know that if they carry on like this, the guests will think they're mad, and it will hinder the advance of the gospel. This is an example of the same principle with gifts being used in an orderly way. None of us, I doubt, would have a problem with that principle - it's important to see that. Because of this, I think it's fair to say that the issue isn't about whether or not there should be orderly use of gifts, but the issue is about whether God's order in the gifts of the Spirit has got anything to do with gender or not. If the answer is 'No'

---

12   I use these terms interchangeably as I'm convinced the Bible does too - see Acts 20, Titus 1, 1 Peter 5, 1 Timothy 3.

13   I'd like to take this moment to say that, in my experience, complementarianism has *never* been about the oppression of women but always about faithfulness to scripture. At the bottom of the complementarianism I've been around I've never detected a desire to silence women out of a place of misogyny, simply a desire not to overlook certain scriptures that seem to suggest some degree of restriction. This is very important because it touches on the matter of motives.

14   It's important to note that the inconsistency of practice among various complementarian churches can be a real source of painful confusion for women members and can lead to disengagement or cynicism. It's important to acknowledge this, and for complementarian leaders to make every effort to be consistent. This is difficult because, at the end of the day, leaders of complementarian churches are also responsible for being true to their own consciences.

then we can put it to bed - let men and women use their gifts in an orderly way, comfortable that 'orderly' has got nothing to say about gender. But if the answer is 'Yes' then we need to explore it.

So, the question is, do we have any texts whereby the use of gifts in the church is linked at all to the role of men and women and the created order? And the answer is a clear 'Yes' - there are three. We have to look at them carefully. I'll be honest, none of them are completely easy passages. I don't want to make them seem more confusing than they actually are, but all have elements that make them *not* 100% straightforward, and all are written by Paul. One of them is explicitly about headship.[15] Because of this, we'll save that one for the next chapter, which is specifically about that. We will focus for now on the other two.

INTERLUDE

Peter, who himself was an apostle, actually admits that Paul's writings aren't always easy to understand (2 Peter 3 v 16)! I find this so encouraging. Peter was not culturally distant from Paul. Peter was not geographically distant from Paul. Peter was not historically distant from Paul. Peter was not relationally distant from Paul. We are. Because of this, I think we must be kind and humble as we wrestle with certain parts of Paul's letters.

We don't know what bits Peter was referring to (whether he was left scratching his beard by the same passages we're going to look at or not!), but it's a comforting thought that Peter, one who walked as close to Jesus as he did, didn't always understand Paul the first time round.

Silence in the Church?

> *Women should remain silent in the churches. They are not allowed to speak, but must be in submission, as the law says.*
> 1 CORINTHIANS 14 V 34

The reason I say that this passage is to do with spiritual gifts is that Paul is talking in this context about prophesying and also weighing prophecy.

---

15   1 Corinthians 11 v 2-16.

At first glance, this is a very surprising thing for Paul to say. Why? Because in the same letter, just a few paragraphs before, he's been giving instructions about *when* (not if) a woman prays out or prophesies. I've never heard anyone pray out or prophesy silently before! The only conclusion can be that he is referring to a certain kind of speaking in church.

What about his reference to 'the law'? Well that's difficult because no one can locate precisely what he's referring to - no one can find the place in the law that he seems to be pointing to. Some say he's referring to Roman law, but Paul's use of the term 'the law' is almost universally to do with God's law. Others say he's referring to the whole of the Old Testament, with its emphasis on female submission to male leadership; for obvious reasons some people receive this and others don't; it hangs on your interpretation of the scriptures.

This sense of inconsistency with his previous point about women praying out and prophesying, and the curious reference to the law, has led some serious and respected scholars to point to this passage as a later insertion, not originally penned by Paul. As a result, they won't even engage with it as scripture.[16] I don't know what to say to that really. I think that as soon as we do that, it seems to me that we embrace a very different way of reading scripture; elements we consider 'out of place' we omit. There must be a better way. Let's try to see what he might be saying by reading on.

> *If they want to enquire about something, they should ask their own husbands at home; for it is disgraceful*
> *for a woman to speak in the church.*
> 1 CORINTHIANS 14 V 35

Here we have a cultural setting where men and women were not used to being together. The women most likely weren't used to the freedom of being able to speak out and contribute. Maybe Paul is simply trying to retain a bit of order by encouraging the women to ask their husbands or fathers any theological questions when they get home, rather than creating a free-for-all at church!

When we consider that chapters 11-14 of this epistle are, for a large part, Paul's attempt at chucking out the bathwater of disorder while holding on to the baby of charismatic church life, this passage begins to make more sense to us. He is doing his best to teach the Corinthians how to do 'all things' but 'in a fitting and orderly way'.[17]

---

16 Gordon Fee - a heavyweight scholar - is a proponent of this view.

17 1 Corinthians 14 v 40.

Bear in mind that the Corinthians' gatherings were pretty wild. Drunkenness and division at the Lord's supper were commonplace. People were speaking in tongues all at the same time with no interpretations. People were interrupting one another's prophecies, and it seems the ladies, animated with their new found freedoms, were asking all sorts of questions in the midst of the clamour!

Maybe Paul is simply trying to keep the contributions helpful and on track in a very exciting and new situation.

Because Paul has already taught about women praying publicly and prophesying in the meetings, where he says it's shameful for a woman to speak in church, he simply can't mean that comprehensively. The context of the statement makes clear that it's specifically about asking questions. In what sense is this shameful? Well, let's bear in mind that many women weren't educated in the ancient near eastern world - for them to be in a context where they were learning was a very radical and liberating thing. As such, they would have been way behind many of the men in lots of areas of knowledge (not intelligence - they are very different things). They would be tempted to continually interrupt for clarity. If wives and daughters kept asking all manner of things in church, it could beg the question as to whether or not the men were taking responsibility for what the Lord said ought to be happening in their homes, whereby God's word ought to be a central part of everyday life.[18]

What was going on indoors? Negligence on the part of dads and husbands? Passivity? It wouldn't be the first time! Maybe Paul wants to put that straight.

Egalitarian scholar Craig Keener is happy to interpret Paul's meaning in this passage to be that all "disruptive questions in an environment where silence was expected of new learners, which most women were" were unwelcome. Keener also makes the point that, as a matter of propriety, women were not supposed to speak to men to whom they were not related, and so such interactions were discouraged.[19]

Very occasionally, when reading epistles, we are met with statements that seem quite out of the blue and leave us, who know so little about the immediate context, quite bemused. It doesn't happen often but it does happen. This is why my response to this passage is so short. I've tried to show what Paul could be getting at, but I have more questions than answers. What we *do* see however, is that the subject of gender is not completely irrelevant when it comes to the use of spiritual gifts in the church. Maybe this is all we can take from it in this moment, but it's something worth noting.

---

18   Deuteronomy 6 v 6-8.

19   Page 171, Discovering Biblical Equality.

The Hinge Passage?

Now for the second scripture that involves both the use of spiritual gifts and gender.

Therefore I want the men everywhere to pray, lifting up holy hands without anger or disputing I also want the women to dress modestly, with decency and propriety, adorning themselves, not with elaborate hairstyles or gold or pearls or expensive clothes, but with good deeds, appropriate for women who profess to worship God.

A woman should learn in quietness and full submission. I do not permit a woman to teach or to assume authority over a man; she must be quiet. For Adam was formed first, then Eve. And Adam was not the one deceived; it was the woman who was deceived and became a sinner. But women will be saved through childbearing—if they continue in faith, love and holiness with propriety.

1 TIMOTHY 2 V 8-15

Paul's first letter to Timothy in Ephesus (where he is serving the church on Paul's behalf) contains what has become essentially the key 'battleground' in the New Testament on the matter of men and women. We find a seemingly clear prohibition concerning women teaching and having authority over men. What do we do with this?

Complementarians see the plain reading of the text and say that it's clear. The place of authority and teaching in the church is for certain appointed men. Egalitarians are adamant that certain contextual and linguistic considerations help us to understand that Paul did not mean what it appears to mean. They see it as an unusual measure introduced into a particular church at a particular time.

If you haven't got a cup of tea or coffee with you, now is the time to get one - because this is going to take a bit of time!

Remember what I said right near the start about the importance of getting to grips with the context of epistles as much as possible? This obviously becomes very important here. We are looking for any evidence that will help us discern *how* to read this passage.

We may know what the words *literally* mean, but we want to find out what exactly Paul wanted the Ephesians to hear, and whether he expected all churches down the ages to hear the same thing!

What do we know about the wider context into which this letter was written? What are the emphases that come through the whole epistle? We're trying to understand the bigger picture in order to get the details right.

What do we know of Ephesus? We know that Ephesus was the centre of Artemis worship.[20] In Greek mythology she was born to Zeus and Leto, and was the twin of Apollo. In certain accounts of the myth, she was born before her twin brother. She was considered to be the protector of young children and women, and a goddess who would both afflict these with disease, as well as bring relief. She was also one of the primary goddesses of childbirth. The ancient temple of Artemis, in Ephesus, was considered one of the wonders of the ancient world. Seeing as the most common rule was that goddesses had priestesses, (while gods had priests), the virgin goddess Artemis was probably served by young virgin priestesses. We see the power and influence of her worship in Paul's visit to Ephesus in the book of Acts, chapter 19, and the riotous uproar caused by his evangelistic success.

In the letter itself, we see some themes that come through repeatedly. Some of Paul's letters are crisis letters and others aren't. The crisis letters are full of corrections and seem to zone in on particular issues in quite detailed ways, whereas the other letters are more generic. This letter has the feel of a crisis letter. Paul goes straight in after the formal greetings with the words:

> As I urged you when I went into Macedonia, stay there in Ephesus so that you may command certain people not to teach false doctrines any longer...
> 1 TIMOTHY 1 V 3

Time and again Paul brings corrections. Leadership comes up a lot. How to discern and appoint good leadership. How to honour good leadership. How to deal with leaders when they go awry. Myths, genealogies, and the futility of getting caught up with stories other than the gospel, are other themes that Paul tackles more than once in this letter. It's a good idea to bear these two themes of leadership and myths in mind as we work through this passage.

Paul starts the passage above by urging the men in the church to pray and live harmonious lives. The word here for 'men' is not the generic word for all people but the specific word for males.

INTERLUDE

What is it with guys and prayer meetings?! Why are prayer meetings normally 75% or higher female in their attendance? It doesn't seem to be a new thing by what Paul writes here.

---

20   Diana and Artemis are the same goddess. The Romans called her Diana, the Greeks called her Artemis.

Men, when will we realise that, no matter how great our biceps are, there are certain things that only God's arm can move? We need to be provoked and spurred on by many of our sisters who know what it is to really pray. I was talking to a pastor recently and he said something so helpful to me: "Those who don't gather to pray, don't understand Who's running the church." I couldn't agree more.

We are, and will always be, out of our depth!

Who is sufficient for these things? Only God. Therefore pray. Pray like it matters. Pray like it means something. Pray your guts out.

Interlude (rant) over.

Next, Paul calls on the women to focus on their inner beauty and to adopt a posture of learning. The word for 'quietly' here could be taken two ways: it could be that Paul is calling for no one to disturb the women in order for them to be able to learn; or it could be that Paul is referring to their own state of mind - to learn peacefully, not to be worked up and restless. We know for sure that it's a different word from the one used in 1 Corinthians 14 concerning women being silent.

He also refers to external decorations. This passage is to do with ostentatious dress for the purpose of showing off wealth. Paul wants none of that.

Because most debates about this passage rush to the prohibition, we miss the significance of what Paul is encouraging the women to do. He is encouraging them to learn - let a woman learn! In a culture where very often women were not considered important enough to invest in educationally, this is a really powerful point.

We learn for two reasons: we learn in order to know; and we learn in order to teach what has been learnt. Surely, Paul has both of these outcomes in mind for the women he is encouraging to learn. Paul wants the women to grow intellectually and spiritually, and I'm sure modern women will find this music to their ears.

Paul calls for submissiveness among the women. This is a word that has also created a lot of discussion. We'll get to it in a later chapter, but for now it's important to say that while in common usage, submission is normally indicative of some kind of defeat; with our gospel lenses on, it's actually a very positive word, one that points us directly to Jesus.

Now for the big one

I do not permit a woman to teach or to assume authority over a man; rather, she must be quiet.
1 TIMOTHY 2 V 12

For some reason, Paul feels the need to add this to his statement about learning peacefully and submissively. It could mean two things. *Either* that she is not to usurp the elders as a self-appointed teacher, or simply that she is not to be in a position of teaching the men and exercising authority over them.

The question is around whether the word for 'authority' means usurp authority or simply exercise authority; linguists differ in their opinions. The reason why there is this difference of opinion is because the usual word for 'authority' (exousia) is not used here, but rather a different word (authenteo). You won't find this word anywhere else in the New Testament.

Welcome to the sometimes difficult world of biblical linguistics!

Because Paul had at his disposal a much more commonly used word for authority[21] and didn't use it here, I believe it is hermeneutically responsible to seriously consider that he was reaching for a different idea than simply 'exercising authority'.

A study of how the word was used in wider literature of the day yields different results depending on who you ask. The reality is that it's used in different ways, sometimes to denote a negative, usurping, violent dynamic and other times simply the exercising of appropriate authority.

If Paul is using the word in the negative sense, it may reveal that he was referring to an unhelpfully strident set of women at Ephesus who were inappropriately trying to take charge. If this were so, then it would remove the difficulty of the apparent universal prohibition, and we would apply this verse by prohibiting particularly underhand and subversive women from entering church leadership - something that is without controversy, I'm sure!

My only issue with this is that I don't think he'd want such women to 'teach or exercise authority over' other women either, in which case why only command them not to do so towards men? I'm also certain that he wouldn't want overbearing men to teach and lead, so why pick on the women? Though false teachers are mentioned in the letter, it seems quite clear that they are men.[22]

---

21   The Greek 'exousia' is used repeatedly in the New Testament.

22   1 Timothy 1 v 20, 1 Timothy 5 v 14-15.

If there was a particular creation-based dynamic between men and women that he thought mattered, then it might make more sense to take this verse to be referring to something beyond a local crisis.

Who, What, When?

> *For Adam was formed first, then Eve. And Adam was not the one deceived; it was the woman who was deceived and became a sinner.*
> 1 TIMOTHY 2 V 13-14

In the passage that we are particularly considering, Paul rests his argument on the order of creation, that Adam was created before Eve and that Eve was deceived.

Thinking back to the story in Genesis, Adam had been given the command about the tree; he had been personally entrusted with this from God before Eve was created. Eve, as we saw earlier, clearly knew about it, so had personal responsibility. In her interaction with the serpent we know that Adam was present, and silent![23] Instead of looking to him and teaming with him, she engaged directly with the enemy, got deceived, and then encouraged her husband into transgression by giving him the fruit.

Complementarians believe that the assumption here is *not* that she was deceived because she didn't have the theological tools Adam did, but that God had entrusted Adam with the command, and Eve, through 'going it alone', was left spiritually vulnerable, and was thus deceived.

If we begin proposing that women are more susceptible to deception, we are in error. Countless more men have led people astray spiritually than women have. It's nothing to do with who's the most clear thinking or pure in heart out of the sexes - neither of us are.

I do think we need to take the creation account seriously. Adam was created first. What happened between that time and the creation of Eve? Two main things. He was entrusted with the command, and he was commissioned to work the garden. These two things, we might say, were his stewardship in a unique way. He was alone for a period of time and couldn't do the job without her. He needed her to fulfil the task. Her creation is a 'Eureka!' moment for him, but does it undo the significance of these two things being given directly to him by God before she was made? Is this what Paul has in mind, particularly the command (as representing doctrine/teaching), which became the subject of Eve's discussion with the serpent and led to her deception?

---

23   Genesis 3 v 6.

Safe Delivery?

But women will be saved through childbearing—if they continue in faith, love and holiness with propriety.
1 TIMOTHY 2 V 15

Without any contextual considerations this statement is, at first appearances, somewhat baffling; why would Paul say such a thing? Let's look at it two ways. Firstly, through highly-contextualised lenses and secondly, without moving beyond what is explicitly stated.[24]

Let's imagine that the backdrop of this letter is, as some have suggested, a scenario where certain women, who were formerly priestesses of Artemis, have found their way into the church as self-appointed teachers. Let's imagine they are introducing some form of syncretism, blending Christianity with Artemis worship. Remember the riot in Ephesus was provoked by the loss of earnings of those who made 'gods' due to multitudes coming to Christ? It's not a crazy stretch to imagine a less violent and more subtle strategy by the locals. Instead of trying to outright destroy Christianity, just blend it with their local beliefs. Let's imagine that is the context. It makes sense of Paul coming in strongly against myths. We know that Artemis was one of the premium goddesses of childbirth. What if some of the women were being taught, or were teaching in the church, things that were a horrible blend of Christianity and Artemis worship? Paul's exhortation to put a stop to such teaching may necessarily involve him calming the fears of many women that if they turned their back on Artemis completely, they would be struck dead by her in childbirth. Maybe Paul is saying that God will keep you safe in childbirth and that there is no need to fear forsaking Artemis. This is feasible, as the word 'save' can refer to more than spiritual salvation; it can simply mean 'keep safe'. Personally I don't think it's a crazy suggestion; the big weakness is that there is so little in the text, that it feels more like conjecture. But perhaps with a verse as unusual as this one, we have permission to use our imaginations a little more than normal!

Now let's try a second interpretation.

Nowhere in the Bible does it teach that any of us are saved by giving birth or for that matter by any good works. Quite the opposite! It's possible that he's initially referring to Eve and how she was, in a sense, redeemed from total judgement through the promise that her seed would destroy the ancient serpent. That promise was actually the backdrop to Adam calling her 'Eve' - giver of life. So maybe it could simply be referring to that. But then it changes from 'she' to 'they', as if Paul widens the point for all women. So I think it's clear that Paul is speaking about more than Eve; he does have the women at Ephesus in view. Let's

---

24   By 'highly-contextualised' I mean moving beyond simply what we find in the text for context and moving into knowledge of the context that we have from extra-biblical sources.

look at another verse from the same letter that says something similarly unusual about salvation - then we will lay them alongside each other and see where we get:

> *Watch your life and doctrine closely. Persevere in them, because if you do, you will save both yourself and your hearers.*
> 1 TIMOTHY 4 V 16

We know that salvation belongs to God, and is by His grace and His grace alone. So what does Paul mean by saying to Timothy he'll save himself and others by being diligent in belief and practice? Surely he's saying to Timothy that if he is faithful with what God has given him to do, then he himself and those he is serving will come into and enjoy the full benefits of salvation. That God will use him as an instrument in his purpose of salvation for the good of his own soul and the souls of his hearers. It's short-hand for saying that God will bring salvation blessings through his efforts, admittedly phrased in an unconventional way.

Let's now think again about the original verse, the one about child-bearing. A complementarian reading might see it like this: A woman is not to lead governmentally in the church. That is something God has appointed certain men to uniquely do, demonstrated in creating Adam first and entrusting him with 'the doctrine'. As those men do this faithfully, it is filled with redemptive power. But there is also something that only women have been appointed to uniquely do. Not all men will be elders. Not all women will bear children. Only men can be elders. Only women can bear children. It's an incredible honour to be an elder. It's an incredible honour to bear children. To be an elder means you get to invest in people for the glory of God. To bear children means you get to invest in people for the glory of God. An elder who serves well will connect with God's redemptive purposes by investing truth in people. A mother who mothers well will connect with God's redemptive purposes by investing truth in people. Not all men are called to be elders. Not all women are called to bear children. These two roles, however, are exclusively reserved for each sex. If you are called to child-bearing and you live a Godly, holy and self-controlled life, God will use this to bring salvation blessings into your life and thus the life of your offspring. You will know the peace of God in this calling, and you will bear much fruit in it.

Speaking personally for a moment, there are some things about feminism that I applaud. I think it's great that male oppression, gender injustices, pay scale inequalities, and abuse and misuse of women are being challenged fiercely and competently. But the increasing denigration of the role of childbearing and maternal, feminine nurture of children is a problem. It can, at times, lead to a restlessness on the part of new mums and the temptation to despise what is surely one of the most precious seasons of their lives. I'll go further - I think it's a demonic ideological stronghold.

A woman can nourish and sustain a baby for about a year and a half through nothing but her own body. She can provide a safe home for future kings, queens, nurses, teachers, philanthropists, musicians, preachers, husbands, wives, mums, dads, divine image-bearers, presidents, artists, businesspeople, architects, cleaners, builders, chefs, creatives and leaders...and that home is her own body. That is sublime. If investing in other people is the highest goal for every one of us (and I believe it is), then nurturing little ones is a contender for the top spot!

In closing let me also say that the place of spiritual mums is absolutely key. When a woman invests in people she brings truth and life in a way that a man doesn't, and can't.

Only a woman can be a spiritual mother. And men and women need spiritual mothers. Even the apostle Paul knew the value of having a spiritual mother in his life.[25] A feminine woman who incubates and nurtures physical and spiritual life is obviously involved in things beyond the scope of a man.

I love the term 'mother in Israel', used by Deborah in the book of Judges. We need scores and scores of spiritual mums in the church that will teach the younger women and strengthen the younger men.

A Creational and Contextual Cocktail?

We're coming in to land on this one now. Perhaps there is a blending of the context with the creation order, some of it timely and some timeless (isn't there always?).

Bear in mind that one of the 'doctrines of demons' that Paul refers to in chapter 4 verse 3 is forbidding marriage. Bear in mind that Paul encourages the younger widows in the church to remarry[26] (something he doesn't do with the widows in Corinth[27]). Let's also not forget that when this was written, marriage was synonymous with having children. Bear in mind also the fear of Artemis striking you down in labour as a result of turning away from her and turning to Christ.

I'm trying to build a picture.

We can see, perhaps, that Paul's comments about women being saved through child-bearing is potentially more closely related to numbers of relevant matters in that particular context. Getting married and having children meant something more here than it might do somewhere else, where these particular poisonous ideas weren't being promoted. Nevertheless, Paul could build his arguments on the story of

---

25   Romans 16 v 13.

26   1 Timothy 5 v 14.

27   1 Corinthians 7.

creation, where we find Adam created first, Eve deceived, and particular judgement and promise around child-bearing. It's worth a thought. It's a blending of the contextual with the creational.

A complementarian would want to ask the question of some women at this point. When women come up against this verse that has a restriction in it, is the issue to do with preaching and teaching per se, or is it more to do with the suggestion that God may have ordained certain things for men only? Let's imagine it's the latter. A legitimate response might be that God has ordained that only women can bear children. Both are incredible privileges. Leading households and incubating life are both noble tasks. Neither is better or more important than the other.

INTERLUDE

Katia Adams, an egalitarian pastor and author, makes the point that if this command was part and parcel of Paul's normal practice, Timothy would have known this. By this point he had known Paul for approximately ten years, so why would Paul have had to write to him about it unless it was only specific to this situation?

I think this is quite a strong point and that Katia is either correct or else it was that Paul, knowing Timothy well, sent him a lifeline.

We know Timothy was no alpha male; he was prone to timidity, frequently ill and had to be told by Paul to not let anyone look down on him. He was also in Ephesus on Paul's behalf as a delegate. It may have served him very well to have something written by Paul's hand that he could read out to the church to quell the trouble-makers, something in a sense to almost hide behind!

But there's more. If we are going down this road, then we should ask how much else in this epistle ought Timothy to have already known? Quite a lot I think! Whether it was about money, or leaders or food laws, I'm pretty sure Timothy, after a decade with Paul, was familiar with his ways.

I think it becomes clearer and clearer that while this letter was addressed to Timothy, it was also very much addressed to the church. Maybe the church was in such a bad way, it was much safer to write the letter to Timothy so that the content wouldn't 'go missing' but would be in safe hands.

———————

Summing Up

When it comes to the Timothy passage, I would say that because the word translated 'exercise authority' is a genuinely very difficult one to decisively interpret, and because it is linguistically feasible that the two commands can be seen as one, I think the interpretation 'I do not permit a woman to teach in a way that tries to usurp a man'[28] is definitely viable. With striking examples in the New Testament of both women teaching, and teaching as part of general 'one anothering',[29] I personally feel comfortable that Paul is happy for women to teach men in the church, provided they are in a good, healthy submissive relationship to the governing authorities (elders). If someone was to say to me, wouldn't that be exactly the same for a man, I would reply affirmatively; you wouldn't want anyone teaching in the church with a view to usurping those whom God had appointed as elders. Which leads to the question, why does Paul particularly pinpoint women? I think that if there wasn't a particular issue with this happening in Ephesus he wouldn't raise it, as he doesn't raise it in most of his letters as a standard point.

But why doesn't he just call out those women and challenge them about their heart attitude? Why does he have to make it about something bigger and bring in the creation story? Maybe they are pushing a female superiority agenda, and he is explicitly reacting to that. I mean by this that they are not just teaching from a wrong motive, but the content of their teaching is about women being primary. This would explain Paul's response. But also, perhaps Paul is protecting a boundary line that He considers to be part of the fabric of created design. Maybe what he sees at work in Ephesus is potentially undermining the way God originally put things in place, i.e. these ungodly women are not just acting sinfully but also in a way that specifically disregards appropriate male headship.

If we take the 'teach' and 'usurp authority' together as one, it's most likely that the content of their teaching was poor and unhealthy, as it's very hard to find a situation linguistically in scripture where the two words would be paired like this if one word was being used positively and the other negatively. So, bad

---

28 Strong's Concordance denotes the word as 'acting of oneself'. This is very helpful as it would fit with the idea of being a self-appointed teaching authority.

29 I draw the reader's attention to the following:
    - Priscilla and Aquila teaching Apollos a better way in Acts 18;
    - Paul's unqualified comments in 1 Corinthians 14 v 26 concerning the church coming together and everyone having something to bring, including a 'teaching';
    - The mixed gender list of 'gospel workers' in Romans 16;
    - The call for everyone in the church to 'teach' and 'admonish' one another in Colossians 3 v 16.

teaching (doctrines of demons[30]) with a view to 'get one over' on the elders (usurping authority) could potentially be in view.

Application

When it comes to application in church life, surely the emphasis ought to be on releasing the gifts in the body of Christ. That is foundational, and is what I would describe as the great secret that unlocks the graceful movement of this beautiful, spiritual body. I'm convinced the enemy does all he can (including using cranky expressions of complementarianism, of which there are loads) to lock up members of Christ's body and hinder the fruitful expression of gifts. This is where the real heat of the battle is.

Seeing as the office of elders is not a gift, is it not possible to imagine all the gifts of men and women at work fruitfully, and with liberty and joy, in a scenario where local churches were overseen by teams of very humble and releasing men? If I was to be a complementarian, this is the only way I could peacefully be so.

My overall response to this argument is that I do think it's clear that stopping someone from using their spiritual gifts is a different matter to stopping someone from using their spiritual gifts in certain ways or settings. Are there any passages of scripture that give the impression that gender has a bearing on the appropriate use of spiritual gifts? There are three and we have looked at two of them. We will look at the third in the following chapter.

All of them are difficult to understand, because they involve either very complex argumentation, or unique phrases, or seeming contradiction. This ought to make us stop and pause; humility required.

No Male and Female?

Before we end this chapter, there is a key verse that egalitarians believe settles once and for all that gender is essentially irrelevant in matters of Christian life and ministry.

> *There is neither Jew nor Gentile, neither slave nor free, nor is there male and female, for you are all one in Christ Jesus.*
> GALATIANS 3 V 28

The context of Galatians was that a nasty division between Jew and Gentile had crept into the churches in this region, a division based on a corrupted gospel. Paul writes the epistle to straighten these things out.

---

30   1 Timothy 4 v 1-5.

The reason that egalitarians think this verse is so key is specifically to do with the term 'male and female', which seems to have been lifted *directly* from Genesis 1. Notice it doesn't say 'men and women'.

The point egalitarian scholar Gordon Fee makes here[31] is that in Christ all things are made new. This means that even the original creation is superseded by gospel realities. Essentially, we should not be simply looking back to Genesis chapters 1 and 2 as our model, but we should be going beyond them! This is obviously a very inspiring idea with much to commend it - what do we think?

Fee here could be open to the charge of holding an over-realised eschatology.[32] Follow me for a minute. Remember the principle of weighing scripture with scripture? When Paul writes Romans (another book where he is addressing gospel unity), three times he uses the phrase 'the Jew first and also the Gentile'. There is an order.

Whether that is purely chronological or whether it refers to more than that, he simultaneously draws some defining lines between Jews and Gentiles, and yet shows them to be in exactly the same position in terms of our need for Jesus and only Jesus to save us.

In the space of a few verses he says "What advantage has the Jew...? Much in every way!" and "What shall we conclude then? Do we [Jews] have any advantage? Not at all!"[33] Genius! He makes the point that all Jews are in the same desperate need for salvation by grace through Christ, but he also acknowledges the distinction. First the Jews and then the Gentiles. Later in the letter he talks about Gentile converts being grafted into a Jewish olive tree. The result is one tree, but there are still these layers to the story.

The point? In Galatians, Paul says there is no Jew or Gentile. It seems clear, however, that this doesn't lead him to the conclusion that there *literally* isn't such a thing as Jews and Gentiles in Christ, or that there is no distinction. Surely, given the context and his writings elsewhere, Paul's point is that there is absolutely no barrier to our fellowship in Christ, that we are one in Jesus, so united that we are intertwined.

Paul says in Galatians that there is no slave or free. And yet in Ephesians and Colossians, he takes the time to help slaves and masters who are part of the same church to relate well to one another. Again, he doesn't do away with all distinctions but it's clear that his aim is to see them come together in deep and unfettered unity.

---

31   Chapter 10, Discovering Biblical Equality.

32   This phrase describes someone who seems to forget there is a 'not yet' element to the Kingdom in this age, and who expects everything 'now'. Evangelicals use the phrase 'now and not yet' to describe the truth that while the Kingdom has been inaugurated in Christ, it hasn't yet been consummated.

33   Romans 3 v 1-2, 3 v 9.

I think it is therefore persuasive that Paul's comment about men and women is exactly the same. He's not arguing for the abolition of gender. He is absolutely opposing anything that would give the impression of a tiered system!

Doesn't it make more sense to say that he is doing with male and female what he is doing with Jew and Greek and what he is doing with slave and free? What he does with those categories throughout his letters is to demonstrate that we are all just as lost without Christ, and all just as saved in Christ. That there is no room whatsoever for unequal privileges or spiritual one-upmanship. We are all filled to the brim in Christ! We are one in Jesus!

The reason I say that this is over-realised eschatology is because the New Testament does a wonderful job of tethering the foundations of the original creation with the heights of the new creation; in this sense, Genesis 1 and 2 are never discarded but blended with all that has come and is coming through Christ. I can't say for certain why Paul used the term 'male and female' but I think it doesn't have enough in it to dismantle the tethering of the old and the new that we see all the way through the New Testament. To make this passage say that Paul literally does away with male and female distinction is, for my money, an overreach that can't be supported.

Chapter Fourteen
Headship Revisited: Complementarian Pillar Five

Headship does not disappear in the new community; Paul is clear that God is the head of Christ and husbands are the heads of their wives. It's not something to avoid but something to embrace and something that exists, in some mysterious way, even between the Father and Jesus!

As we have done in the previous chapter we are going to look at a New Testament passage where the themes of spiritual gifts and gender intersect:

> I praise you for remembering me in everything and for holding to the traditions just as I passed them on to you. But I want you to realise that the head of every man is Christ, and the head of the woman is man, and the head of Christ is God. Every man who prays or prophesies with his head covered dishonours his head. But every woman who prays or prophesies with his head covered dishonours her head—it is the same as having her head shaved. For if a woman does not cover her head, she might as well have her hair cut off; but if it is a disgrace for a woman to have her hair cut off or her head shaved, then she should cover her head. A man ought not to cover his head, since he is the image and glory of God; but woman is the glory of man. For man did not come from woman, but woman from man; neither was man created for woman, but woman for man. It is for this reason that a woman ought to have authority over her own head, because of the angels. Nevertheless, in the Lord woman is not independent of man, nor is man independent of woman. For as woman came from man, so also man is born of woman. But everything comes from God. Judge for yourselves: Is it proper for a woman to pray to God with her head uncovered? Does not the very nature of things teach you that if a man has long hair, it is a disgrace to him, but that if a woman has long hair, it is her glory? For long hair is given to her as a covering. If anyone wants to be contentious about this, we have no other practice—nor do the churches of God.
> 1 CORINTHIANS 11 V 2-16

I've read a lot of different perspectives on this passage, and the scope of interpretations is truly mind-boggling. You will find that it is one of the most discussed and dissected in the New Testament; I can almost see the apostle Peter scratching his beard! With that in mind I won't play the sage; I won't pretend to have the final interpretation of it comprehensively nailed. Instead, I want to pull out the main threads which we will all hopefully be able to see are clearly in there. Here we go.

In short: it's about *headship*. The context of the passage concerns women praying and prophesying in congregational gatherings. In the passage, Paul specifies that headship exists between God and Christ, Christ and men, and husbands and wives (or men and women - linguistically it could be either, but it's more practical to apply in marriage), and that headship is rooted in the story of creation and is therefore a transcendent idea and not culturally bound. Finally, head coverings, hair and angels all come into it.

Heads and Tales

There is debate about what the Greek word for 'head' (kephale) means. Depending who you ask, you'll hear different things. The reality is that the word seems to be used in a number of different ways, so it's best to think about what definition most adequately fits the immediate context of the passage. Apparently it can mean 'prominent' or 'chief','source' or a literal 'head'. Here it is obviously not referring to a literal head.

Firstly, let's try out 'source'.

"Christ is the *source* of man..." I'm not sure how Christ is the source of man, unless the term 'Christ' is being used to describe the LORD when He created Adam in Genesis 2. This seems to be a strange use of the title Christ - but it's possible.

"Husband is the *source* of wife..." At first glance that seems straightforward: this is what happened in creation - *she* was taken out of *him* and so, in a sense, *he* is her source.

"God is the *source* of Christ..." This could be referring to what theologians call the 'eternal procession of the Son' or to the incarnation, where God's Spirit overshadowed Mary and Christ was brought forth from God.

There are a few problems with translating *kephale* as 'source'. In the first couplet, the term 'Christ' seems a bit out of place in the context of the creation story. As we consider the second couplet another problem arises - follow me here: God made both Adam and Eve directly, with His own 'hands', so, He is just as much the source of Eve as He is of Adam - but if we are contending that *Adam* is the source of Eve because she came *from* him, then it follows that the *ground* is the source of Adam because he came *from* it. God made Adam out of the ground and made Eve out of Adam. For 'head' to mean 'source' then either God is the head of man *and* woman (because He made both), or the ground is the head of Adam and man is the head of Eve. Neither of those are consistent with where the passage is going.

Next, let's try 'prominent' in terms of a 'firstness' that represents some kind of unique spiritual authority.

"Christ has *prominence* over man…" No problem.

"A husband has *prominence* over his wife…" He was created first and, as we studied in the creation chapters, I believe there are strong signposts to him carrying a unique, spiritual authority, so yes.

"God is before Christ…" Interesting. That there is some kind of 'firstness' that the Father has in the Trinitarian relationship seems to be agreed, though there was of course never a time when the Father was and the Son wasn't. The fact that the word 'Christ' here is used instead of 'Son' makes me wonder if this is specifically referring to the relationship between the Father and Jesus during His time on earth, in that sense then yes, the Father is before Christ. There is also the reality revealed in 1 Corinthians 15 v 28 that when the end comes Christ will Himself be subjected to the Father.

Finally, does it work to use the word *kephale* here to mean 'chief'? I think it's clear that it doesn't. To conclude, I think that head as 'prominence' works best.

INTERLUDE

The Kingdom of God takes everything we are familiar with and turns it on its head. As I'm writing about prominence, I can feel the discomfort of so many men and women I know, but here's the thing: in Christ, *first* looks like *last*. Whilst it does mean 'first', it also specifically manifests as 'last in line'. Jesus, the firstborn over all creation, voluntarily becomes *last of all,* servant of all; His life poured out for the world. While saying that apostles are first in the church, Paul explicitly makes it clear that God has deliberately placed apostles *last in line,* so that they are like the offscourings of all things, the scum of the earth.[1]

The Kingdom of God is full of surprises. We mustn't jump to our own cultural conclusions when we come up against certain words and terms based on what they usually mean in our cultural contexts. Instead, we must allow our minds to be renewed: *first* looks like *last*. *First* doesn't *deny* the authority and responsibility of prominence but it *manifests* in sacrificial service.

It seems that Paul wanted the Corinthians to remember that the first woman came from the first man and that this is significant. He linked this with how the women in the church adorn themselves, particularly

---

1   1 Corinthians 4 v 13.

when it comes to speaking under the Spirit's influence. Paul wanted them all to remember that, while the women were now co-heirs with the men, this didn't undo the firstness of the man that we see in the first two chapters of Genesis.

Symbolically speaking, head coverings and hair at this time touched on themes of independence, gender distinction and sexual modesty/availability. He wanted the wives to signal that they are not independent of their husbands because without Adam there would be no Eve. We can only guess but perhaps the women, with their newfound Christian freedoms, were tempted to push themselves ahead of men or strike out alone, despising them in some way, so Paul wanted to advise them against that. Or maybe the men, adopting an over-realised eschatology, were encouraging the women to do away with head coverings or were even starting to wear them themselves.

For us, having millennia of Christian history behind us, it can be very difficult to imagine or relate to some of the difficulties these young, predominantly Gentile churches were experiencing. I think many of us would be shocked if we were teleported into their gatherings! Most of us tend to belong to fairly respectable Christian churches, where most people know how to behave and how not to. These churches, and particularly the Corinthians, were not like that!

Image and Glory

In verse 7 Paul makes a statement that, at first glance, is puzzling: that "woman is the glory of man". While it upholds the Genesis 1 teaching that both men and women are in the image of God (it doesn't say that woman is the image of man), it introduces a previously unarticulated truth: that man is the glory of God and woman is the glory of man. What does it mean? In order to understand, it's vital that our interpretation must work in both directions; we must be able to say of God and the man what we say of the man and the woman, as the phrase is used identically.

I think the clearest way to understand is this: a woman being a man's glory translates to her being created to bring honour to her metaphorical head, her husband. In Corinth, she will do this by wearing a head covering when she contributes publicly in the church service as her way of saying that she respects his headship. It translates the man being God's glory as his being created to bring honour to *his* metaphorical head, Christ. In Corinth, he will do this by *not* wearing a head covering when he contributes publicly in the church service.

Why should the woman honour her husband in this way? Paul answers in the two following verses, 8 and 9: she was made *from* him and she was made *for* him.

We've looked at the first part of that phrase already but it's important to recognise that this latter part could be misused in all kinds of ways. I believe it simply means that how she adorns herself, and how she relates to her husband, matters uniquely because her purpose is wrapped up in helping him; she can be uniquely helpful. It then follows that she can be uniquely *unhelpful*, and Paul wants to make sure that doesn't happen.

Of course, a man can be uniquely damaging if he either dominates or abdicates in his marriage. They *both* have a unique contribution, and can therefore be uniquely constructive or uniquely destructive in the areas and purposes for which God has brought them together.

Verse 10 introduces a couple of things that need clarifying. Firstly, the Bible you read may well say that the woman is to wear a symbol of authority on her head or that she has authority over her own head to wear a covering. All translations agree that the word 'symbol' is not in the original; it simply says 'authority'. So this verse can be taken two ways: either she is to wear a symbol on her head that speaks of being under her husband's authority; or she has the authority to make the right decision concerning what to do with her physical head in light of headship. Either way, Paul is urging the wearing of head coverings (something that was culturally very meaningful in this regard in Corinth), but the way we interpret the use of the word 'authority' can impact the tone and feel of what he is asking them to do. It would not be wise to take this ambiguous phrase and build too much on it with regards to how authority works in marriage. We will, however, endeavour to unpack this as we work through the book and meet more explicit passages.

One final reason Paul gives for a woman wearing a head covering is 'because of the angels'.

What does he mean by referring to the angels? Here are two ideas: Paul could be referring to actual heavenly beings, who we know watch the church keenly.[2] Alternatively, he could mean human 'messengers' (this is what the word 'angel' can also translate as), who would seemingly come to check out the church and report back to various bodies, whether Jewish or Greek. Cogent arguments can be made for both.

We know that principalities and powers look on at the church and see the wisdom of God in her. If 'the angels' see gender confusion or ignorance, there is a problem - the wisdom of God is not being displayed; the church is no longer telling the right story. This reflects badly on both the people whose destiny it is to judge angels in the future, as well as on the Lord Himself as we are the members of His body.

We know that in both Jewish and Greco-Roman cultures what a woman did with her hair mattered; as I said earlier, matters of modesty, sexual availability and propriety were tied up with it (pardon the pun). If

---

2   Ephesians 3v10.

these angels refer to human messengers from outside of the church, then the church, wanting to avoid unnecessary controversies, could reasonably ask for cultural protocols to be followed in order to both get on and live a quiet life and be as much of a blessing to one another as possible, while still 'in the body'.

Whatever Paul had in mind in this passage, it's clear elsewhere that the church has a huge and weighty responsibility with regards to spiritual forces and realities that exist invisibly alongside us. How we deal with issues like men and women is important. I don't believe we are dealing with earthly realities that God has simply loaded with spiritual meaning - as if that wouldn't be enough to make us tremble! - but somehow our earthly identities mirror heavenly realities that are eternal.

C. S. Lewis puts it like this:

> "We cannot shuffle or tamper so much. With the church, we are farther in: for there we are dealing with male and female not merely as facts of nature but as the live and awful shadows of realities utterly beyond our control and largely beyond our direct knowledge. Or rather, we are not dealing with them but (as we shall soon learn if we meddle) they are dealing with us."

Switching it up?

In verses 11 and 12 Paul plays a masterstroke by pointing out that, just as woman originally came from man, now man comes from woman. He does this, it seems, to keep any of his readers from moving his ideas into something caricatured or abusive and in order to emphasise the interdependence of men and women. Whilst the woman is only here because of man in the beginning, men are only here because of women now. It's clear that Paul does not want his teaching of male headship rooted in the creation story to create a scenario where men lose sight of their absolute need for women. Alongside her being made for him is the reality that his life - although he had God - was 'not good' without her!

Surely Paul's point in these verses is not to undo what he has said in previous verses. The fact that the present-day man now comes from the woman doesn't mean that she is now his head; if that were the case there would be no point to the whole of the passage! It also demonstrates that Paul almost certainly didn't have 'source' in mind when he referred to headship, because despite woman now being the source of man it's clear from the passage that she is not now his head also.

Whether Paul's application is to do with wearing her hair up or down, or some sort of covering, or his and her hair length, these are points of application that I would be happy to approach as more culturally bound. I think that timeless and binding spiritual truths can co-exist with timely applications that aren't binding for all people at all times.

That said, we should at least make the point that Paul's concerns about hair length seem to be linked in some way with what we might call 'gender clarity'. Whether or not a man or woman should have long or short hair seems to be rooted in the idea that men should be recognisably men and women should be recognisably women. We shouldn't present ourselves in ways that would create confusion, but clarity. In doing so, we send a message to the outside world that we are in agreement with who God made us to be.

If gender matters and if gender means something spiritually, then *clarity is vital*. Wherever we create a confused situation we confuse the spiritual meaning and message of male and female, and we begin to tell a different story to God's story.

To conclude: I agree for the most part with the egalitarian point that Pentecost ushered in an age without discrimination around the *gifts*. But I think a layer is added by encouraging appropriate gender dynamics in order to tell the story of creation as faithfully as possible.

Chapter Fifteen
Roman Numerals: Egalitarian Pillar Six

Paul's list of co-workers in Romans 16 is approximately 25% female. Given the patriarchal backdrop of the wider society, this is quite extraordinary. This points to the kind of scenario, in different cultural circumstances (like ours today), where we could easily imagine a 50/50 gender split of gospel ministry.

Romans 16 - you don't hear many preachers or commentators highlight its significance. But if you wanted to taste the relational atmosphere of the early church, this chapter is right up there. It's common for Paul to greet a handful of people in his letters, but here, at the end of Romans, he greets 27 individuals as well as numbers of different house churches. The warmth and affection that jump off the page are breathtaking. These people, with Paul, have been through the fire and the water! Let me repeat the above point; approximately 25% of those on the list are women. These people are gospel workers with Paul, people of stature in the churches, people with authority.[1] All of this within a patriarchal backdrop.

In the New Testament there are ten references to 'workers' outside of the Romans passage (where there are four). There are many what we might describe as 'big hitters' on the list: Apollos, John Mark, Barnabas, Luke, Titus, Epaphroditus, Timothy and Philemon to name some! These are trans-local ministers of the gospel. There is no reason to think those on the list in Romans 16 are fundamentally different.

For egalitarians this begs the question: if this was the case back then, what should it look like now? Surely we should be seeing women in the thick of gospel endeavour, carrying their share of the most senior leadership in church life. Imagine a Christian organisation where this wasn't happening. At their feet, an egalitarian would lay the charge of having drifted from New Testament culture.

---

1   In 1 Corinthians 16 v 15-16 Paul refers to fellow workers and instructs the church to submit to them, making it clear that 'workers' were considered to be leaders.

Gender Breakdown

I do think that if we find ourselves, as Christian ministers, in a male-dominated atmosphere and culture, we are in danger of both undermining the creation mandate of Genesis 1 *and* not faithfully reflecting the culture of the New Testament. I think this passage in Romans 16 puts a very helpful spotlight on all complementarian church streams, and invites from them a clear response.

How might a complementarian respond to the challenge of Romans 16? They would have to acknowledge that those mentioned who are women are clearly workers. Sure, there are some people listed where it doesn't explicitly say this is so, but it's clear that Phoebe, Priscilla, Mary, Tryphaena, Tryphosa and Junia are all in the 'worker' category.

Phoebe, we are told explicitly, was a deacon. We know that Priscilla, along with her husband Aquila, together straightened out the doctrine of a fledgling apostle (Apollos) and 'risked their necks' for Paul's life. It also seems that Junia (along with Andronichus who may have been her husband) could well have been an apostle.[2] Mary, Tryphaena and Tryphosa are all referred to in light of their labour for the gospel. As far as I am concerned, labour for the gospel is service and service is ministry. They were ministers for Christ and His gospel.

Please note that when Paul writes his second letter to Timothy, he says this:

Do your best to present yourself to God as one approved, a worker who has no need to be ashamed, rightly handling the word of truth.
2 TIMOTHY 2 V 15

See what Paul does - he associates being a worker with handling God's word rightly. To work for the gospel, of necessity, involves inspired and empowered speech. The point being, these women didn't just give the notices, cook the food and make the room look nice by their interior design skills, long eyelashes and nice dresses. Complementarian leaders would surely do well to acknowledge, and with vigour, the esteemed

---

2   Without going into all the ins and outs of this one, suffice to say that there has been considerable controversy around whether or not it's 'Junia' - a woman's name, or 'Junias' - a man's name. Of late, it seems that most people agree it's the former. Settle this, and there is another controversy around whether or not this person was 'great among the apostles' implying they were themselves an apostle or whether, as the ESV puts it, they were 'well known to the apostles'. No one seems to agree, and everyone seems to insist they're right! Honestly, I'm somewhat jaded by reading too many people simply propping up their own preference. I'm assuming she was a woman and I'm not making a call on whether she was an apostle or not, but acknowledging, nevertheless, how immensely esteemed she was by Paul. I hope this is not seen as avoidance; that is not my motive - what is one to do when those who supposedly know best say opposite things?! In the FAQs at the end, I will look at the question of women apostles.

place of these women ministers for Jesus and His gospel. My personal conviction is that they would also do well to search out, support and release any sisters of like giftedness and godliness in their churches.

Here we have a mix of men and women, working alongside Paul to serve the churches and advance the faith, men and women who carried delegated authority and leadership responsibility. None of those things would undermine the convictions of most complementarians.

Open Doors and Open Hearts

Let's consider again how the complementarian understands what it means to be a head, and think about how they might respond to the challenge of Romans 16. Headship is representative responsibility from God, for the good of a household. There is the household of fallen humanity of which Adam is the head. There is the household of redeemed humanity, also known as the church, of which Christ is the head. The household of faith, the church, has been organised by God into local congregations, households within a household if you like. Complementarians believe that elders serve in a headship role in that they oversee the flock and will be held to account for its condition, and the members are called to submit to them;[3] it seems clear they function as household representatives. Then there are literal households, families, of which husbands/fathers are the heads. A complementarian should have no problem with gifted women serving among the churches, providing they weren't in a headship role.

From that perspective, a complementarian who was seeing things straight would want to see as many gifted women as possible released into ministry. The man cannot fulfil the entrusted task of the Great Commission without the woman. Healthy leaders would have their own lists of dear brothers and sisters, mothers and fathers, sons and daughters who served alongside them for the sake of the gospel.

So, the big question. Does this passage give the green light for women to serve in all functions of church life? For so long and in so many circles, church ministry and gospel labour have been seen as the domain of men (and maybe occasional uber-gifted women). In light of this, egalitarians would feel - maybe justifiably - that any attempt to use this list to endorse male headship is little more than a poke in the eye for godly, gifted women.

But. Exegetical arguments on the egalitarian side for any of these women serving as elders are pretty thin. Normally it will be Priscilla who is pointed to on this list as the closest to that. But there is no explicit evidence. It's also true that other than Peter, we have no other named elders in the New Testament, so the fact that Priscilla isn't explicitly mentioned as one is not confirmation that she wasn't. But we do need

---

3   Ezekiel 34, Hebrews 13 v 17, Acts 20 v 28.

more than arguments from silence. Other than her, most egalitarian arguments seem to be based entirely on Junia, and for the reasons outlined in the footnote earlier, I don't think that's enough.

So, Romans 16 shows us a mixed gender team of gifted people working alongside Paul. It doesn't, however, necessarily show us a mixed gender team of elders. This brings us very naturally onto the sixth complementarian argument.

Chapter Sixteen

Oversee Don't Overlook: Complementarian Pillar Six

The early church was overseen by male elders. The qualifications for elders that we find in Timothy and Titus are aimed explicitly at men. These men are to copy Jesus, who sacrificed His life for the sake of the flock.

No one would deny that the lists for the qualifications of elders in 1 Timothy 3 v 1-7 and Titus 1 v 5-9 are aimed at men; specifically, the charge of being a faithful husband comes to mind. In 1 Timothy 3 v 11, women (wives?) are specifically introduced, confirming that up to this point men had been in view. This is important because some egalitarians make much of the fact that language back then was androcentric.[1] The explicit and additional introduction of women at this point, however, makes clear that, up to this point, Paul had men exclusively in mind when referring to the role of elders.

The egalitarians who concede that Paul is referring to men often push back that it's not binding, but concessionary. Their point is that Paul's exhortations and instructions are simply a reflection on how things would have been back then, and certainly not a heavenly directive. An egalitarian might point out that the early church honoured the wider culture where it could. It did this in order to avoid unnecessary persecution and maintain a good reputation with outsiders. This explains why the letters, here and there, feel like the wider culture: androcentric and patriarchal. They would go on to say that times have changed and therefore so must we!

Today it is incredibly offensive in the West to prohibit anything on the grounds of gender alone. If we want to embrace the principle of causing least unnecessary offence in the wider culture, then we surely must adjust our practice around elders. We must let the women of appropriate character and gifting serve in this role. I actually think that it's an argument worth listening to and taking very seriously. If the tonevv of the New Testament and what some people consider the controversial verses on gender are based solely

---

1   This means that when referring to men and women, masculine words would have been used, much like the way we might refer to a group of men and women as 'guys'.

on what was culturally acceptable back then, I would say that we need to make sure all our practices now are gender symmetrical.

Big Deal or Small Deal?

We have to work out how big a deal it is that men are elders. How much transcendent meaning is packed into it? If it is incidental and fundamentally without much meaning, if it's based simply on the cultural norms of the time, then it would be the wiser thing to open the office of eldership to appropriately qualified women.[2] If, however, the Bible arranges gender matters as it does for spiritual reasons, then it would be a grave mistake to embrace total symmetry. I've tried to demonstrate up to this point that I think there is way more than culture that is at work in the gender asymmetry we find in scripture.

Having said that, I also think it's important to be as helpful as possible in our wider culture, without giving away anything that pertains to our faithful witness.

So here is the question. To be simultaneously committed to being as helpful as possible to the wider culture and faithful to the Bible, how far might one go with regards to women and eldership? What even is the role of an elder? Well...surprise, surprise - people differ in their views! If anyone's been around the church for a few years, they will realise that churches in different denominations are governed in a variety of ways. For example, some churches have a pastor who is supported by a board of elders. Other churches are led by a team of elders who are also referred to as pastors. Some churches are led by a senior pastor who has other assistant pastors or lay elders alongside them.

The key question, in light of representative responsibility, is this: who is carrying the can? As we saw back in Eden, where does the doctrinal stewardship rest? Bear in mind that the oversight of souls, Biblically speaking, is essentially about making sure people rightly understand and believe the right things and then lovingly and trustingly obey God by practising them.

I believe that the Biblical pattern for church government is a team of elders who, together, carry the can as overseers of souls.[3] The buck stops with them; they steward the doctrine in a local church. They are the representative heads who will give an account to God for the condition of the congregation. An eldership team may have a team leader, someone who is more gifted as a leader, but the Bible teaches that all elders carry the oversight of the church together.

---

2   In this scenario, the qualifications would be the same as those for the men that we find in 1 Timothy and Titus.

3   Hebrews 13 v 17, Acts 20 v 28, 1 Peter 5 v 2.

This is the bottom line for me as to why I believe elders ought to be men.

If a church is set up in such a way that elders don't carry the final responsibility but a senior pastor does, then I think, in that scenario, men and women could be elders. I would say, however, that I don't believe a Biblical idea of eldership is in view in that scenario.

As an aside, because eldership is never *explicitly* called headship in the Bible (I think we see it to be implicitly and clearly the case as shown above), some decide that they are complementarian in the home, but not in the church, where Jesus Himself is explicitly the Head. I can at least follow the logic: Jesus is the Head of every church, now let's get on and set things up how we like regardless of gender, safe in the knowledge that He is in charge.

I'm not sure whether a church that did this would continue to tell our multi-layered and rich story as faithfully as she might: the story of creation, where Adam and Eve were charged to rule creation together, with Adam as doctrinal steward and Eve as essential helper, and the story of salvation where Christ, as the second Adam, lays His life down for the flock. I think we would end up flattening things out and losing something along the way.

Given that there is no evidence for women elders in the Bible, but instead a clear expectation that they will be men, coupled with our responsibility of telling the God story as faithfully as possible, I believe the most faithful course of action is to appoint men as elders.

However, in my humble opinion, given the wider cultural developments in the West, complementarian churches who cannot and do not articulate their position with both truth and beauty, well…I think their days are numbered. People will vote with their feet if they don't realise what's actually going on here; without a powerful story and a life-giving model of what God has in mind with this, people will only see prohibition.

What a tragedy that would be.

INTERLUDE

The church has a knack of being about 10-20 years behind the world. We followed in terms of divorce rates and now sit at about the same level. In fact, ours may now be higher, but if so that's probably only because Christians still get married!

The Western world is travelling full speed down the road past egalitarianism, and on its way to interchangeable androgyny. I fear that beneath this equality banner there travels an interchangeability agenda. Wouldn't the enemy love this?

In the next couple of decades, I believe that the kind of men this produces will begin to trouble a generation of women that want more. And vice versa. I imagine that there will be some kind of wake-up moment. Wouldn't it be almost tragicomic if the church followed the world down this road and found itself waist-deep in gender uniformity at the same time the world woke up and started looking for answers; there goes the church again, trailing behind a failed and fallen system instead of shining like a city on a hill.

If churches that believe in male headship continue to appoint teams of godly men to oversee them, they are being consistent with what they believe. But hear this: they must care enough about this to be willing to pay the price inside and outside the church. They must also learn - and quickly - to tell the story well.

I will also add that if elders of complementarian churches are not exemplary and wholehearted in their passionate investment in women, I believe they are in sin and will also find their churches in significant trouble before long.

I do believe these matters of gender hang as much on what we understand to be masculine and feminine behaviour as they do on church structure - maybe even more so. Because of this, when we get to the end of the seven pillars, I will begin to articulate how I see godly masculinity and femininity, i.e. what it means for a man to be faithful to God's design as man, and what it means for a woman to be faithful to God's design as woman.

On that sober note, let's look at the seventh pillar of the egalitarian perspective.

Chapter Seventeen
Contextual Competence: Egalitarian Pillar Seven

Headship and submission dynamics taught in the New Testament are no more than culturally binding. They were written in order to protect the church in that age from charges of disorder in the wider culture. They are not timeless reflections of God's Kingdom. We must read the epistles with a keener eye for context.

There is much about the epistles that can frustrate us, because we desperately want to fill in the gaps. We have 101 questions. Why is this line of argument being so powerfully brought to bear? Why has he articulated this in this way? Why is he softer in this letter than another letter? What does he mean by that word? How many of us would give our right arm to pick the apostles' brains! This human side to the Bible is something we love - the circumstantial backdrop, each author's particular style, the earthiness that makes the Hebrew scriptures unique among all other religious writings.

But then, there is what we might call the divine side. That it's inerrant. That it's sufficient. That it's perspicuous. We believe the Holy Spirit inspired and oversaw these writings and preserved the doctrine in a way that equips us to know the mind of God for all that we need in our time. We know that we can't know everything. But we can know enough to be faithful.[1] And so while we need to consider context, we mustn't overplay it to the point where we find ourselves editing out or essentially rewriting scripture. We must also be somewhat cautious about our own personal corruption. There are certain scriptures that, to put it bluntly, make life difficult for us!

When you are shepherding a congregation, you know that a large percentage of people really don't want the Bible to be saying certain things that it does. Whether it's about forgiveness or about honouring the government or about the sanctity of life, or financial prudence or sexual purity, or caring for the poor or male and female. From that perspective, it does seem somewhat suspect in our age, when there is a huge furore around gender and sexuality, that 'suddenly' certain scriptures that seem to make some quite clear

---

1   Deuteronomy 29 v 29.

delineation concerning gender and sexuality are being held up as either culturally constrained or misunderstood for the last 1900 years. There is something in that which may perhaps lack a bit of honesty.

The reality is that each generation will have different battles. What does it mean to be faithful? Opinions and trends will come and go, there is nothing new under the sun, but to be faithful to the living and enduring word of God is our holy duty. To be mindful that our life is but a breath[2] and that our natural beauty, like the grass and the flowers, will both wither and fade,[3] but that His word stands forever; this is wisdom. So yes, let it not just be permitted that we understand the context of different parts of the Bible; we must. But in order to obey, not in order to escape.

One relevant passage we haven't spent much time on specifically is Peter's teaching on marriage in his first epistle. Let's study this with a keen eye for context.

> *Wives, in the same way, submit yourselves to your own husbands so that, if any of them do not believe the word, they may be won over without words by the behaviour of their wives, when they see the purity and reverence of your lives.*
> 1 PETER 3 V 1-2

Here Peter starts with 'likewise' because he's been talking about how all believers are to submit to various governing institutions and then slaves to masters. Then he picks up with marriage, both generally and with a specific focus on wives whose husbands are either not disciples or at least not walking in obedience. He says that all wives are to be subject to their husbands, and are to win over those who don't obey the word by their conduct, rather than their words.

The word for 'be subject to' - *hupatosso* in Greek - is the same word used when referring to governing authorities and slaves to masters. In each case, Peter speaks to the person being called to submit. He doesn't write to the master to make the slave submit or to the husband to make the wife submit. He never does that, and neither does Paul. They address the person who is called to submit and ask them to do so. This is one of the ways that abuse is guarded against. All of us have choices to make and have the agency to do so. None of this is forced.

---

2   James 4 v 14.

3   Isaiah 40 v 6-8.

Don't Trip!

The call to submit can feel unfair for many women. It can become what the Bible calls a stumbling block, something that causes us to trip up spiritually. Let me show you how this works. In our part of the world, when we're doing marriage prep with a couple, it's always this matter of headship and submission that takes most attention and time and causes most questions and bother. We try to give it the attention it deserves because it's both biblically important *and* culturally sensitive.

Conversely, I heard a while ago of a marriage prep course in a non-Western culture where some of those attending began to protest because the leaders were emphasising the point that biblically speaking, men and women are equal. They were giving this truth the attention it deserves, because in their context, this element is both biblically important *and* culturally sensitive. So you have these nuanced biblical truths causing upset and anger in different cultures because, as I said earlier, none of us are processing this stuff in a vacuum; the word of God is challenging our cultural norms and assumptions. It's not comfortable.

This is where we need to be very aware, not just of the context of the things written in scripture, but of our own context. We need to understand what's going on in our own hearts. Generally speaking, the non-Western Christians referred to above would have had no problem with the teaching on headship and submission, and generally speaking the British Christians would have had no problem with the teaching on equality! This is one of the reasons why it's so good to travel; it helps us not just understand others better but also understand *ourselves* better. But it can still be difficult to accept that this is what's going on, that our struggle is borne out of cultural norms - surely, we say, the Bible just *can't* mean *that!* And so we hunt around for interpretations of scripture that fit our cultural norms; that way, if we can find some, we can feel both godly and comfortable at the same time. If only.

There's an added problem. Because for the most part, in the West we're very rich, we're also very proud. I don't think it's always intentional - more of a default. And so we have this cultural elitism. We refer to other parts of the world as 'developing' as if we're waiting for them to catch up with us in every way. Sure, we may be more developed in terms of infrastructure or tech, but in every way? There's something deeply suspect about that assumption. It's so proud. And so when our culture is challenged, we assume that any change would be some kind of backward step. We love to describe ourselves as 'progressive'.

And it can become a stumbling-block. Stumbling blocks are a fascinating and rather scary subject in the Bible. They're both good and bad, depending on the part they play.

Jesus says that if someone causes a little one (a young believer or a child) to sin (literally 'causes them to stumble'), it would be better for that person if they had tied a millstone around their neck and jumped into the sea. An example of how bad they can be.

Jesus, however, is referred to as the 'stone of offence' in the exact same sense. There's something about Him that has the ability to cause us to end up flat on our backsides. Why? Because He's Lord, and He only comes as Lord, and He's not changing for anyone. And He's utterly impartial, which means that no one gets away with nonsense, regardless of how beautiful or charismatic or charming or rich or resourceful they are. No one. He's the great leveller. That's an example of how good stumbling-blocks can be.

So, this talk about wives submitting to husbands is a cultural stumbling block for many in the West - men and women. And we have to ask the question: is the Bible really teaching some kind of authority asymmetry in marriage by God's design and for the good of both? If we see that it is, ours is to pick ourselves up off the floor and walk forward in obedience. That's how we change.

Transcendent Beauty

> *Your beauty should not come from outward adornment, such as elaborate hairstyles and the wearing of gold jewellery or fine clothes. Rather, it should be that of your inner self, the unfading beauty of a gentle and quiet spirit, which is of great worth in God's sight.*
> 1 PETER 3 V 3-4

Similar to the Timothy passage, the apostle Peter encourages women to shun ostentatious clothing and to focus on their inner beauty. He wants them to grow in quiet confidence, not worried and anxious about too many things but confident in God. This idea of 'quietness' came up in Timothy when talking about women. What is this particular word referring to? It's not so much about silence (unlike the 1 Corinthians 14 passage we looked at); here it's more to do with being undisturbed in your spirit, living in that place of stillness. We see a similar idea in Isaiah where it says:

> *In repentance and rest is your salvation; in quietness and trust is your strength.*
> ISAIAH 30 V 15

Here we see a quality of stillness that arises from confidence in God, and Peter says that in God's sight this quality is very precious. Why? Well, I imagine that whenever any of us have that inner stillness that comes out of confidence in God, we're not going to speak or act from the wrong place; God is going to be glorified and people are going to be blessed.

But maybe for a woman, it takes on a whole different layer of meaning. In preparation for completing this book I wrote to quite a few women asking them to put into their own words what femininity and masculinity meant to them. Interestingly, in conversation with one woman, she confided, sadly, that at the heart of her own experience of being a woman was a sense of not feeling safe, that there was a vulnerability that had to be reckoned with. Being a woman in what is often 'a man's world'[4] can be fraught with anxieties. To find that place of settled confidence and trust in 'Abba', whereby the temptation to take control in an ungodly way is resisted, is understandably very precious in the sight of God. Note the context of Peter's exhortation to these women. It's not to simply appear orderly to a patriarchal world. He talks about that which is precious in God's sight. This is transcendent.

It's Frightening - Don't be Afraid

For this is the way the holy women of the past who put their hope in God used to adorn themselves. They submitted themselves to their own husbands, like Sarah, who obeyed Abraham and called him her lord. You are her daughters if you do what is right and do not give way to fear.
1 PETER 3 V 5-6

This is one of my wife's and my favourite passages on marital submission, because Peter acknowledges that it's frightening to submit yourself to someone imperfect. Submission is not about unconditional obedience; that's reserved for God alone. A complementarian would say that it's about a posture of voluntary, faith-filled yielding to whoever is your head, in this case, your husband. It's something you offer from a place of faith. It's not something that someone makes you do against your will. It's something that you, and only you, can give - no one can give it for you or on your behalf; there is 100% agency. Peter describes a wife's submission as an adornment, something she adds to herself in order to be more beautiful to her husband. That's an amazing thing to think about (we'll get to the guys' bit in just a moment).

When a husband knows that his wife has got his back, is *for* him, cheering him on, receiving him with all her might and bringing all that she has to help him, ready to honour him with vigour and enthusiasm, it makes him ready to take on the world. Suddenly, just maybe, he can do what God has put in his heart. What if her act of submission is one of the keys that unlocks his true strength?

I remember having lunch with a Christian man who was quite effeminate in his manner, and whose sexuality was for him a matter of some pain and confusion. My wife and I had noticed how sometimes, unhelpfully, certain women seemed to treat him more like one of their girlfriends. We suspected this didn't help him.

---

4   By this, I mean a world where men are often at an advantage due to either corrupt systems or wrong attitudes, not that God made this world to be a man's world.

Over lunch, quite out of the blue, he confessed there was one woman in the church who, by the way she treated him, actually made him feel like a man. What an extraordinary admission. It revealed to me how helpful (and unhelpful) we can be to one another, and the unique power we have as men and women to assist each other in growing up into who the Lord says we are.

Some have questioned Peter's use of the story of Abraham and Sarah here. They point to the only recorded instance we have of Sarah calling him 'lord' and show that it wasn't really in the context of her submitting. This is true. But I don't think that's what Peter is doing here. I think he is essentially referring to Sarah's submission to Abraham, and then taking this way of addressing him as an example of that. It is universally acknowledged that she submitted to him in following him through thick and thin on their faith adventure. We looked at that earlier in the book. Her reference to him as 'lord' is simply another example of her submissive posture.

With regards to submission, it is not passive, weak or degrading. The gospel we believe in and celebrate is based upon the submission of Jesus to His Father's will. Jesus' act of submission in going to the cross is the most extraordinary thing that has ever taken place in the history of the planet. It was and is and will ever be spectacularly awesome and unimaginably powerful. We will sing about it forever. The trust! The courage! The fearlessness! The cost!

> *Jesus paid it all*
> *All to Him I owe*
> *Sin had left a crimson stain*
> *He washed it white as snow.*[5]

All of this treasure is brought to us through His submission and commitment to the Father's plan.

Understanding and Honour

> *Husbands, in the same way be considerate as you live with your wives, and treat them with respect as the weaker partner and as heirs with you of the gracious gift of life, so that nothing will hinder your prayers.*
> 1 PETER 3 V 7

Here Peter says some things that need attention and understanding. He starts with a 'likewise', but doesn't go on to tell the husband to submit. So what is the 'likewise' about? He's developing his teaching on what godliness in relationships looks like. In the fifth chapter of the same letter, Peter uses the same word,

---

5   Hymn written in 1865 by Elvina M Hall and is public domain.

'likewise', within the pairing of how elders are to serve the church and how younger people are to relate to the elders; his instructions to both parties aren't identical or symmetrical but the 'likewise' seems to denote that he is calling upon both parties to act in a godly way.

Peter says to husbands that they're to live with their wives in an understanding way. This means that they are to get to know them, to try their best to understand them. Not to fear listening to them and letting them talk. The truth is that men can be afraid of this. A woman's internal world can be an overwhelming place for many men. She seems to sense and perceive things from angles and directions that can, quite frankly, leave many men dazed and confused. A woman is uniquely wired for relationships - she was created for companionship. She understands relational dynamics in ways that are often utterly beyond men. When a woman wants to talk about what she is experiencing and seeing in ways that require more of men than they sometimes feel they have, it can be tempting for a man to shut things down and move on. For a man to try to understand and get to know his wife, so that she can feel known and honoured by him, as the passage says, this is a great service that he can do for her. If he will face his own fears in doing so, there is great reward.

Now what about the 'weaker vessel' bit? The general observation that men, in the main, are physically stronger, is no great controversy. He is exhorting men never to use their physical strength to take advantage of, or to dishonour their wives. This might sound obvious, but the domestic violence statistics are not encouraging. It's worth saying loud and clear to the men: never use your superior physical strength to harm or control the women that God has put in your life for you to protect and love.

Beauty means something profound for women and strength does for men; both are, in a sense, their unique stewardship from God as men and women. It's important to see how the Bible looks to redeem these attributes and re-cast them spiritually. This rescues women from the trap of fixation with how they look externally. This releases them into the quest for inner beauty, which is a manifestation of godly femininity. This also rescues men from the trap of fixation with how they look externally. This releases them into the quest for godly strength, which is a manifestation of godly masculinity.

Neither of these are meant in a crass or exclusive way. We are all, men and women, beautified through God's salvation[6] and we are all, men and women, to be clothed with spiritual strength to engage in spiritual warfare.[7] I'm just saying that if you look across the world in every culture you will see an emphasis: women are made, generally speaking, more beautiful than men, and men, generally speaking, stronger. This is not

---

6   See Isaiah 61.

7   See Ephesians 6.

wrong, but it can quickly go wrong as we fall headlong into idolatry over these things. When we turn to Christ, feminine beauty and masculine strength can be redeemed - that's the point.

From this perspective, it's a good thing when nurturing and training young men and women to speak into their anxieties and fears in this regard, and to lift them to this higher paradigm.

In the same way that men can be stunned into silence by the beauty of a woman, and a woman can be powerfully comforted by the strength of a man, men can also be killed by poorly stewarded feminine beauty, and women can be destroyed by poorly stewarded masculine strength. When men allow Jesus to teach them how to harness their strength for the purpose of being loving and understanding, a very powerful thing happens - similarly when women allow Jesus to teach them how to love and serve others with their beauty. Let's be very, very clear - women are not weak - unless something has gone wrong. Secure men are looking for strong women. One of my wife's most attractive attributes is her strength. And just in case there are any guys out there who are feeling a bit sensitive, let me also say, for the record, that neither are men innately ugly!

But there are these emphases. If all we think about with men and women is equality, we're sure to overlook the controlled strength of men manifesting in sacrificial service, and the inner beauty of women manifesting in quiet confidence, and what these point to (hint: the gospel). This would be a huge loss.

When Daughters are also Sons

Peter also wants the husbands to know that their wives are heirs of the grace of life, just as they are. For us this sounds obvious, but when this was written it was the sons who would inherit the family riches. God has sons and daughters and they're both heirs.

And so, Peter says, if you think you can treat your wife unfairly, throwing your weight about, well - you've got another thing coming. Your relationship with God will be impacted: you will see it in your prayer life, you'll know it, something will be deeply wrong because God Himself will be resisting you.

As we've walked through this passage, I hope you can see that in Peter's words, there are elements that need clarifying and highlighting, both because of the context he is writing in and because of our own context, but the main content stands. He is drawing together issues of creation - comparative physical strength and beauty, and he is drawing together the Old and New Testament, connecting Sarah and Abraham with husbands and wives. Arising out of those, he is appealing to them to conduct themselves spiritually, lovingly, fearlessly - these are timeless matters that don't change from context to context.

As I've said earlier, many scriptural commands are also given with the wider context in view, with one of the purposes being not to bring the church into disrepute. We have to be keenly aware of that, and adopt the same principles today. This is why I said earlier that if it can be shown that these commands concerning men and women are given essentially to placate the wider patriarchal culture of the day, then we must relegate them today as *only* contextual. It just seems to me that the arguments transcend that and are rooted in creation and the gospel.

Contextual Consistency

It's also very important to notice that Peter was actually and specifically challenging Greco-Roman culture in this passage by giving women with unbelieving husbands the freedom to follow Christ when the prevailing culture said that wives had to follow the religion of their husbands. He was therefore not just going along with cultural practice.[8]

As we consider this, and these other elements, the idea that the apostle was for the most part, simply giving a nod to the wider culture begins to look more and more like a house of cards.

My conclusive response to the seventh egalitarian argument is, yes, we have to give very good attention to the context in which the passage was written, and as importantly to our own context, but never at the expense of the actual content. In a nutshell… context - yes; content - even more so.

This brings us to our final argument from the traditionalist perspective.

---

8   Thanks to David Devenish for this insight.

Chapter Eighteen

Bigger Story: Complementarian Pillar Seven

The relationship between a husband and a wife is way bigger than itself. It tells the transcendent story of Jesus and the church. Two united as one flesh has always been about the gospel! Interchangeable roles and symmetrical submission in a marriage will never tell this story faithfully.

It's quite difficult to step outside of our own understanding of what marriage looks like and imagine the kind of scenario more typical in Bible times. Consider for a moment: it was not at all unusual for a husband to be a decade or two older than his wife, and for them to marry when she was a teenager, and for her never to be educated. Not only this, but she was considered his property. He essentially had the power of life and death over his family.[1] To compare what we have in the modern West with what I've just described as essentially the same thing - "marriage" - is almost beyond comprehension. It's a sobering moment that helps us realise how much, without thinking about it, we consider life in Bible times to be similar to life now, when it really wasn't.

Paul was writing into a very different culture, and calling for Christlike headship on the part of the husband and church-like submission on the part of the wife. In that culture it would have been a huge ask of the husband to manifest leadership in a self-sacrificing way, when, most likely, he was simply used to getting things his own way. For the wife to submit to him as a leader would have been completely expected, but then to submit to his sacrificial service and love would, I imagine, have been quite disorientating.

At least they would have had no problem with the idea of a marriage that *didn't* have interchangeable roles; both having a unique contribution based on their gender would have been expected. As our wider culture moves towards an increasingly egalitarian model, there is no question that this complementarian model of marriage, this idea that the man and the woman do not have entirely interchangeable roles, brings equal challenge to both men and women. It's not just women who struggle with it. Men are nervous of overstepping, or accidentally domineering, or becoming 'toxic', and so they often struggle to manifest qualities

---

1   Think Abraham and Isaac in Genesis 22, and Jephthah and his daughter in Judges 11.

that complementarians would be championing in husbands - initiative, vigour, presence. Easier to wait. Or hide.

Women surrounded by a feminist atmosphere are often stuck in a 'show yourself equal' vibe, and rather than simply enjoying the strength of their husband, they can feel a pressure to demonstrate why they are 'just as ___ as their husband' (fill in the gap) and this can suck the joy out of things.

 Another challenge is that a gospel that rests on a relational dynamic between two non-equal parties (Jesus and us) finds its closest mirroring in a relationship between two equal parties (man and wife). So what I am championing here is not without its challenges! But it's good to ask the question: what is it that makes a Christian marriage a Christian marriage?

Practising virtues like unselfishness, loving communication, humble service, etc., are all a really good start. But I think there's more, and according to Paul, it's this: the husband plays the part of the self-sacrificing Jesus and the wife plays the part of the radiant church. Of course he's not supposed to act like Jesus in every way (Lord of Lords, Judge of the world etc.), and she's not supposed to act like the church in every way (worshipping, unquestioning obedience etc.). Paul is clear about what is supposed to happen. He is supposed to serve her in sacrificial love for her spiritual good. He is supposed to feel a sense of responsibility for the spiritual condition of his wife and for them as a unit, and she is supposed to welcome that wholeheartedly and let its impact propel her into further holiness and passionate running alongside him as his partner and helper. Will they make sacrifices for each other? Of course they will. Will they bless one another? You'd hope so! Will they do all kinds of one-anothering? If it's healthy. But there is this extra layer. Let's get into the text.

> Do not get drunk on wine, which leads to debauchery. Instead, be filled with the Spirit, speaking to one another with psalms, hymns, and songs from the Spirit. Sing and make music from your heart to the Lord, always giving thanks to God the Father for everything, in the name of our Lord Jesus Christ. Submit to one another out of reverence for Christ. Wives, submit yourselves to your own husbands as you do to the Lord. For the husband is the head of the wife as Christ is the head of the church, his body, of which he is the Saviour. Now as the church submits to Christ, so also wives should submit to their husbands in everything. Husbands, love your wives, just as Christ loved the church and gave himself up for her to make her holy, cleansing her by the washing with water through the word, and to present her to himself as a radiant church, without stain or wrinkle or any other blemish, but holy and blameless. In this same way, husbands ought to love their wives as their own bodies. He who loves his wife loves himself. After all, no one ever hated their own body, but they feed and care for their body, just as Christ does the church— for we are members of his body. "For this reason a man will leave his father and mother and be united to

his wife, and the two will become one flesh." This is a profound mystery—but I am talking about Christ and the church. However, each one of you also must love his wife as he loves himself, and the wife must respect her husband.
EPHESIANS 5 V 18-33.

I've started at verse 18 in order to help us to understand the context of the passage. It's about being filled with the Holy Spirit. Even though in your Bible there is probably a gap between verse 21 and verse 22, and then most likely a heading that says something like 'Husbands and wives', don't be fooled! That gap and that heading are not part of scripture but have been added by people trying to be helpful.

Headings, chapters and verses *do* help us when we want to reference certain passages and find what we're looking for in what is - admittedly - a very big book. But it's often also very *unhelpful* in how it subconsciously trains us to read the Bible by piecemeal, splitting up whole, flowing letters into 'bits and pieces'. Rant over.

What follows is a description of what the Spirit-filled life looks like, both in church gatherings and then in our relationships in day to day life. We see here that appropriate submission is part of the Spirit-filled life, that the life of the Spirit powerfully touches the dynamics of our various relationships. What follows are three different kinds of relationships - husbands and wives, parents and children, slaves and masters.

(LONG) INTERLUDE

Here in Ephesians 5 and 6, as well as in Colossians 3, and then again in 1 Peter 2 and 3, we have the two apostles addressing what were known then as 'household codes'.[2] The household code was a concept coined by Aristotle, who laid out in great detail how he thought households ought to work in terms of the various roles and functions that were to be upheld. Core to this code was the role of 'paterfamilias', the senior man of the house. It seems clear from the way Paul and Peter write that they are deliberately reframing how things should work in the home within a 'household code' framework.

The differences between what they do and what Aristotle does are huge. Typically it would be the 'head' of the household that would be addressed, and the emphasis would be on the importance and necessity of him exercising authority over all others in the home. Paul and Peter differ from this in that they address both parties in various relationships. Not only this, they address the party with least power first, thus ensuring

---

2   Episode 651 from the podcast Biblethinker.org was helpful on household codes.

their agency. Then, as if that wasn't revolutionary enough, the exhortation to those with the power is not for them to exert it, but instead for them to use their position for self-sacrifice rather than self-service. So there is no doubt, this is a radical reframing of the household codes.

However, a standard egalitarian response to this would be that this is, as well as a radical reframing, an example of divine accommodation. They would take encouragement from the way that the apostles, through the inspiration of the Spirit, creatively subvert the power dynamics of the household code through gospel dynamics of humility and self-sacrifice. But they wouldn't, for one moment, want to hold on to any vestige of male headship as a satisfactory destination. Egalitarians would be waiting for a time when total 'liberation' from all these dynamics could be received by the wider culture, and when that time comes, do away with anything that potentially gets in the way of total mutuality. Egalitarians would want to take the examples of slaves and masters (included in these passages) and use them to show how, in the same way, the perfect scenario is for the abolition of such an institution, and that the perfect scenario for husbands, wives, parents and children would be similarly revolutionary.

What do I think of this?

Firstly, I think it's clear that slavery exists as a very different institution than the other relationships. Husbands, wives, parents and children are built firmly into the creation narrative and design - slavery is part of the fall (see chapter 3 for a fuller treatment on the matter of slavery). Therefore, before we proceed any further, we ought not to approach these various relationships as like for like. But if we believe in the abolition of slavery, then the notion of divine accommodation on these matters ought to give us pause for thought. If it's applicable to masters and slaves, then it may be, in some way, to husbands, wives, parents and children.

I think we would all agree that the Bible doesn't teach the abolition of marriage or the family. It's important to say that, because straight away it demonstrates that we are not to approach these three different pairings of relationships identically. So, husbands and wives and parents and children are to continue as household relationships, but upon the foundation of God's good creation. Now let's compare those two.

Ought the authority dynamic between parents and children to be done away with? I don't think anyone with their head screwed on is arguing for that. Therefore, we can all happily say that the commands put forward concerning parents and children stay as they are. This shows us that at least one of the household relationships described can remain as it is plainly read.

Our reflections on the differences between masters and slaves (perfect scenario = abolition) and parents and children (perfect scenario = as it's written) show us that each set of relationships can and ought to be approached on its own merits, meaning that our assessment of what a fully redeemed marriage looks like can be assessed without reference to the other relationships.

The reasons given for the submission of wives to husbands are different from the other household code relationships. They are either based on creation or salvation. As such, to call it divine accommodation is, I think, mistaken.

Over, Under and One Anothering!

Back to the three pairings we find in Ephesians 5 and 6. What Paul seems to do in all three relational situations is to call one party in each relationship to submit, and then the other party to make it as easy as possible for the first party to do so. Let me show you what I mean: Wives submit to your husbands: Husbands love your wives sacrificially. Children obey your parents: Dads, don't provoke your children to anger. Slaves/servants obey your masters as if before God not men: Masters treat your slaves/servants as if before God not men, with no threatening.

There is another way of understanding this passage. The egalitarian perspective takes the phrase in verse 21, "submitting to one another", and says that it is to be applied in the sense that everyone in the church ought to submit to everyone. The egalitarian perspective would point to Jesus laying down His life for the church, and husbands modelling their love for their wives on that as a kind of 'submission' in terms of the humility that is being expressed. It's really important that we explore this carefully, because complementarians say that in verse 21 Paul *isn't* telling everyone to submit to everyone, but is clearly calling wives to submit to husbands (explicitly in light of them being their head), children to parents, and slaves to masters.[3] The complementarian would say that submission has at least *something* to do with authority and that for everyone to submit to everyone is therefore nonsensical. That we are all most definitely to *prefer* one another is a certainty,[4] but preference and submission are different things.

Complementarians would say that submission *is* about spiritual authority and would then ask: was Paul telling parents to submit to their children? They would answer "No". Was Paul asking masters to submit to their slaves/servants? Again, they would answer "No".

---

3   Please refer to the opening pages of this book for comments on the New Testament perspective on slavery.

4   Philippians 2 v 3-4.

Likewise, they would say that Paul was not telling husbands to submit to their wives.

Egalitarians would want to firmly point out the word for 'submit' is different from the word 'obey' which is used in Ephesians concerning the relationship between parents and children and masters and slaves.

Complementarians would concede this is true,[5] but they would want to make clear that while the nature of the marriage relationship differs enormously from those other two relationships and therefore it would look nothing like that, still, the sense of some kind of authority asymmetry remains.

Asymmetrical Submission

It would be a good idea at this point to refer to the way the rest of the New Testament uses this particular Greek word for submit - *hupotasso*.

Every single instance, potentially bar one, is used with regards to an ordered authoritative relationship, sometimes positive, sometimes negative, whether it's citizens to authorities (Romans 13 v 1, Titus 3 v 1, 1 Peter 2 v 13), Jesus to His parents (Luke 2 v 51), creation to vanity (Romans 8 v 20), the whole collective of spiritual forces to the exalted Christ (1 Peter 3 v 22), demons to believers (Luke 10 v 17), the spirits of prophets to the prophets (1 Corinthians 14 v 32), all things to Jesus (Philippians 3 v 21, 1 Corinthians 15 v 27, Ephesians 1 v 22, Hebrews 2 v 8, 1 Peter 3 v 22), believers to Father God (Hebrews 12 v 9), younger believers to the elders (1 Peter 5 v 5), wives to husbands (1 Peter 3 v 5, Colossians 3 v 18, Ephesians 5 v 21-24, Titus 2 v 5), the fleshly mind to God's law (Romans 8 v 7-8), servants to masters (Titus 2 v 9, 1 Peter 2 v 18), Jewish unbelievers to God's righteousness (Romans 10 v 3), believers to God (James 4 v 7, Hebrews 12 v 9), and the apostles to false brothers (Galatians 2 v 5), and the Son to the Father at the end of all things (1 Corinthians 15 v 28).

It's fairly compelling. All of these are what we might describe as relationships that carry differing degrees and types of assymetry. They are all very different, but that's what they have in common. Four times wives are explicitly told to submit to their husbands;[6] you will never find it the other way round.

There is one passage that is perhaps somewhat ambiguous:

---

5   However, as we saw earlier, Peter uses the same word, 'hupotasso' for citizens and governments, slaves and masters, wives and husbands.

6   Ephesians 5 v 22 and 24, Colossians 3 v 18, 1 Peter 3 v 1.

You know that the household of Stephanas were the first converts in Achaia, and they have devoted themselves to the service of the Lord's people. I urge you, brothers and sisters, to submit to such people and to everyone who joins in the work and labours at it.
1 CORINTHIANS 16 V 15-16

Egalitarians see the above passage as arguing for a more generic 'subjection', a more mutual non-specific submission. Paul urges the church to be subject to the household of Stephanas, who were the first converts in Asia, and also to every fellow worker and labourer. It sounds quite generic, right? It sounds like Paul is saying to the church that they are to be subject to these various people. However, I would say that it seems from reading the New Testament that those who served among the churches as 'workers' carried authority or stature in the church. It is perfectly consistent and pretty certain that those whom Paul is referring to in 1 Corinthians 16 v 16 are leaders that serve among the churches, in which case, the call to submit to them would fall in line completely with the rest of the scriptures' exhortation around submission.

What is common in all of these *hupotasso* references listed above, sometimes negatively and sometimes positively, is the theme of order and some kind of authority. There are different kinds of authority. Christ has all authority and we obey Him unquestioningly. In these other relationships, we have authority at work in different ways. In specifically Christian relationships, the authority is spiritual, and redeemed, and often nuanced.

Remember that spiritual authority is the God-given liberty or jurisdiction to serve and protect another/others in ways appropriate to the relationship, acknowledged in the heavenly places (meaning that God Himself, and angels and demons of all ranks take note of it - it's real). It's vital to relate authority to protection and not to punishment. It's a bit of a rookie error to hear the word 'authority' and jump to ideas of oppression, abuse, punishment, fear, lack of ease etc. This is much more closely related to our fallen experience of how people often go wrong than it is to the scriptural idea.

Symmetrical Submission

Egalitarians would want to push back on the above from a different linguistic angle.

Considering 'one another,' this term pretty much always means exactly that - a two-way activity. Even in the immediate context of Ephesians 5, we see that being filled with the Spirit will lead to:

...speaking to one another with psalms, hymns and songs from the Spirit...submit to one another out of reverence for Christ.
EPHESIANS 5 V 19A, 21

In the same sentence he uses the same phrase 'one another' twice, firstly for when they are addressing one another with songs, and secondly when submitting to one another. Would he use the same phrase in the same sentence to mean different things? It would be a bit surprising.

If Paul, talking about mutual submission, is referring here to a selfless humility which he undoubtedly does call the Christian community to across the board,[7] while he would be using the word 'submission' in a very unusual, even unique, way, I get it; just as Christ, being in very nature God, didn't grasp it but made Himself nothing, we are to model ourselves on Him.

I suppose we could blend the two ideas together and say that Paul could be talking about a general attitude of humility across the board, followed by an explanation of some specific applications in differing relationships. I could happily live with that.

Frequently Neglected...

It's actually an important moment to talk about a passage of scripture that is often overlooked but is vitally important, and particularly favourable to the egalitarian view of things with regards to marriage and the idea of mutual submission and authority:

Now for the matters you wrote about: "It is good for a man not to have sexual relations with a woman." But since sexual immorality is occurring, each man should have sexual relations with his own wife, and each woman with her own husband. The husband should fulfil his marital duty to his wife, and likewise the wife to her husband. <u>The wife does not have authority over her own body but yields it to her husband. In the same way, the husband does not have authority over his own body but yields it to his wife.</u> Do not deprive each other except perhaps by mutual consent and for a time, so that you may devote yourselves to prayer. Then come together again so that Satan will not tempt you because of your lack of self-control. I say this as a concession, not as a command.
1 CORINTHIANS 7 V 1-6 (EMPHASIS MINE)

This is an important passage because the complementarian perspective on marriage, the idea that a husband has authority as 'head' of the home, is in these verses potentially blown out of the water. Because

---

7   See Philippians 2 v 3.

here, we see the mutual authority that I have seriously questioned, explicitly articulated. The husband has authority over his wife's body and the wife has authority over the husband's body.

The Corinthian believers, it seems, were what we might call 'super-spiritual'. And sometimes super-spiritual people are a bit funny about physical things like food and drink, and especially sex, even sex within marriage. So Paul has to help them to realise that it's actually part of their spiritual protection to be making love regularly as husband and wife.

That's the context. Now to the point about having authority over one another's body.

How does this square with previous comments I've made about everyone submitting to everyone leading to a chaotic scenario? Complementarians would either go quiet with no response (which apparently they frequently do), or they would say that within the headship dynamic a wife and a husband both have liberty or free access to one another's bodies sexually, and that neither has a trump card or special privileges when it comes to sex, but instead there is a mutual liberty for both of them. When a husband desires his wife he has the freedom to initiate sex, and when a wife desires her husband she has the freedom to do the same; there is no sense that one has to wait for the other to make the move as if one had more liberty than the other. It's also not OK to simply hold yourself back from the other as if your body was your own.

As we saw earlier, there is a very similar dynamic in the Song of Songs, where both lover and beloved are not backward in coming forward in their desire for intimacy with one another.

So, maybe the authority dynamic in Christian marriage is mutual only when it comes to sex…? Katia Adams, in her book 'Equal', says this doesn't stack up because sex is never 'only' sex! Sex obviously touches upon all kinds of powerful elements in a marriage, to the point that it makes most sense to say that if the authority dynamic is mutual in a Christian couple's sex life, then it must be for the whole marriage.

It's a good point. But could it also be true that because sex *is* so powerful, and because sex *has* been so badly abused since the fall (rape, assault, prostitution), Paul gives it special mention as a way of ending selfish sex in the Christian home?

Could it also be a direct reference to Genesis 3 v 16? Linda Belleville, a leading egalitarian scholar, takes the phrase, "your desire will be for your husband" to be talking about inordinate sexual desire on the part of a woman. She takes "But he will rule over you" to mean that the man will impose his will sexually. If that is what Genesis 3 is getting at, this could be Paul's way of specifically undoing fallen sexual dynamics in marriage.[8]

---

8   This seems like a bit of a strange theory but I thought it was worth mentioning.

That Paul makes special mention of this matter to the Corinthians is also worth noting, because as you read through the first letter to the Corinthians, it becomes very clear that so much of what Paul is trying to do among them is to help them understand the spirituality of their bodies, whether it's with regard to food and drink, sexual activity or physical resurrection. They need special help and attention when it comes to all things physical, and so Paul spells out to them that concerning sex, all married church members have permission from God to enjoy and give enjoyment to their spouse.

A further complementarian theory is that this command specifically protects against polygamy. If each husband and each wife have rights over the other's body, they can't go and marry someone else also.

An egalitarian might read that explanation and not be completely satisfied - the contextual issues might be correct, and that may be why Paul is bringing it up with the Corinthians, but putting that to one side, what does it actually mean that the man is the head and yet in this matter they have mutual authority? Why? How?

Let me be clear: I do not think that the Bible teaches that there is or ought to be unilateral authority on the part of the husband in a marriage; this passage makes it clear that this cannot be the case. I believe that dynamics of mutuality are what we ought to be shooting for. Maybe it's best to put it like this. A husband and wife have authority over one another. A husband also has a particular authority on her behalf: a liberty to serve and beautify her, and with that a particular representative responsibility for them as a unit.

At the end of the day, Paul must be consistent with himself. Sure, he will emphasise and phrase things differently depending on the context he is writing into but, under the inspiration of the Holy Spirit, he is in deep and harmonious agreement with himself.

Head, Shoulders, Knees and Toes

As a husband works this out by playing the part of Christ in sacrificial service of his wife,[9] she has been uniquely charged with playing the part of the church in receiving this wholeheartedly. Let's explore this a bit further by returning to Ephesians.

What does the image of Christ as the Head show us from this letter? Remember our work on 'head' *(kephale)* earlier, and my conclusion that we have to see it in its context. I argued that in 1 Corinthians 11, 'prominence' seemed to be the best explanation of the use of the word.

---

9   It's important to make the point here that we are not talking about the husband running around at his wife's every whim or simply doing whatever she asks. The sacrificial service of Jesus for the church is for the good and holiness of the church - the same is true of the husband's service of his wife.

Earlier in Ephesians we are told of Christ, that the Father:

> ...placed all things under His feet and appointed Him to be head over everything for the church, which is His body, the fullness of Him who fills everything in every way.
> EPHESIANS 1 V 22-23.

Here in the first chapter of Ephesians, we see Christ as 'head over all things'. Here this means that He is 'chief'. Remember that this was one of the other ways the word *kephale* can be used. We read of His exaltation above all authority and power and dominion - the main idea here is authority.

Interestingly though, within this specific image, the 'all things' *doesn't* include the church. Follow me here. Of course Christ is Lord of the church - I'm not questioning that. But let's look carefully at the image. Christ, as chief over all things, is given *to the church,* which is his body. This image is of Christ organically united with the church (head and body), with all powers under His feet. This means those powers are also under us, because His feet are part of His body!

So, Christ's headship is about His being chief in chapter one, but it's specifically about His chiefly rule over all of creation *with us alongside Him in this role.* This is consistent with Christ sharing His victorious demon-defeating authority with us.[10]

Throughout the rest of Ephesians, Christ's headship is focused on His unity with the church as His body. The ancients understood that all nourishment and growth of the human body came from the head, and so the image is used in chapter four metaphorically, to talk about Christ helping the church grow by bringing gifts to her of the apostle, the prophet, etc.

The headship of Christ in this image is primarily to do with nourishing. Again, if we follow the meaning of 'prominence' this also makes sense: He is nourishing His body out of a sense of responsibility for it.

It's exactly the same in Ephesians 5 when Paul talks about marriage. Let's follow Paul's logic. He says in verse 23 that the husband is the head of the wife, even as Christ is the head of the church. They are one flesh, completely united. Similarly, as the church submits to Christ, wives should submit to their husbands. As we saw earlier, 'submit' is an authority-laden word. The church yields to Christ's prominence and to His nourishing; He is responsible, and He does us good. A wife ought to yield to her husband's sense of responsibility for her good.

------

10   Luke 10 v 17, Romans 16 v 20, Mark 16 v 18, 2 Corinthians 2 v 14.

Husbands are to love their wives. Just as Christ loved the church sacrificially for her beautification, a husband ought to love his wife as his own body. Jesus nourishes the church because we are members of His own body. Husbands are to love their wives with whom they are one flesh.

This whole idea of the husband as the head and the wife as the body is wedded so tightly to the image of the organic unity of Christ and the church, that it's genuinely bewildering to me how anyone could suggest that headship and submission are nothing more than a nod to the culture.

Foot Washing Prohibited?

Note that the wife's submission to him is her receptivity to this - as active and demanding as his doing of it. Let me demonstrate. Jesus, we are told, "knowing that the Father had given all things into his hands",[11] strips off his outer garment and washes His disciple's feet, but Peter will have none of it. Is it an act of authority on Jesus' part? No. But it's an act of service that comes from a place of knowing His authority. The complementarian would say that this is a good way to describe a husband's role, an act of service that comes from a place of knowing his authority.

But look what happens. Peter won't receive this. He would have felt much more comfortable if the tables were turned, but it's not the time for that. Later on he will do this - in fact Jesus is doing it for his disciples in order to explicitly give them a model of what they will do, but before that, they need to yield. To receive His service is Peter's act of submission. The same for wives. They are to let their husband lay his life down and serve them spiritually, to receive and encourage this. What will the end result be? According to this passage, their radiance, joy and holiness. Of course the marriage becomes a place of mutual give and take but it exists alongside this dynamic.

What do I mean by 'serving spiritually'? I think it's primarily about taking responsibility for the spiritual quality of what they have together - of making time and space to be with God together and learning how to follow Him as a unit. Note this: they learn together - it's not a teacher and a pupil! I'm just saying that he takes responsibility for this in a unique way.

Paul connects the creation story with the salvation story in Ephesians 5, and says that the one refers to the other. The one flesh union of Adam and Eve is compared to the one flesh union of Jesus and the church. This brings together the grand idea that the organic unity and asymmetry we see in creation and in the gospel are to be mirrored in marriage.

---

11   John 13 v 3.

Mutual honour. Mutual respect and release of spiritual gifts. Mutual liberty physically. Particular steward-ship given to the man for serving and beautifying the woman and feeling a sense of responsibility for her. Particular stewardship given to the woman to gladly receive this and enthusiastically help him. Because he starts by giving and she starts by receiving, you might say there is a leadership of sorts here, but not one that would negate mutual initiative, undermine equality or stifle a healthy one-anothering that is at the heart of all Christian relationships.[12]

In Everything?

In verse 24 Paul says that the wife ought to submit to her husband "in everything". What does he mean by this? It's clear that it isn't literally everything, because elsewhere Paul grants wives with non-Christian husbands the liberty to continue walking in their new faith and not going along with their husbands' vari-ous beliefs or religious views.

Phrases like 'as to the Lord' and 'in the Lord' are helpful because they create both a sense of expansiveness and exclusivity. A wife's submission to her husband is to be expansive in the sense that she is not to adopt a posture of challenging and questioning that comes out of an unwillingness to submit, but instead is to welcome him as her head wholeheartedly and as an act of worship. It's possible for a wife to hamstring her husband by harbouring an attitude that essentially undermines him. It can be subtle or not, but however it manifests, it's both powerful and harmful. This will need to be repented of in a deep way if their dynamic is to flow and if he is to realise his true calling. God requires that she, with her whole being, welcomes him. But there is this exclusivity in the sense that she is always to guard her own conscience before the Lord and not submit to any ideas, plans or behaviours of her husband that will compromise her spiritually and cause her to dishonour the Lord.

Drawing it all Together

I think it is clear as we've explored the use of the word *hupotasso* (submit) in the New Testament, that it's less likely that Paul is talking about submission in a generic sense, as we never find that in the Bible any-where, and much more likely that he is talking about submission in specific ways in specific relationships. This however, doesn't mean the same thing for each kind of relationship. A marriage is not a relation-ship between parents and children, which is not a relationship between slaves and masters, which is not a relationship between God and us, which is not a relationship between us and the law etc. They are all fundamentally different.

---

12   See FAQs on how a marriage can work in this way when the woman has a more typical leadership personality than her husband.

Just because the issue of submission comes up in each relationship, the nature of the relationship and what is being commanded will determine what that submission ought to look like. For marriage it's fairly straightforward. Husband, put your wife first for the glory of God. Wife, wholeheartedly receive him. Husbands, take responsibility for what you are as a unit. Wives, welcome this with enthusiasm and help your husbands in every way you can.

We have, understandably, spent a lot of time on marriage in this chapter and hopefully shown how, as a relationship, it has a unique calling to point beyond itself to the greatest story ever told. As for other male and female relationships, while they don't have the calling on them to represent the relationship of Christ and the church, they will still be relationships where men and women interact as gendered beings. The most straightforward - and frightening - way to unpack what this might look like, is by thinking through what masculinity and femininity are when they are at their most healthy. Let's go where, currently, even angels might fear to tread.

Chapter Nineteen

The $10,000 Question: What are Masculinity & Femininity?

When I first became a believer I had literally no idea about most things. I was lashed with deep spiritual wounds that left me over-sensitive and in constant pain. I was also dragging around the weight of habitual sins that had me eating out of their hands. I'd spent years opening all the wrong doors and closing all the right ones. I was a mess.

By the grace of God, I got saved into a church that took discipleship really seriously.[1]

Before I knew it, I was being taught, invested in, modelled to, entrusted with and deeply loved. I was in a spiritual family of fantastic mums, dads, brothers and sisters. As part of this, good men came alongside me and taught me about being a good man. Looking back, was some of it cringy and caricatured? Yup. But most of it was really, really good. There was an objective standard to grow up into, a higher calling, something exciting and transcendent: the goal of being a godly man.

There are two particular ways of *not* growing into a man. The first is by staying a boy; the Bible spends most of the time on this kind of contrast. This is because, as we have been saying all along, men and women are essentially the same, and we are all typically in much more danger of staying as spiritual infants than somehow growing into a gender morphed expression of our true selves.

But the second way of not growing into a man is by refusing to step into the gendered reality of who God has made us. You don't hear so much on this one anymore. Why? I think there is a loss of clarity that has led to a loss of confidence that has led to a loss of communication. I think the loss of clarity in the church is due to unhelpfully caricatured and essentially toxic models of complementarianism being taught and modelled, as well as an aggressive feminist agenda in the wider Western culture that will stop at nothing until it wins the day.

This agenda is collapsing all gender distinctives in the name of freedom and equality. I think that in the same way our culture has taken love and now re-interpreted it as acceptance ("If you loved me, you would accept me as I am"); equality regarding gender has now been re-interpreted as interchangeability. This

---

1 Shout out to Dartford Community Church, which was then called Dartford Christian Fellowship! Forever in your debt.

militant spirit has struck fear into the heart of the church. I think the church is afraid of being seen by the outside world as regressive, oppressive, archaic, ignorant, and (most stingingly of all) unloving.

I will here attempt to bring some clarity. It won't be perfect and that's OK. I'm trying my best.

Sexual Symbolism

Where the manhood of a man and the womanhood of a woman are most obviously observed in their interaction is in their sexual intimacy. From the very first pages of scripture, the maleness and the femaleness of humanity are connected to their ability to multiply the divine image. They were naked and unashamed.

The story of creation unravels without sexuality, from the commission of chapter one to the delight of chapter two, to the promised redemption of chapter three; all of it rests on their sexuality. It is a physical reality and also a spiritual reality, which means that it speaks of things beyond itself. This means that you don't have to have sex to be able to be part of the story; it's way bigger than that. This is one of the reasons why, I believe, the Song of Songs is right bang in the middle of the Bible - a book with hardly a mention of God in it![2]

There is a spirituality about sex that is not supposed to sexualise our spirituality, but enrich it through powerful and wisely handled imagery. I'm reaching for a spiritualised sexuality, *not* a sexualised spirituality.

 SELAH

A man is most obviously a man when he is intimate with his wife. And vice versa. In this moment it can only be a man with a woman and nothing else. This moment provides the ultimate distinctiveness. No getting away from it. Therefore, I think it's reasonable to take this most distinctive of acts to explore if it might be pointing us to a deeper understanding of the soul of a man and the soul of a woman.

God Himself repeatedly uses the relationship between men and women, and particularly marriage and sexual union, in vivid terms, to talk about His relationship with His people, right through both testaments; biblical content on this is plentiful. We find no reticence on God's part, but instead quite the opposite. Please take a moment to read Ezekiel 16 to get a sense of what I mean. You won't just find it there, it's literally everywhere, particularly through the prophets.

---

2   Just once explicitly in 8 v 6, although some commentators think that it's God speaking in the final sentence of 5 v 1.

The overlapping realities of the sexual and the spiritual are both vital to grasp and potentially dangerous. As the Hebrew religion was officially established at Sinai, its sexual ethic was revolutionary. With a complete absence of ritualistic sexual activity, it was unique in its time. The need to warn against homosexuality, bestiality, adultery, rape and other sexual deviancy was vital, as this nation was placed in the midst of nations enslaved to other 'gods', who demanded all manner of ritualistic sexual activity.[3]

And yet there was nothing prudish about Judaism. Its commitment to a creation narrative that climaxed with naked and unashamed image-bearers multiplying and filling the earth with God's explicit blessing was anything but!

In Hebrew thought, the physical is not regarded as unspiritual or irrelevant. There is instead a reverence for all that God has made, and a determination to enjoy His creation within the boundaries that He has set.

Why do we so often come across sexual imagery when reading the Bible, particularly with regards to the relationship between God and His people? Because marriage, as both a covenantal and exclusive relationship, and sex, as an intimate, exquisite and ecstatic union, serve as powerful images of what the redemptive relationship between Yahweh and His people ought to look like: covenantally and exclusively faithful (no other gods) and intimately exquisite.

It is surely no coincidence that in the relationship between God and His people we all, men and women, play the feminine role. We are the pursued and He is the pursuer. He moves towards us and we respond to His initiative with open hearts.

When we get to the New Testament, the imagery becomes extraordinarily vivid with regards to the sexual relationship and pregnancy. We read that those who are born of God have His 'seed' abiding in them:[4] The Greek word used here is 'sperma'. Peter uses the similar idea of God 'sowing' His seed in us (His living and abiding word), and causing us to be born again.[5] Moving to the book of Romans, we read again of both creation and us 'groaning' with labour pains, pregnant as we await our full redemption.[6] Moving back a chapter in Romans, we are faced with the allegory of us being married to the law and it being a barren marriage

---

3   It's important to note that behind false man-made gods that have no real existence are demonic powers that most definitely do. These powers love to watch humans corrupt themselves in all kinds of ways, deriving sordid pleasure from seeing those who bear the image of God degrade themselves as part of their idolatrous worship. It's a gross thought, but it's unfortunately true.

4   1 John 3 v 9.

5   1 Peter 1 v 23.

6   Romans 8 v 18-25.

with no way out except death! We then die to the law in order that we might "belong to another, to Him who has been raised from the dead, in order that we may bear fruit for God".[7] In all of these passages we are, one way or another, the impregnated wife. This is a very powerful and consistent image in scripture. God moves towards us with life and vigour, and we receive Him with faith. The end result? New life, or fruitfulness. There is a movement here, a flow, a direction of travel that is asymmetrical and very fruitful.

When a Picture Paints a Thousand Words

Now we have paved the way for legitimately using sexual imagery to describe spiritual realities, let's look at this subject together. Because I'm talking here about masculinity and femininity, I'm taking the image of sexual intercourse, but moving it beyond sex and marriage in order to think about the development of the gendered soul, and how we relate through that to the members of the opposite sex.

What's happening in the moment of intimacy between a husband and wife? A number of things. He is passionately giving of himself and she is passionately receiving him. He is moving out of himself with prominence. She is welcoming that part of him into herself, expecting both pleasure and life. He leaves something of himself with her and she, from and within herself, incubates new life. Neither is passive, and the result is ecstasy and life.

Before I take these images and transpose them beyond sex itself and into a picture of masculinity and femininity, I want to make two things clear. Firstly, these expressions obviously manifest in a unique and physical way in marriage, but I am suggesting that it's a pointer to other healthy male/female relationships as expressions of gendered souls. Secondly, as we see maternal attributes in Father God and in Jesus, there are, within a healthy man or woman, two sides. Both men and women, in God's design, have masculine and feminine sides to them. This is to be celebrated, and this is what guards us against caricatured expressions of gender.

The point is that a spiritually healthy man in a non-crisis situation will lean more into and express more of the masculine, and a spiritually healthy woman in a non-crisis situation will lean more into and express more of the feminine. If there is some poor spiritual health or if there is a particular crisis situation (or both), you may see a different manifestation. Let's explore those two things for a minute or two.

---

7   Romans 7 v 4.

Born Broken

We'll start with thinking about our spiritual health. All of us are born in Adam, meaning that we are born under sin. So we're all fallen from day one. But there's more. All of us also come from our parents (and their parents, etc.), who carry their own specifically fallen traits. To say that we don't inherit some of these strikes me as about as foolish as saying we don't inherit personality traits or physical features; of course we do. Add to this that we are born into a fallen world, and experience all manner of dark and traumatic situations. These three things should leave us in no doubt that all of us come to Christ, no matter how young we are, very broken and in need of serious restoration.

Part of this brokenness will very often be around the area of gender. Why do I say this?

Because it's such a key part of our imaging of God and of our story-telling destiny, that Satan will most certainly have it in his sights. Therefore, if when I begin to unpack masculinity and femininity and you find yourself thinking 'That's not me', I'm asking that you won't immediately dismiss what I'm saying. Instead I'm asking that you will bring before God what I have said, and ask Him if He might be pin-pointing something that needs a bit of mending or healing or restoring or cleansing.

Identity Crisis

The second thing is to do with crises. In crisis situations, large or small, it may actually be appropriate to lean into the 'other' side of ourselves - that which is less natural, for the good of others and for our own survival.

Let me give an example. Imagine a recently widowed woman with young children. There may be a season where she will need to lean into her masculine side a bit more than she would have done before the death of her husband, in order to nurture her children as healthily as possible. Children need the masculine and the feminine. It could be that over time, God provides new men in their lives via the wider family and/or the church or that she remarries, but for a season she will need to lean into something that might feel a bit foreign, in order to get the job done as well as possible. I think it's fascinating that Paul, in a crisis situation with the Galatians, talks about himself in maternal terms as if he is pregnant with them, and in labour pains waiting to see Christ fully formed in them. Something is going badly wrong with them, and he takes on this posture. Also with the Thessalonians, where he could only stay for a few weeks due to persecution, in the midst of 'much conflict', he says that he and his co-workers (all men on this trip) were like nursing mothers taking care of them, and also like fathers exhorting and encouraging and charging them. I love that there is none of this collapsing of motherly and fatherly roles into one thing, but also an acknowledgement that they were able to manifest both kinds of service and leadership! This is part of God's incredible design.

But it can also get weird.

Some men and women have had to manifest and emphasise the opposite of their truest self through significantly dysfunctional relationships in life. The way significant others have acted has left them with no option, even if they didn't know quite what they were doing. Some people are brought up by parents who wanted them to be the opposite sex. Some daughters are brought up without a dad or with poor paternal models and they learnt the hard way that no man was going to lovingly serve them. This vacuum and the coping patterns learned through it could hinder them peacefully receiving appropriate male love, or cause them to learn from it to inordinately crave any male love they can. Some sons are brought up without a dad, and their mum demanded them to be the man of the house way before they were ready, and in their immaturity they reached for masculinity and came out macho. Some men and women married someone who changed overnight, leaving them all at sea and having to be something they never expected. The list goes on and on.

All of these are crisis situations that can have a serious impact upon the soul. We have to act in a certain way and then it becomes habitual. We then start to believe and tell ourselves and others it's who we are.

I believe the days are coming when the Church will rediscover her healing gift and we will see incredible restoration from the Lord. It requires us to stop defending ourselves and let the Lord come in with His liberating truth.

The Signposts

Now that we have looked at spiritual health and crises, and how those things impact how we express our masculine and feminine traits, let me begin to unpack how I see the wider application of the initial points made about masculinity and femininity above.

Firstly, he is passionately giving of himself, and she is passionately receiving him. A masculine man will passionately give of himself to the women in his life - he will not wait for them to give to him first, and neither will he give with conditions; his posture is that he gives. This can look like all kinds of service; physical help may be particularly welcome as he tends to be stronger, but all sorts of service would be appropriate. It goes without saying therefore that he is not passive. Please note: passivity is a sign, not of femininity, but of broken humanity. Passivity is a terrible thing in the life of both men and women.

A feminine woman will gladly receive this service and won't feel threatened by it, or feel the need to show what she can do from a place of insecurity and competitiveness. Our distinctly gendered souls are most clearly seen in relation to one another, and receiving happily from worthy men is a vital part of the feminine soul.

A godly man knows that a woman is his equal - he has no desire for her to prove it. So she can relax and enjoy his giving. For a woman to welcome this offer of service with open arms is very feminine, and is a great blessing to a man.

Next. He is prominently moving out of himself toward her. She is welcoming that part of him into herself, expecting both pleasure and life. To be prominent is to take a risk. You could get shot down. Much easier to wait for someone else to make the move. I think there is a prominence that is very masculine - remember I have said that I think it's the preferable way the term 'kephale' (head) should be interpreted. Not for one minute am I referring to showing off or pushing yourself forward out of selfish ambition, etc. I'm primarily reaching here toward the idea of the man moving appropriately and pro-actively towards the women in his life for the purpose of serving them.

If a woman welcomes that when it comes her way, this is very feminine, and she ought to expect that these God-given relationships will bring much joy and life to her. Am I saying that a woman can't take initiative relationally with men, no - that would be a caricature, but if she were to do so from a place of wanting to prove something or fearing that nothing would happen if she didn't, well this can be something that can begin to cut across her femininity and cause her to lose something of her true self.

I believe we have a crisis in masculinity. I believe that this will always lead to a crisis in femininity. Because we have a crisis in masculinity, and it's not just in the world but in the church, we have fewer and fewer men in the church, and those we do have are often too scared to embrace masculinity by expressing controlled strength in case it turns out to be toxic, or in case someone gets upset. But my plea is for men not to apologise for their God-given prominence; that will not serve women. Instead, be first by being 'last', sacrificially serving the women in your life.

Next up. He leaves something of himself with her and she, from and within herself, incubates this new life. Isn't it a fascinating thought that for centuries, one part of the church has so esteemed one woman that they have almost made her a fourth person of the Trinity, and yet that same church has never, up to this day, conceded that a woman can be the senior leader of a church.[8] How is it that a church can do this? Though I don't agree with the whole dynamic described above, what I appreciate is the way the motherhood of Mary is so highly esteemed. It is the same in religious Jewish culture, where a woman having lots of children and giving the most energetic years of her life to nurturing them is not for one minute seen as some kind of 'waste'.

---

8   This insight is taken from the C S Lewis article called 'Priestesses in the church' and, while I don't agree with a key part of its premise, I do believe it contains some fascinating insights.

I've already spoken about the highly esteemed role of bearing and nurturing children, but here I'm taking it beyond the physical, and wanting to draw out this feminine quality of receiving what godly men bring to the table and then incubating it with discernment and wisdom. The act of love-making can have a direct nine-month long impact on a woman. She has received what has been given, and this life then grows inside of her, nurtured and cared for. Then she will usually suckle and sustain that life for another six months to a year. Eve is the mother of all living. While not all women will do this physically, I believe that spiritually there is the ability to nurture the life that men can bring by their headship, and build it into all that it should be. This also may be why our pastoral teams are often full of women - they know how to journey with people and see them develop to full strength, through care and attention.

I think it's so important that male leaders extol the virtues of femininity in women, particularly women leaders. If they don't, women leaders will hear the message loud and clear - "In order to lead, you have to act like a man." This is a tragedy. I believe that if men affirm women in their femininity, women will increasingly feel able to express all their gifts, but from a place of rest, knowing they are delighted in and truly valued. In this scenario they will increasingly not view masculinity as a threat or an irrelevance, but will themselves begin to extol the virtues of masculinity in men. I think, in a very positive sense, this could release something akin to the spiritual equivalent of splitting the atom!

 SELAH

Avoiding the Weird

As I turn to some other elements of masculinity and femininity, let me emphasise again that all of these attributes are good and godly, and to be desired in all people - I believe it's what we lean into, what we emphasise, what we most consistently draw upon that builds creation-designed and gospel-signposting gender quality between us.

The other important thing to say, and this will also keep us from straying into bizarre caricatures, is that masculinity and femininity are chiefly concerned with the way we relate to the opposite sex. I think we go wrong when we begin to talk about these traits in ways that leave no bandwidth for the different ways that God designed us within our own gender. It's best to consider these traits within the context of how we relate to one another, rather than simply saying, "Men are like this" or "Women are like this".

Unique Stewardships

Earlier in the book, I also spoke about the unique stewardship of men and women. I said that for women it is beauty, and for men it is strength.

The vast majority of little girls fizz and pop when a father-figure finds them beautiful! It means something very profound for a woman to be considered beautiful. As far as I'm concerned, this is at the heart of femininity. She is Eve - what a queen! Look at Adam's response when He first sees her! Look at Jesus enduring the cross and despising the shame of it for the joy set before Him - being united with His bride!

God's plan is to use this desire and take her on a journey of beautification that is way deeper than anything a visit to the spa could achieve. Her call to trust God, and then certain worthy men with a quiet confidence and strength, is a thing of absolute stunning beauty in the eyes of the Lord. For her to want to look nice while she is on this journey seems to me to be the most natural thing in the world.

But let her discern the line between what is helpful and what isn't with regards to her appearance. If she is taking her cues from the world, she will be deceived. Satan is in charge of the world and he is the great misogynist. Remember Genesis 3, where we are told that there will be enmity between Satan and the woman. The enemy hates women with a particular hatred, because through her came the Messiah. He wants to capitalise on a woman's desire to be beautiful, and then trap her in it by making her an object of lust. If she is deceived in this way, then the enemy can use the woman's beauty in such a way as to be kryptonite to men. Needless to say, this is not helpful.

If her genuine focus is on holiness and her inner person, she is very unlikely to get this wrong, as her conscience will be working well, and her ears will be attuned to the Holy Spirit's guidance. But it is a powerful thing, and it's good to be aware of it. It's a stewardship, which means it's something that, as a woman, God has entrusted her with, and she is accountable for what she does with it.

Similarly with men and their strength. Most young boys want to show how strong they are. Some get this knocked out of them via abusive parents or bullies - reminiscent of the baby elephant. Tied to a small tree at a young age and powerless to escape, by the time it reaches adulthood, though it could uproot the tree in a moment, it remains passively captive and psychologically imprisoned. A young man in touch with his masculine soul is vigour personified. Sure, it will express itself through different personalities and temperaments, but it's there.

The call to take sacrificial responsibility, with all the risks involved, sparks the masculine soul. Higher testosterone levels mean that strength brings with it a deep sense of meaning for men. It's their unique stewardship. Strength manifesting gently in the treatment of women is a gift in the life of women, and it can create a sense of life-giving safety and joy. Uncontrolled masculine strength brings chaos and fear into the soul of a woman. The denial of strength (hiding) is not the answer. The cultivation of the fruit of the Spirit is. It is a powerful thing, and it's good to be aware of it. It's a stewardship, which means it's something that, as a man, God has entrusted him with, and he is accountable for what he does with it.

If we were to embrace what I'm suggesting up to this point in the book, what might it look like as men and women in the church community?

Chapter Twenty
Getting Practical!

Below I've used key words as triggers to lead us into certain dream scenarios...

Celebration

It's right that we celebrate the gospel of Jesus Christ and make much of Him. It's right that we celebrate one another as individually gifted members of Christ's body. I want to suggest that it's also right that we celebrate one another as men and women and not be ashamed of that. We are so familiar with women in the media rolling their eyes at apparently clumsy or ignorant men. Likewise, we don't have to look far before we pick up patronising or lewd tones when men speak about women. We are the church - the redeemed!

Wouldn't it be wonderful if women spoke well of men as men, celebrating their strength and vitality and their spiritually fraternal and paternal qualities? Imagine women who gladly received the masculine contribution of men into the life of the church. Imagine a community where women felt the freedom to publicly champion strong and godly men, and imagine a rousing response from other women in the congregation, ready to pray for them and encourage them.

Imagine a church where the men were obviously thrilled with the sisters God had given them, where every woman felt like a VIP around them![1] A church where women didn't constantly have to strive to be seen or heard. A community where the women inherently knew, by the way their brothers and fathers around them treated them, that they were seen as equals. Where the equality and unique insights and perspectives of women were celebrated by men in the life of the church, and not just conceded.

Proliferation

When we read the New Testament, we see a great diversity and dynamism around ministry. It wasn't a lone pastor leading a church with a few volunteer helpers. It was apostles, prophets, evangelists, pastors and teachers serving among the churches, and it was elders and deacons serving local congregations all as team ministries and not lone rangers. We should be looking for the proliferation of ministry, both in the local church and across the churches, male and female senior leaders and effective ministries serving together as friends and spiritual family.

---

1   I found this phrase in John Benton's 'Gender Questions'.

I would suggest that local churches consider elders, deacons and other perhaps non-specified, but gifted and trusted, brothers and sisters to be something of a leadership team in the local church. When matters specifically pertaining to faithfulness to God's commands are in view, the elders would have a particular responsibility and contribution, but on other matters, the wider team would be consistently and wisely drawn upon.

We need to also encourage ranks of women thinkers who are called to be theologians, to study and prepare for this task. Men need the help of women; it's a creation ordinance. I don't believe men are any more gifted or any more suited to theological studies than women. I don't believe that women are more likely to be deceived theologically.

Therefore, I envision churches where teams of certain men carry final responsibility for the doctrine taught and obeyed in their congregation. I envision those men being helped by gifted male and female theologians as they grapple with doctrine. I envision teams of gifted male and female teachers instructing in that agreed doctrine throughout the church.

As long as those men and women are in good relationship with and submitted to those elders, I love this vision.

Imagine a church where everyone was expected to contribute something, a community so dynamic that growth and development were part and parcel of the entire culture and where everyone was encouraged to use their God-given gifts, so that neighbours would be loved, the poor would be served and the church herself would be beautified.

Honour

Honour is a deeply biblical concept. It means to prize or value. It can happen in all kinds of directions and is not necessarily a reflection of authority dynamics. Of course we are most familiar with the command to honour our parents. Here, the one giving honour is in subjection to the one being honoured. Jesus says that the Father will honour those who genuinely serve Jesus.[2] Here, the one being honoured is in subjection to the one giving honour. The church, God's household, is to be a place where significant honour is afforded to everyone by everyone.

Imagine a church where men honoured women as co-heirs, and fiercely resisted anything that gave the impression that the women were in some way beneath them. Imagine a church where men honoured the

---

2   John 12 v 26.

unique help that is brought to them by women. Imagine a church where women felt honoured and welcomed at the table with men.

Imagine a church where women honoured men as household heads, and prayed for their protection in it. Imagine a church where women appreciated strong and tender men who were first to lay down their lives and last to hide. Imagine a church where men felt supported and championed by women.

Reliance

As a final thought, it's clear in the garden that the man, after being given the task of caring for the garden, is unable to fulfil it without her - the situation without her is not good. He needs her. Can I just say that again? He needs her. There is an appropriate reliance that men are to have upon women. Their perspective and input are essential to the fulfilment of our mission together.

Imagine a church life enriched by male and female perspectives. This means that if the elders are men, they will be relying heavily on gifted women in the church to fill out their perspective and feed into key situations and decisions; why wouldn't they? This is a world away from abdication. This is humility.

The elders must make key decisions and take responsibility for them. All well and good. But to do so without due process, without listening to trusted men and women in the church who aren't elders, strikes me as foolhardy and will most likely lead to unnecessary mistakes and defeats.

I would hope to see men and women, spiritual mums, dads, brothers and sisters, growing up as a wonderfully fruitful church family. The older men would have specific things to teach the younger men, because gender matters, and we grow up into our true selves through seeing models of those a few years beyond us. The older women, likewise, would have specific things to teach the younger women.

Having said that, I don't think for one moment that this ought to hinder or quench the flow of the Spirit from spiritual mothers to sons and spiritual fathers to daughters - we all need one another, and an environment that becomes segregated for one reason or another would, as far as I am concerned, lead to strange growth. We are family.

Chapter Twenty-One
Affirmations and Denials

This is a helpful exercise as it turns up the contrast - what am I saying and what am I not saying?

I affirm that men and women can only legitimately express the image of God together and fundamentally need one another.

I deny that in God's Kingdom there is to be any sense of competitiveness or power struggles between men and women.

GENESIS 1 V 26-27, GALATIANS 3 V 28.

I affirm that both true equality and meaningful asymmetry are foundational to a healthy male/female dynamic.

I deny that true equality and meaningful asymmetry are contradictory.

GENESIS 1 & 2.

I affirm happy and integrated interdependence between the sexes in God's Kingdom.

I deny that independence or codependence between the sexes is a healthy expression of male and female.

ROMANS 16 V 1-16, GENESIS 3 V 16.

I affirm that headship is a spiritual reality that exists and that it is modelled between the Father and Christ.

I deny that headship is simply a cultural construct that is a carryover from a fallen patriarchal society.

GENESIS 1-3, 1 CORINTHIANS 11 V 2-16, ROMANS 5 V 12-21, EPHESIANS 5 V 18-33.

I affirm that headship is part of God's good created order and not a result of the fall.

I deny that headship, when properly expressed, is damaging to those being served but is instead life-enhancing.

GENESIS 2, 1 CORINTHIANS 11 V 2-16, EPHESIANS 5 V 18-33.

I affirm that headship is to do with a very specific expression of spiritual authority.

I deny that headship is to do with worldly authority or that it provides any room whatsoever for those on the receiving end to be mistreated, abused, dismissed or controlled.

MATTHEW 20 V 25-28, EPHESIANS 5 V 18-33, GENESIS 2, 1 PETER 3 V 7.

I affirm that a husband has God-given authority on behalf of his wife and their marriage.

I deny that a husband has God-given authority over his wife.

1 CORINTHIANS 7 V 3-4, EPHESIANS 5 V 18-33, GENESIS 2-3.

I affirm that headship denotes representing someone or some people other than yourself before Christ and being specifically accountable to Him for their welfare.

I deny that headship removes the personal and direct accountability of each of us before Christ, and that we all remain directly accountable to Him for what we do.

2 CORINTHIANS 5 V 10, GENESIS 3 V 9-11, 17-19, ROMANS 5 V 12-21.

I affirm that headship is only appropriately expressed through Christlike, loving, sacrificial servant-hood - any other expression is inappropriate.

I deny that headship involves lording it over, dominating, or taking advantage of those being served.

JOHN 13 V 1-17, MATTHEW 20 V 25-28, EPHESIANS 5 V 18-33.

I affirm that headship exists for the good of those that are being served.

I deny that headship exists for the advantage or selfish gain of those serving.

EPHESIANS 5 V 18-33.

I affirm that the Bible contains sufficient content to equip us to understand the mind of God concerning male and female.

I deny that a culture which has expressly rejected the God of the Bible can lead us to the right conclusions concerning what we are as male and female and how we are to relate.

2 TIMOTHY 3 V 16, 1 JOHN 5 V 19, ROMANS 1 V 19-20.

I affirm that Christ is the head of man and man is the head of woman.

I deny that all men are the head of all women, but only as heads of households.

1 CORINTHIANS 11 V 2-16, ROMANS 5 V 12-21

I affirm that all Christian men are themselves being served by some kind of headship - sons to dads, congregation members to elders, all believers to Christ.

I deny that - in normal circumstances - a man will be under the household headship of a woman.

EPHESIANS 5 V 18-33, HEBREWS 13 V 17, 1 CORINTHIANS 11 V 2-16.

I affirm that the appropriate response to headship is voluntary and joyful submission, as seen in the relationship between Jesus and the Father.

I deny that submission, when expressed voluntarily, is synonymous with defeat, control or abuse.

HEBREWS 13 V 17, 1 CORINTHIANS 16 V 15-16, EPHESIANS 5 V 18-33.

I affirm that Christ is directly the Head of all believers, male and female.

I deny that men have any special access or preferred status over women in the family of God, but that both are co-heirs of eternal life, 'sons' together in God's family.

EPHESIANS 5 V 18-33, 1 PETER 3 V 7, GALATIANS 4 V 6-7, ROMANS 8 V 15.

I affirm that headship should lead to the full expression of all gifts in the body of Christ, both male and female.

I deny that headship should create a situation in the body of Christ where only men get to use their spiritual gifts.

1 CORINTHIANS 12-14, ROMANS 16 V 1-16.

I affirm that marriage is a partnership of equals marked by complementary mutuality.

I deny that marriage is a relationship involving unilateral authority.

1 CORINTHIANS 7 V 1-5, GENESIS 2.

I affirm that it is a sacred responsibility to ensure the spiritual gifts of men and women in the life of the church are employed fruitfully.

I deny that it's the will of God to hinder the fruitful employment of the gifts that He has given to men and women.

ACTS 2 V 17-18, ROMANS 16 V 1-16.

Chapter Twenty-Two
Some Short and Relevant Reflections

On the Doctrine of God

While we know that God transcends gender, we also know that He has revealed Himself to us as Father. This is a transcendent revelation, in the sense that it makes up part of inspired scripture. I am not saying that God is a man; the Bible is clear that He isn't.[1]

C S Lewis put it like this:

"God Himself has taught us how to speak of Him. To say that it does not matter is to say either that all the masculine imagery is not inspired, is merely human in origin, or else that, though inspired, it is quite arbitrary and unessential...without drawing upon religion, we know from our poetical experience that image and apprehension cleave closer together than common sense is here prepared to admit; that a child who has been taught to pray to a Mother in Heaven would have a religious life radically different from that of a Christian child."[2]

The revelation of God as Father matters because it's a self-disclosure. We serve a God who has revealed Himself in scripture as Father and perfectly in the person of His Son, Jesus Christ, who is called by the prophet Isaiah - Everlasting Father. He is the ultimate Father; fathers on earth are a dim shadow of a transcendent reality that exists in sublime and unfathomable places, places currently beyond our full apprehension. At the centre point of the highest of heavens, in the throne room of glory, the One who exists there, enthroned as King, is Father.

Within His nature is a feminine side that we all appreciate and love and need; He uses maternal imagery in places to express His ways; these images make us feel especially nurtured and cared for. But this is God, not a goddess. If we press further and ask why, there are no answers. The secret things belong to God and the things revealed belong to us and our children so that we can obey Him.[3] There are certain matters where we simply put our hands over our mouths. It's good for us.

---

1   The incarnation of Christ obviously brings a significant asterisk to this statement!

2   From the C S Lewis article, *Priestesses in the church?*

3   See Deuteronomy 29 v 29.

On the Unique Stewardship of Men

I have argued that there is a united voice throughout the Bible that God has entrusted a certain thing uniquely to the man. What is that thing? It is God's commands - the dos and don'ts. In Eden, it was a single command that Adam received. At Sinai, the Law was given and the Levitical priesthood had a responsibility to teach it and steward it.[4] In the church, the twelve apostles and the elders guard the gate in a similar way. The dos and don'ts are for all of us, but household representatives are held particularly accountable. It is at the heart of what it means to be the 'head'.

I believe it's written into God's created order. I think we see the wisdom of God in it, as it requires men to be courageous when they are often tempted not to be, and it requires women to trust men when they are often tempted not to. It pulls us out of the worst versions of ourselves and reveals God's deep wisdom concerning what is best for us. If this is God's way, it simply HAS to be for the flourishing of both sexes.

This is not to say that men and women ought not to be involved in doctrinal study, theological grappling and teaching; I long to see this! It's simply that elders carry household representation for faithfulness with revealed truth in the life of a local church.

On the Demonising of Authority and Submission

I think it's important that we scrutinise our own understanding of and attitudes to authority and submission. Is authority inherently bad? It can't be because God has created a world where authority exists. Is submission inherently bad? It can't be because it's the appropriate response to authority. Because of this, we must be careful that we don't automatically view these concepts negatively. We must think about them carefully in order to avoid abuses, but we must not let the idea of abuse shape how we think about them.

When we consider that the work of Jesus Christ was one big act of submission to the will of the Father, and when we consider the extraordinary consequences of this, it's slightly bizarre that believers are often so squeamish around the idea. The most influential and prized man to have ever lived was the most submitted. The man who has achieved and accomplished more than anyone else was the most submitted. The man who has been exalted to the highest place was the most submitted.

SELAH

---

4   2 Kings 17 v 27, Malachi 2 v 1-9.

Bear in mind also that Satan hates authority and refuses to submit to God. God's word says that rebellion is as the sin of witchcraft - heavy stuff. Satan loves disorder, disobedience and chaos. Authority is about order, and God is a God of order. He is also the God who is love. We mustn't fall for the idea that authority is inherently unloving or immoral.[5]

Wherever you get to on husbands and wives and elders, make sure you're not looking at it through warped lenses; make sure your mind is firstly renewed to a true understanding and valuing of authority and submission.

On the Cult of Personality

What if our fixation with the individual has led to a cult of personality, whereby we so regard and worship our own particular 'wiring' that we can be tempted to disregard general principles of godliness in case they undermine our sense of self?

I do think this fixation with self is creating a new religion: I am the object of worship, my desires, feelings, likes and dislikes are the essential commandments, and only those who agree with me can join. This is a religion that we must not try to synchronise with the Christian Faith - it would be a disaster. Jesus tells us that if we want to follow Him, we need to deny ourselves every day. Now of course this doesn't mean that we deny our God-given personalities. But we have to accept that our God-given personalities have been warped and polluted by sin. This means that to embrace everything about ourselves would be a serious act of folly.

Beware the mindset that mistakes everything about ourselves as 'fearful and wonderful'.[6] In Christ we enter a relationship of incremental, lifelong transformation. The job's only done once we see Him face to face.[7] One of the things we have been saved from in Christ is that fallen version of ourselves that wants nothing to do with obeying Him. Only as we submit to the bigger story will we find the love, peace and spiritual power that we long for. Our true selves will flourish in such an environment.

---

5   Thanks to Mike Winger of Biblethinker.org for this sentence.

6   I am referring in this phrase to Psalm 139 v 14.

7   See 1 John 3 v 1-3.

On Heads and Bodies

When thinking about Jesus as the Head and the church as the body, and taking that as a parallel with regards to husbands and wives (see Ephesians 5), has it occurred to any of us that a head simply cannot oppress or 'tread down' its body. Why? 'Cos a head ain't got no feet! The body has the feet. Now I know it's only an illustration but it actually serves a worthy point.

Although a head does have a directional role with regards to the body, other than that, it's all organic unity, interdependence and mutual care. For a head to strike out against a body is utter nonsense. And vice versa of course.

Bear in mind that Jesus brings His body to be seated with Him in the heavenly places, that together they may rule over the powers of darkness and place them underfoot! It's a wonderful image of how men and women are to rule together over the powers of darkness and to be in profound and interdependent unity as they do so.

On Headship as Prominence

It's interesting that 'God is the head of Christ'. Theologians get very nervous about pressing into this truth in case it takes us somewhere unorthodox, and rightly so.

We know for certain that the Father and the Son are co-equal, the Son being:

> *God of God*
> *Light of light*
> *Very God of very God*
> *Begotten not made*
> *Being of one substance with the Father*
> *By Whom all things were made*[8]

Yet there is a 'firstness' that the Father has, whether in His eternal begetting of the Son or in His sending of Christ into the world and granting Him all authority.

---

8   Taken from the Nicene Creed.

We are told that at the consummation of all things, the Son, to whom all things have been subjected *by* the Father, will, once everything has been gathered under His feet, "be made subject to him who put everything under him, so that God may be all in all."[9]

What we see here is that the Son, in His rescue mission, culminates His activities by placing all things - even Himself - under the Father![10] At no point does this compromise or undercut their equality.

But there's more. While there is an inherent 'firstness' that the Father has, what does the Father do with that? He exalts the Son and wills that the Son has the pre-eminence in all things - He puts the Son first. The Son, in turn, is looking to take all that's been given Him by the Father, and in a sense bring it back to Him.

If men, being created first, have a prominence through their 'headship', what are they to do with that? If they are looking to the Father and the Son as a model, they will lift up and promote gifted and godly women! How will the women respond? They will shine responsively in a way that lifts up and promotes godly men. Both are, in one sense, doing the same thing, but there is a movement to it that matters, because it reflects something of what we see between the Father and the Son.

On the Two Great Commands

The two great commandments involve love - loving God with all that we have and loving our neighbours as ourselves. The second is *like* the first but it's *not* the first and it's not *exactly* the same.[11]

The Western value system demands that the rights and wants of the individual must be indulged at all costs. Believers must hold the line and insist that our first priority is to love God. If we lose sight of loving God as our priority, we will, with that, lose the ability to love our neighbour well. Not only this. We will also open the doors to the powers of darkness. As we put others, instead of God, first, we will become enslaved to the dark desires that grow out of the rebellious and wounded parts of people; we will end up with something we didn't bargain for. We must not indulge everyone's wants in the name of love. The way we ensure against this is by prioritising God and putting first what He wants, trusting that this will result in genuine human flourishing.

---

9   1 Corinthians 15 v 24-28.

10   The same word for 'submit' or 'be subject to', *hupotasso* is used in this passage.

11   See Matthew 22 v 39.

Chapter Twenty-Three
FAQs

Does Male Headship in Marriage Mean the Husband is the Leader?

This is a really fascinating and important question. I think it's hard to answer in terms of a straight yes or no, because leadership is a gift as well as a position. In our crazy world, some people have the position of leadership without the gift and some have the gift without the position. Some have neither and some have both!

Different husbands and wives are diversely gifted. Natural leaders tend to be clear thinking and decisive. There is no question that some wives carry these attributes more than their husbands. I don't believe that in a healthy marriage, either partner needs to become someone God hasn't made them. Sure, we all need to mature and die to ourselves, but that's a different thing. To curtail our God-given personalities with their accompanying gifts is not called for.

I believe that a wife ought to be free to manifest these qualities in marriage. But if she believes what I'm proposing in this book, it will have an impact on how she does so. It will be tethered to a submissive spirit that yields to the reality that her husband has been entrusted with a particular spiritual authority for them (note not 'over her'). A godly husband who has a leadership gift will want to make sure he is manifesting leadership qualities in such a way that his wife feels honoured and understood and loved. A godly husband who doesn't have a leadership gift will still want to engage fully in taking responsibility for the spiritual nourishment of his wife and carrying a unique sense of spiritual responsibility for the state of the marriage. Likewise, a godly wife will want to make sure she is manifesting leadership qualities in such a way that her husband feels honoured and respected. Both will be considerate to their spouse. Both will be considerate of the spiritual reality of headship. He will sacrificially serve. She will respectfully submit.

Asymmetrical gender quality.

Was the apostle Paul a misogynist?

Did Paul have a problem with women? Was he trying to undo the liberating work of Jesus with women? These are some of the charges that have been laid at his feet from certain quarters. Let's take a look.

Paul is the one who tells us there's no male and female in Christ.[1] This is a very radical verse and one that a misogynist would never write! As we have seen, Paul is the one who introduces us to female deacons[2] - a key leadership office in church life.

If we take the passage in Acts 6 as a prototype for the ministry of deacons, there is no denying that it was an office in the Jerusalem church reserved for men.[3] As the role developed, it seems clear that women were permitted, but here's the point: the apostles closest to Jesus in earthly terms, chose seven men, while Paul - the New Testament writer who gives us the really meaty verses concerning male headship - clearly affirmed the office of deacon for both men and women.

What I'm not doing is saying that the Jerusalem apostles and Paul were in disagreement, I'm simply refuting the idea that somehow Paul took things in a more conservative direction than Jesus when it came to the treatment of women in the church.

As we have also seen earlier, Paul's list of key gospel co-workers affectionately and passionately greeted in the letter to the Romans is approximately 25% female. This is phenomenal, especially when you consider the reality of the Ancient Near East and the Greco-Roman world! This is a world where women are typically excluded from much of the action. Not so Paul's team of co-workers. Paul also relies heavily on the wife and husband team of Priscilla and Aquila as beloved and key co-workers.[4] I phrase it 'wife and husband' and not the other way round, because her name usually comes up first when they're mentioned, probably highlighting that her contribution to the ministry was more prominent due to her specific, individual gifts.

Paul is happy to begin His Spirit-led gospel work in Macedonia among a gathering of prayerful women, whereby Lydia is the first to come to Christ and host Paul and Silas. We also know that certain women were the hosts of certain house churches. It seems to me that Paul's emphasis on women in ministry leans clearly in the direction of permissiveness and appreciation. Restrictions are only *emphasised* in contexts of crisis and disorder.

Can women be apostles?

Firstly, the majority of churches in the world don't believe in modern-day apostles, so straight away it's all a bit controversial! Assuming you do, you then need to decide how to define that role. It's not as easy as it

---

1   Galatians 3 v 28.

2   Romans 16 v 1.

3   The Greek word used in Acts 6 v 3 is 'Aner' which is talking about males.

4   Acts 18 v 26, Romans 16 v 3-4, 1 Corinthians 16 v 19, 2 Timothy 4 v 19.

sounds, because it's quite a general sort of word that literally means 'sent one' and can be used of any sort of ambassadorial role.

It's used definitely to describe the Twelve and Paul. But 1 Corinthians 15 v 7 suggests that it's also used to describe a group of disciples beyond them. Then it's clear elsewhere that Barnabas is considered an apostle.[5] Paul also refers to Apollos as an apostle.[6] And then of course we have Junia (see chapter 15, footnote 2).

In our own modern day context, some argue that it's legitimate to use the term 'apostle' to describe Christian pioneers (missionaries, church planters, etc.) because they are involved in the apostolic work of laying foundations, reaching new areas and establishing churches. So you see the difficulty.

In an apostolic 'movement' or 'network' or 'family' of churches, the term 'apostle' is usually applied to those who carry the most senior role of responsibility among those churches. If that family of churches was complementarian, the term 'apostle' would most likely be reserved for men, for the sake of consistency and clarity.

There are things that apostles are particularly gifted in: preaching and defending the gospel, laying foundations in a church, straightening out bad teaching, pressing into pioneering situations, developing leaders and caring for the poor. There are some women who are definitely gifted in these various ways. If we had a wider scope of use for the word, then such women could be described as apostles.

Because there are no explicitly named women apostles in the New Testament, it's legitimate to argue that, from the perspective of narrative theology, the argument leans towards it being an office for men. But someone may push back that this is merely an argument from silence - usually the weakest kind of argument!

While we would all agree that being a Christian isn't about titles, and if it becomes so then we've lost our way, we must also recognise that words like 'elder', 'deacon', 'apostle', 'prophet', 'evangelist', 'pastor', 'teacher' and others, are used in the Bible as a way of positively identifying where the Lord has placed people in His body; it's not wrong to name things.

So where do I land on this? I don't enjoy fence-sitting, but I think I have two things to say that, together, potentially place me on either side of it.

---

5   Acts 14 v 14.

6   1 Corinthians 4 v 6-13.

On the first side of the fence, I'd say that if we were using the term 'apostle' in its broadest sense and considering the way that the Lord clearly uses women in such activities as pioneering, caring for the poor, teaching and defending the faith and nurturing leaders, I could see how calling a woman whom God was using in these ways 'an apostle' would fit. One of the (numerous) dangers in not doing so, is that you can end up calling a particular man who's not as obviously apostolically gifted as a particular woman 'an apostle' while not repeating the favour for the woman. This seems to be a situation where reality is being avoided as well as some sort of injustice being committed - not good. Really not good.

On the other side of the fence, sailing as closely to scripture as possible, I can find no clear examples of women being designated as apostles. To me it seems that this role, while wider than the Twelve and Paul, did not consist of a large circle of people. There also seems, among these apostles, to be a degree of spiritual authority among the churches that would be potentially problematic if a woman were to be an apostle who served among male-governed churches.

Given the above arguments, I think there are two options for practical application, neither of them perfect.

The first is by calling women gifted in these ways apostles, while making clear that the doctrinal plumb-line in a family/network of churches would be the final responsibility of male apostles in that family. Someone might protest that this apparent 'tiering' of apostles is difficult to justify Biblically, but in 1 Thessalonians 2 v 6 Paul refers to not just himself but also Timothy and Silvanus as apostles. So what? Well, we know that Timothy was also a delegate of Paul in Ephesus, meaning that he was sent on his behalf, so here we seem to have a clear example of two apostles, Paul and Timothy, one of whom seemed to manifest a seniority of sorts. Therefore, if we can live with a sliding scale of apostolic grace and function, this could be a potentially fruitful option.

The second is by not calling women gifted in these ways apostles (on the grounds that it simply raises too many difficulties regarding the authority dynamic between apostles and elders), but still acknowledging a degree of 'apostolic gifting'. This could help us with Andronicus and Junia in Romans 16, who may have been husband and wife and who we might describe as an apostolic couple, potentially serving among the churches as a spiritual mother and father. The main problem here is that we don't find anyone described explicitly in the Bible as simply 'apostolic' whereas we do find apostles. Nevertheless, seeing as we are happy to describe people as pastorally and evangelistically gifted without similar biblical precedent, it may be a helpful, if somewhat pragmatic, way forward.[7]

While we are here, I'd like to make the point that when we consider what are known as the 'Ephesians 4 ministries' - apostles, prophets, evangelists, pastors and teachers - complementarians seem divided on whether women can be described in these ways. I think it's clear that women can be prophets and evangelists. Regarding pastors and teachers or pastor/teachers, Paul may here be referring to elders. If we allow for the fact that he may not necessarily be referring to elders, then I think we have the freedom to use these terms for women who serve the body of Christ with significant pastoral and teaching gifts. Perhaps consistency of terminology, as well as leaning into generosity, are the keys here to keep from unnecessary confusion and pain. We do have to acknowledge that the Bible is not written as a systematic theology, but is a collection of various genres of literature written by various authors over a period of time, that together create a rich and varied tapestry of consistent truth. But this explains why sometimes the lines are not as clear as we might like.[8]

Shouldn't husbands and wives be elders together?

The reality is that every elder's wife (or husband if you're in an egalitarian church) has a different mix of gifts and sense of personal call. Some of them may seem to be very suited to serving as elders, others not. The Bible is clear that part of the calling to eldership involves a desire for it, that's one of the ways you know you're called. This desire can't simply be created; it's God-given. It therefore seems safer and wiser to suggest that while every elder and their spouse will, to differing degrees, 'team it', I think it's best to let each person be appointed to eldership on their own merits, rather than based on who they are married to. I think this keeps the elder's spouse free from a lot of unnecessary pressure.

---

7   There has in recent years been some teaching suggesting that everyone in the church has some measure of at least one of the gifts mentioned in Ephesians 4 (apostle, prophet, evangelist, pastor, teacher). I personally do not subscribe to this view. The phraseology here makes it clear that certain people are given 'as gifts' to the church, by Jesus. I believe healthy churches ought to be exposed to, and be positively impacted by, all of these ministries (so that 'each one receives grace'), but I believe that these ministries are particular individuals who have been given to the church, as gifts from the ascended Christ.

8   Many people think the Ephesians 4 ministries occupy something of a distinct place in the church. This is because the people themselves are described *as* gifts in this passage, contrasted with the idea of people that *have* gifts, which describes all believers. As such, some people would consider these ministries to have a scope beyond the local congregation and called to serve the wider body of Christ. These people, generally speaking, wouldn't automatically consider Ephesians 4 pastor/teachers as elders, because elders are set apart to serve a local congregation.

I do think that where you have couples who are both clearly gifts given by Jesus to the church,[9] good thought needs to be given as to how to express those gifts fruitfully, while clarifying who carries the oversight responsibility for the church. Some wives will help their husbands by being very involved with them in ministry, others will be helpful in other ways. Let's bear in mind that I have argued that Genesis gives us a picture of teamwork that still leaves room for differing degrees of responsibility and stewardship.

Can Women have High Powered, Leading Job Roles?

This one won't take long: absolutely. I think the Bible is chiefly concerned with households. Are corporations, organisations and nations considered households? No.[10] There may be other considerations for a woman in this kind of role,[11] but at its heart I don't think it poses any problems theologically.

Doesn't Complementarianism Erase Equality?

In what sense does a complementarian consider men and women to be equal in Christ? Particularly if women can't be elders, which seems to not just speak, but *shout* of inequality! Let's think about different kinds of equality. Equality of worth. Looking at the amount of attention that Jesus gives to women, it's really very difficult to argue that God sees women as worth less than men. The Father has made us co-heirs with Christ and calls us by name, men and women. The Spirit is poured out without discrimination. I think that equality of worth is beyond debate. Equality of image-bearing. Nothing in the Bible suggests that either the man or the woman more clearly represents the image of God, but that together we bring the fullest picture. Equality of roles. Under a more complementarian pattern, a woman's role in the home and church would be just as influential as the man's, but their influence would be worked out in different ways.

This raises a very important question. Is equality the same as 'interchangeability'? The answer, of course, is 'no'. Egalitarians would agree with this. They are not arguing that men and women are the same, but

---

9   As I said earlier, I don't believe that everyone is given to the church in this way. Of course we are all called to be very meaningfully connected to a local church and use our gifts, but Ephesians 4 v 11 talks of people that Jesus gives to the church as gifts. For these people, they can't shake the fact that by divine ordination they are given to the church, and thus the church takes up an inordinate amount of their passion and thought and time.

10   The leadership of the nation of Israel is somewhat unique because they represented God's own nation similarly to how the church does now, and so it was something of a household. I will avoid, at this point, the deeply felt debate concerning the nation of Israel in the purposes of God. Please take my comment above in the most simple terms. Maybe one day we can explore this in more depth!

11   Things like how to manifest her authority in a feminine way, how to value her time with small children if she has them or plans to have them, how to keep the dynamic with her husband healthy (if she is married), and how to navigate potential gender prejudice graciously but firmly, etc.

they are arguing that they see no reason why men should remain 'in power'. This is a vital issue that needs addressing: how do we power-share while honouring the headship reality?

Genesis 1 shows us power-sharing as we look after creation. Genesis 2 shows us some things that suggest a less symmetrical dynamic. If the man is entrusted with the command in a unique way, he is also granted the power to do this effectively. But likewise, if the woman is entrusted with the unique role of helping the man, then she also has the power to do this effectively. Agency is never removed. Free will and good conscience are always honoured. If we can learn to work much more intentionally in mixed gender teams, then I think a lot of the heat will be removed from the equality question. We'll be too busy happily and fruitfully serving Christ together!

If Elders are the Stewards of Church Doctrine shouldn't they be the ones who Preach on Sundays?

This is a reasonable question. As a starter for ten, it's very important that we don't take our model of church services and then imagine the early church was exactly the same, and then attempt to make Biblical truth fit perfectly with the way we do things; the way we do things may need to change! When we read Paul's first letter to the Corinthians, we find perhaps the most detailed description among all the epistles of what the early church gatherings looked like. What seems clear is that instead of a sermonic centrepiece by one person, there were, interspersed throughout their time together, all kinds of contributions, including teachings, by all kinds of people.

Our way of arranging church services seems to have sprung up from the Reformation, and this begins to make sense of why. Up to this point, the church had become doctrinally skewed and was also stuck in the mire of superstition and wacky ideas that had no basis in scripture; what was needed was some solid gospel preaching and Bible teaching. With this backdrop, a sound sermon by a schooled preacher was the felt need of the church. Now don't hear what I'm not saying; I believe in preaching, and providing the person is sufficiently gifted, I don't mind long sermons at all. Paul himself preached for so long once, that someone dropped off and fell out of a third storey window! Release the huge preaching gifts in the church to preach their hearts out. But. It's also imperative that the gifts among the body of Christ are exercised in a way that begins to reflect what Paul writes about to the Corinthians - when you gather, everyone's got something to bring!

So, given that I do believe the elders are the stewards of the doctrine taught and lived in the local church, what suggestions do I have for expressing this manifestly, as well as pursuing dynamic charismatic church life? I will focus on Sundays because that is when, for most churches, the whole congregation gathers together, and it's the elders who have oversight for the whole congregation.

Why not arrange some Sunday services differently, so that every other week or once a month, instead of one person preaching for forty minutes, a number of people either come prepared with something shorter, or more room is made for spontaneous teachings. In this scenario, everyone would realise that what is going on is not how only an elder could function, and you would have the elders present obviously presiding over things.

Why not make sure that when strange doctrines and accompanying attitudes and behaviours creep into the church, it's the elders who step in and refute the false ideas and bring corrective discipline to the wrong conduct? This would be a very clear way of making clear to the congregation that the elders guard this element of church life.

Why not, in releasing other gifted teachers to teach on Sundays, make sure that the elders stand before the congregation and endorse and pray for this person before they preach, so that it's clear that whoever is preaching is doing so on behalf of the elders. It would also be advised that the elders would look over the prepared material of non-elder preachers beforehand in order to be able to peacefully endorse what is going to be said. It may also be helpful for the elders to provide the fundamental sermon outlines, though for some preachers this could stifle their gift somewhat.

I also think it's legitimate for only the elders to preach on a Sunday - at least it's consistent and clear. But if this were the case, I would strongly encourage both consistency in this (not getting men who aren't elders to preach) and the training and prolific releasing of gifted teachers in every other area of church life (evangelistic events, Bible studies, small groups, youth and kids, men's and women's events, specialist equipping etc.).

Why Can't Justice and Kindness Simply Prevail?

Behind this question is a belief. The belief is that the egalitarian route is by far the kinder and more just way of doing life in Christ. In terms of the question above, yes! Let's believe the best - that complementarians and egalitarians are both reaching for justice and kindness.

It's important that we don't import our own ideas of these concepts into the conversation and make that our starting point. We trust that God, being ultimately just and perfectly kind, will have, in His word, prescribed a way of living in community that most properly reflects this. From that perspective, the matter remains, at its heart, an exegetical one. What does the Bible teach? If we can do our most thorough work there, we will more likely end up with the most just and kind route through.

To not demonstrate that kind of confidence in scripture would be a significant statement for an evangelical Christian. An egalitarian would say that power dynamics and people being what they are, a church that reserved its most senior leadership position for men, would inevitably feel male dominated. To marginalise women who are, along with men, co-heirs of eternal life would mean that in one fell swoop, injustice and unkindness have surely won the day. A complementarian would point to the united voice in scripture concerning the male and female created order, and protest that if we sidelined that, we would be giving something beautiful away. We would now read our Bibles with either suspicious or editorial lenses and would no longer simply let the scriptures speak. What kind of justice and kindness is that?

As a very moderate complementarian, it's vital that I sit with the egalitarian perspective and let it search me out. If the Bible teaches that headship is a reality and that it's something God has entrusted to husbands, fathers and elders, then what does it look like to exercise this in such a way as to bring maximum life and joy for all involved? In literal terms, I love to hold doors open for women. Not because they are unable to open them themselves (!) but because for me, it's a simple way of expressing my preference for them. What does the spiritual equivalent look like? How could I, and other men of influence 'open the door' so wide for women that they don't simply find themselves with ample opportunity to exercise their gifts, but feel enthusiastically invited to do so by men they respect? What if those men were to search them out to co-labour with them, in order to hear from them and be profoundly helped by them? What if those men affirmed and served those women in such a way as to make them really feel their value and worth? Might that be something that carried the kind of redemptive power in it that somehow outshone a scenario where both were simply at the table? Might that strike dead the Genesis 3 dominion that lies at the heart of fallen man? Might it strike dead the Genesis 3 desire that lies at the heart of fallen women? It would at least help!

It's at this point that I think difficult but important questions should be asked. If lurking at the bottom of the egalitarian perspective is a fear of male oppression, while that may be tragically understandable, could we consider it a good foundation? If at the bottom of complementarianism there is a desire to keep things 'male', could we consider it a worthy foundation? I think we can clearly see that the answer to both questions is a resounding "No". But it's vital that we search our hearts.

Can a Woman Truly Champion Complementarianism?

It's clear that some do, so the initial answer is "Yes". But behind the question is the reality that for many women, to champion this perspective is to place them firmly in the category of the treacherous. They are seen as turning their back on their own, replacing their hands and the hands of their sisters back firmly in the chauvinistic bonds that were finally starting to loosen. The oppression and liberation narrative is a powerful one. To champion the complementarian perspective, as a woman, is not for the faint-hearted.

My honest perspective is that the strength of female negative response to this is a blend of three things: firstly the Genesis 3 curse (fallen women do not want to have a man as their head); secondly the innumerable instances of negative experiences at the hands of men that are both shameful and tragic; and thirdly the external pressure of secular feminism.

Considering for a moment, the second element, whether for women it's men dismissing them, leering at them, attacking them, shouting them down, bypassing them or objectifying them, men, for the most part, have not done well. This is why, as I said earlier, while none of us are perfect, I think it's vitally important to say that as believers, our head, Jesus, is the only model for true headship, and no son, daughter, wife or church member ought to submit to someone violent or abusive, or someone leading them into ungodliness.

Does the Story of Ahab and Jezebel have Anything to Say About this Subject?

Nestled in the Old Testament records of the kings, we encounter a terrifying figure called Jezebel, who was queen of Israel alongside the disastrous king, Ahab.[12] A devoted worshipper of Baal and Asherah, she was an inciter of evil, a murderous thief, and a seductress. The spiritual power she wielded reduced mighty Elijah to a depressed and near suicidal wreck.

If we heard no more of her, she would simply be another 'Don't be like this' figure in the Bible. But we do. In the book of Revelation, Jesus speaks to the church in Thyatira, rebuking a woman in the church, whom He addresses as 'that Jezebel'. This woman is enticing the church into idolatry and encouraging sexual immorality. Deja vu. It seems that this woman is not actually called Jezebel but because of her spiritual traits, Jesus calls her that, and in doing so elevates Jezebel to more than just a historical figure.

Many Christian leaders in pentecostal and charismatic circles have developed this idea to the point where they would say there is a particular demonic 'Jezebel' spirit that manifests in certain people, and is marked by a desire for power at all costs, coupled with a murderous seductiveness.

Given that in both cases the Jezebel figure was a woman, and in the Old Testament account she was wreaking particular havoc on certain men and their inheritance (Ahab, Elijah, Naboth), and also because in some church circles the label 'Jezebel' seems to have been attributed very freely to any woman who shows the remotest sign of strength, it's worth exploring whether or not men and women, in their dynamics, need to be particularly watchful in this regard.

---

12   See 1 Kings 16-21 and 2 Kings 9.

If there is a specific demonic spirit that goes by this name, while I don't think it will necessarily be confined to women, I do think women who are tempted around power, and attracted or attached to weaker men, need to be particularly watchful here. Those two things could create a vulnerability, and so if you are a woman who ticks those boxes (don't feel condemned, we all have our struggles), keeping a right heart before God and being deeply and genuinely accountable to trusted and truthful people are requisite for keeping things clean. Having said that, where the label is used by men against women who show leadership qualities or strength, this is much more a comment on those men's insecurities than it is on the women in question; let's avoid such unhelpful behaviour. I will say this: because the male/female dynamic is so key to the image and purposes of God, the matter is most certainly spiritually charged. Carelessness in this matter can open the door to demonic powers that wreak havoc. This is way beyond merely psychological and behavioural; male and female cuts to the heart of spiritual things.

What Does a Healthy Complementarian Marriage Look Like?

The complementarian would want men and women to note that headship is not primarily something men *do;* it's a reality that simply is. How it's expressed we'll get to in a minute - but that would be a headline for a complementarian. The teaching is that it's a spiritual reality rather than a verb, which means that whether you believe it or not, it's still true.[13]

Ephesians 5 v 21-33 is not trying to argue for the reality of this headship. Paul is actually concerned with how a husband expresses it, in order that it might look like Jesus and therefore be life-giving.

The wife is the delight. The beauty. The radiant one. The pursued and cherished one. And also...the submitted one. Not the passive one. Not the defeated one. Submission isn't about that. Submission to an enemy involves defeat. Submission to a tyrant involves passivity. Submission to a lover involves delight. It's the willing giving of yourself to the tender strength that is being given to you.

Husbands. Here is how you 'do' headship, what it looks like in order for it to qualify as appropriate. Love your wife. Give yourself up entirely for your wife. Beautify her with your sacrificial love. Win her over completely. Let her know she is the only one for you. Die to any others that have tried to get a hold on your heart. All by the power of the Holy Spirit - not your own resources. All at the expense of your own comforts, priorities, wants, laziness, lusts, selfishness and greed. Paul assumes that the husbands do pretty well at loving themselves. Now get on and treat your wife in the same way.

---

13   Contrary to postmodern thought, the inconvenient thing about truth is that it's true even when we don't believe it!

Wives, respect your husbands - with your thoughts, and your conversation with him and about him. Let him know that he is highly esteemed. Next we get to a very brief exhortation that appears near the end of the letter to the Colossians - nothing new, but it hopefully helps to bring the point home.

> *Wives, submit to your husbands, as is fitting in the Lord. Husbands, love your wives, and do not be harsh with them.*
> COLOSSIANS 3 V 18-19

Again it's clear. It's the wives who are to submit to their husbands, it's not something the husbands offer their wives, because that wouldn't tell the right story. This is why Paul says it's fitting in the Lord - it fits with creation and it fits with the gospel.

Husbands, there it is again - LOVE YOUR WIFE! How many times do we need to hear it? This is the key. Let your wife know that you know and understand and cherish and value her. Oh and one more thing; that means no harshness. Nothing that could lead her to feeling embittered.

I heard a story once of a husband who was getting a bit fed up with his wife. In fact, he was getting so fed up that he decided to write down everything that was annoying him about her. He told me that as he was writing the list he felt a kind of ice come over his heart. Immediately he stopped writing that list and in fact completely did away with it, and simply resolved that he would sacrificially love her with determination and resolve. His testimony was that this resulted in the protection of his own heart, and her flourishing in all sorts of new ways. Husbands…your wife is your dream girl; end of story.

Sometimes there are what I would call bizarre caricatures that can arise around this matter of headship in marriage. You hear people talk about it as if the husband makes all the decisions or has to initiate everything that happens, and other tragic tales. Let me make it very clear that there is nothing in the whole of the Bible to suggest that this is what a godly marriage ought to look like.

Below is an example of how our marriage works when it comes to decision making. In the day to day, we either usually agree or defer to one another's particular wisdom and strengths in light of what a particular decision is about. Also, by default I will, out of sacrificial love, defer to Davina's wishes on matters that aren't a big deal. Why not? It's good for me. But sometimes we disagree on important matters. After 25 years of marriage, having grown more and more into one another's image (!) and being deeply aligned in our values and mutually submitted to scripture, these instances are thankfully rare, but sometimes it happens. For myself and my wife, the first thing we'll do is reflect carefully and prayerfully to see if either of us, for whatever reason, is just being stubborn or insensitive, or anything else ungodly. The Bible says that the wisdom from above is reasonable[14] - that's something that we will both need to make sure we are manifesting.

After that, our consciences may be clear but we still don't see eye to eye. If it's a matter that's too important for one of us to humbly give way to the other, we will look for trusted counsel.

Once we've done that, if that counsel has not shed any new light on the conversation, then, because it's a decision that is significant and has maybe been a bit fraught, I will explicitly take final responsibility for the decision. PLEASE NOTE: That doesn't mean we'll necessarily end up doing what I wanted - I may make the call to go with her choice - but it does mean that the buck will stop with me, for better or for worse. The aim is that that will be a blessing for her; that by taking a burden rather than adding to it and in stepping up in that moment she will not feel in any way disempowered or patronised, but *blessed*. To be honest, in these rare moments she has usually *asked* me to do this! There it is.

99% of the time we simply pool our various insights and wisdom and gifts in order to make good choices, and give each other a lot of grace when we get it wrong. In this sense it's helpful to see the headship pattern as foundational, it's there and it's there to protect, but the moment by moment dynamics of the marriage, while strengthened by that, are focused on this mutuality, this partnership. Two people with different, complimentary gifts, listening to one another, dignifying one another, preferring one another.

What do I Mean by the Word 'Prominence'?

Earlier in the book I said that I believe 'prominence' is the best word to describe what the New Testament means by the word 'head' (kephale). Also note that in one of the previous FAQs I said that it seems likely that Priscilla had a more prominent gift or ministry contribution than her husband Aquila, which is why, unusually for the time, her name is usually mentioned first.

In light of these two comments above, am I being consistent? What do I mean by the head of a household having prominence? Thinking back to the creation story, where Adam is created first, entrusted with obeying God's commands before Eve is created, and then held primarily accountable for their disobedience, I am suggesting that prominence is about God charging a man with prominent spiritual responsibility as head of a household.

How this plays out is that a man would feel this sense of responsibility and not hide (other than in God!), nor be passive or selfish, but sacrificially give himself for the good of those he has this responsibility for.

---

14   James 3 v 17.

I would also expect any woman on the receiving end of this service to feel blessed, and take it as a sign that she is deeply loved and valued. I would hope that this would motivate her to bring her gifts to help him in what God has called them to do together, because he needs her help and without her things won't be good.

It's a two-way motion but it's asymmetrical, as spiritual realities embedded in creation and the gospel play out in distinctive ways.

Headship equals firstness equals prominence. Prominence of responsibility *NOT* prominence of gift.

What Does this Teaching say to the Widows and the Fatherless?

Throughout the scriptures we find repetitive references to the widows and the fatherless. God has a very special concern for them. Here are some examples:

> *Do not move an ancient boundary stone or encroach on the fields of the fatherless, for their Defender is strong; he will take up their case against you.*
> PROVERBS 23 V 10-11

> *Sing to God, sing in praise of his name, extol him who rides on the clouds; rejoice before him—his name is the LORD. A father to the fatherless, a defender of widows, is God in his holy dwelling.*
> PSALM 68 V 4-5

If I were to ask you what it is about the widows and fatherless that draws the compassion and protection of the Lord towards them in this special way, what would you say? You might say that they are particularly vulnerable, and I would agree, but then I would ask you why that is. The answer is that both have had their 'head' taken from them.

The man who was to lovingly protect them has been taken from them and this has left them vulnerable. In these instances the ultimate Head over all, the Lord Himself, is stirred to compassion and is swift to proclaim Himself as their protector with a fierceness that causes us to tremble. This is headship.

A man is supposed to protect those under his care. Not oppress, but protect. Not abuse, but protect. Not desert, but protect. Not forsake, but protect. Not dominate, but protect. Not fight against, but fight for. This, I believe, is what he is called to do by God. It is a spiritual responsibility. His presence is supposed to bring a sense of safety, so that confident flourishing might take place. This is headship. This is being a household representative.

Wives and children and church members, in ways appropriate to the relationship (a husband and wife looks different to a church and elders), ought to delight in and welcome this. It is vital in a world of bullies and oppressors and serpents and con-artists and those who take advantage and intimidate. A man's headship ought to say to those types, "You're not coming in here - end of story." Whether it's heretics or womanisers sliding into the church, creeps and bullies in school or neighbours from hell, headship done well in these situations brings wisdom, strength and a sense of safety for those in the household.

Our society has very many households without dads for all kinds of reasons. We mustn't pretend that this isn't a vulnerable situation - that would be naive. Before I say any more about this, let me make it clear that I have tremendous respect for the amazing job that single parents do, the majority of whom are mums; my three siblings and I had only my mum at home from the age of eleven, and I live in constant gratitude to her for her resilience, resourcefulness and other-worldly patience!

But the reality is that we were in this situation as a result of failed marriages - it was not at all ideal. I will never forget the feeling of intense vulnerability when a group of young men came to our house to attack me when I was a teenager. That there was no one present to protect me, that I was supposedly the man of the house, that I clearly was not ready; it's a very dark moment I'd rather forget.

I don't write this to discourage, but instead to help us face reality and to bring some encouragement. I do believe that God gives special grace to such households, and as I look back now, through all the difficulties, I see that my mum was helped and strengthened by some brilliant men in the church, who really made a difference. Men who sat with me when I was tripping out on LSD, men who helped renovate our garden, men who invited me to football games, men who showed an interest in me, men who didn't give up on me when I was a total clown. This was God's provision to me, my mum, my sister and brothers. I believe this was God's zeal, God's passion, His own fierce headship determined to protect us and see us through tough times. And this is the beauty of the church - that there are men in the church whom God will stir by His own Spirit to step in and play something of that role in the lives of fatherless households.

Our God understands the realities of life in a fallen world. None of us have it all sewn up, all of us walk with a limp. This particular gap, this lack of a man in the mix, God takes very seriously - it matters to Him. He cares deeply about it, and if this applies to you then you can be 100% sure that He is attentive to your cry, and though there may be tears in the night, trust me, there will be joy in the morning.[15]

Could I say something similar to the motherless? Yes I could, but it wouldn't be exactly the same. Growing up, I had friends whose mum had left and they were at home only with Dad. It was a similar situation to

---

15   Psalm 30 v 5.

mine but also very different, having its own unique contours of pain. If they had been in the church, I can imagine armies of women stepping in to mother those children in ways that move me as I think about it now 35 years later; a tsunami of care and nurture and feminine strength would have crashed in on their lives! We're back to Genesis 1 and 2 all over again - men and women woven together in beautiful interdependence to bring in the full image of God.

To the widows and the fatherless, this teaching says that God's eye is on you in a special way. His jealous love for you will not be dampened, and you can count on His support and faithfulness. He is your head and He takes it very seriously. Even if you can't understand why things have worked out as they have, He is good and His love for you endures forever.

What does this Teaching say to the Unmarried?

For reasons good and bad, I believe the church of the future will have more single people in it than it has in recent history.[16] I hope that what I've laid out in this book will prove to be a happy signpost to all people, regardless of marital status.

This is because Adam and Eve are, at the same time, not just the prototype husband and wife but also the prototype man and woman. This means that what we see in the garden has something deep and profound to say to all of us. There are, if you like, 'echoes of Eden' that resonate in each of our souls - it's way deeper and higher than whether or not we're married. I believe there is a transcendent meaning as well as a powerful counter-cultural result in the emphasis. For men to feel a sense of need for gifted and godly women in their lives is a beautiful thing and, likewise, for women to feel valued and drawn in alongside such men to bring their gifts into the mix.

For a woman to be recognised and delighted in, according to her true design, and for her to champion decent, releasing men has world-changing power. She is to be known and understood and not dismissed. He is to be respected and helped and not despised. For her voice to be heard and her perspective to be valued is vital. For his strength and vitality to be celebrated is vital. For them to find unity in their differences is a key that will unlock enormous Kingdom potential.

---

16   The bad reasons are a growing fear of marriage, fear of commitment, relational neurosis and widespread sexual confusion in Western culture. The good reasons are the toppling of the idol of marriage and the dismantling of the idea that unless you are married you are somehow incomplete or disqualified from true maturity and senior responsibility in the church.

What Does Headship Look Like Day to Day?

Thankfully, it's actually a lot simpler than you might think. The devil loves us to complicate things and get us in a muddle. As with most (all?) things to do with the faith, the heart is the crucial matter. If, whether you are a man or woman, you believe and confess this teaching of male headship, and if you commit to seeing it work itself out, the hardest work is done.

All men are, first and foremost, under the headship of Christ, and so they know what it takes to meaningfully trust Him. Also, most men have men other than Jesus - imperfect men - to whom they are submitted, whether their own dad when they're young or church leaders when adults, and therefore empathy ought to be high.

Also if you're a man, you will take very seriously your role as head concerning your wife (if you are married), your children (if you have them) and all those who are looking to you for leadership (if you are a pastor). You will be proactive, gentle, patient, sacrificial, servant-hearted and kind in your dealings with them. You will also pray for them regularly and passionately. This is manifesting good headship; you are being like Jesus. If you are a man you will be learning how to face down your own fears and deal with the temptations you face to go quiet and deny your strength, or to bully and lord it over by abusing your strength. You will learn to manifest your strength in gentleness, immovability in the things of God, and fervent prayer.

If you are a woman, first and foremost, you are under the headship of Christ, and so any other submitting that you do will be done in the context of loving and looking to please Jesus. You will not submit to anything that would cause you to disobey Christ. As it's Him who has called you to submit to your husband (if you're married), or your father or your church leaders, then your act of submission is done happily because it's unto the Lord and with a 100% clear conscience. If you are a woman then you will be looking to express all your gifts and all your strength so as to be a particular help to the men in your lives. Because you believe in this, you will learn how to do it intuitively over time, looking to bring all that you have to the table and serve Christ by helping the men that God has put into your life - husband, fathers, pastors.

What if the Men won't Make Room for the Women?

It's unfortunate to have to address this question, but I have included it as I believe that in some situations this is the case. Let's be honest. While being the same sex doesn't necessarily mean we get on, I think there is a level of innate understanding between those of the same sex.

Men can have a surprisingly negative impact on women just by being a little bit thoughtless or by not taking time to listen carefully. Women can have a surprisingly negative impact on men by honing in on every detail, particularly when it comes to relationships and who said what. We can wind each other up! This has meant that in some churches, good and godly people have been squeezed out on account of their gender.

Men can feel that in some ways it's easier and more straightforward to have a leadership conversation just among other men; it seems simpler and we just sort of steamroll through things. When women are in the mix they say things we would never think of, and sometimes what they say are inconvenient truths! Don't get me wrong - it doesn't always work in this direction, but in my world it can tend to, so I'm honing in on it. While it might be easier and feel more simple to make decisions as guys, I think it's time we woke up to the fact that, in light of Genesis 1, we need the woman's voice in the mix. We will have to adjust and we will have to unlearn and relearn certain things, but it will be worth it and it will be fruitful. There is a better destination than where we currently are.

Let's do this.

Chapter Twenty-Four
Hearing the Woman's Voice

It's been quite a journey. I wanted to end by letting the voices of women speak directly in this book. They may not all agree in a detailed way with the conclusions I've come to but they are all women that I trust and respect. I asked them to do their best to define femininity and also, if they had the inclination, to comment on how they viewed healthy masculinity. This is what they said. Their voices are the last ones to be heard - seemed right.

Femininity to me is…the natural expression of women. It is distinctive because it exudes a powerful essence of what it is to be a woman - strong, soft, passionate, devoted, tender, protective, free, and at times vulnerable. I appreciate masculinity when men show strong, confident leadership, yet are protective, perceptive and sensitive enough to read a room and adjust accordingly. Humility is key, as arrogance diminishes the strength from true masculinity, I think also passion is an attribute, and determination.

A (LONDON UK)

———————————

To me, femininity is an honour and part of God's design. Being distinct, created deliberately second in God's perfect creation order, but not second best or worth less, just distinct. Distinct perspectives, feelings and thoughts. In our femininity we are a perfect match and complement to our Adams. Working better together than alone. As women we rejoice in that distinctiveness and are proud to be called daughters by our King…the world and religion struggle with the rightful place women hold as co-heirs in Christ. As always, only God gets it perfectly right.

It is way more than a social construct. Our femininity is innate, not put upon us. It's not about power or value. It's about being made by God in a way that's unique to us. The world and religion struggle with the rightful place women hold as co-heirs in Christ. As always, only God gets it perfectly right. We are simultaneously the weaker vessel and the Proverbs 31 woman and there is no contradiction. Femininity is part of the original plan and I thank God for making me a woman. The good men in my life have the courage to lead. They protect, love and nurture the women, children and other men in their lives. They balance strength with humility. They can be tender hearted and vulnerable and yet strong and certain. They neither abuse their strength, nor are they too passive. Healthy masculinity feels safe, both in family and church. The language matters though, doesn't it? You rightly added the healthy to masculinity as it's a loaded term. Just like when we say complementarity and headship in our family of churches, other Christians hear patriarchy and female oppression. A few times in discussions, I have felt that I was defending a concept to people that to me feels healthy, balanced and God-given that the opposite sex viewed as a codeword for subjugation but at closer examination our stance was not that far apart. Often, headship and masculinity are judged based solely on the worst examples we encounter of male dominance, misogyny and chauvinism, not on the flourishing for both partners if it's done well, and the freedom that lies within the Godly order. We are not alike and that is good. We have different temperaments, strengths and feelings. It makes for a richer life together. Can language ever be redeemed or do we need new words? Who knows.

N (GERMANY)

———————————

Femininity is like a lioness. Physically she looks distinct from the lion. She takes care of herself and looks her best, but without becoming vain or obsessed. Her nature is nurturing, graceful and gentle, yet she has a fierceness that fights where necessary. The pride is her priority as she cares and connects, and although she is smaller, she knows how to roar.

To me, the answer to 'what is healthy masculinity?' has got to be found in studying the person and life of Jesus, Who was created fully male and Who lived a life without sin. My observation is therefore that 'healthy masculinity' is not about being the most muscular or handsome. Isaiah 53:2 says about Jesus, 'He had no form or majesty that we should look at Him, and no beauty that we should desire Him.' Although not muscular, Jesus was strong in character and never gave in to temptation (Hebrews 4:15). Isaiah 61 and 42:3 describes Jesus' approach towards the vulnerable and weak: 'A bruised reed He will not break, and a smouldering wick He will not snuff out.' We can also read stories such as the feeding of the 5000 and the provision of Peter's tax. These passages describe someone who is strong in heart and character. He is gentle, yet a protector, defender and provider for those in His care, especially the weak and vulnerable. To me, this is healthy masculinity.

A (CAMBRIDGE UK)

———————————

The first word that came to me is strength. I would say especially with family members, a lot of women in my life have been or are very resilient. It isn't something you'd notice at first glance, but when you understand what enables them to be who they are and give, in the way they do, there is a strength there that enables them to stand. I think it could be different to more obvious, maybe masculine, strength (maybe). It is inner and therefore more humble strength, and it gives a depth of character because of the things it has weathered. I think there is gentleness or grace that disguises it, so it isn't on show at all times. A quiet strength.

D (LONDON UK)

————————

I think true femininity is beautiful. It is strong yet gentle, decisive yet humble, assertive yet full of grace. It does not force itself upon others, yet it stands out. It is fiery and passionate, yet tender. It is a woman's full embrace of God's unique design of her, and a Holy Spirit empowered attempt to live that out for God's glory.

I really appreciate: men who truly listen and seek to understand; men of conviction (not the criminal kind!) but worn with humility, not arrogance; those who show genuine care and seek to build up and encourage, rather than correct and be right; those with empathy (this makes such a difference); men who are secure in who they are in Christ, and not trying to prove something; men with strength of character but who are humble enough to be learners too; men who are decisive; those who know they need others (both women and men) and seek to call out the gifting in those around them; and those that ask questions in pursuit of genuinely knowing others. I love it when men live from a place of strength in who they are in Christ and what He's called them to, while knowing they are not the whole picture, and that genuine and equal partnership (with men and women) is vital for them and others to fulfil their calls.

E (POLAND)

————————

As I began to think about this question, it surprised me how difficult I found it to answer. Femininity is so multi-layered and can be seen, or not, in many aspects of life: from manner and character, to style and beauty, both physical and aesthetic. I think to some degree it is innate and to another degree learnt/constructed. Biblically I think there are varied examples of femininity...some characteristics I would say are: gentleness, being servant hearted, nurturing, and kind; but these are not in opposition to strength and resilience. Then I thought surely these traits are, or should also be, true of masculinity? Perhaps it is the combination and obviousness of them that varies between femininity and masculinity.

A (NEW ZEALAND)

When I consider the word femininity I think of an inner beauty, the evidence of which is gentleness and gracefulness - but that does not mean she is a 'push over'! She may have strong opinions and be a leader in her own right but, nevertheless, she maintains her sense of poise and peace, quietly confident in who she is. The other attributes that come to mind are: caring and nurturing; empathy; and a vulnerability that is not so evident in a man.

Regarding masculinity: an inner strength so that I feel safe, protected, cared for and supported. Compassionate, loving, patient - and with children too. A sense of humour!! This might sound like a funny one, but to maintain a sense of humour in the everyday pressures, etc. of life is so important.

A (NORWICH UK)

Femininity is displaying strength from the heart, whereas true masculinity is providing protection through innate strength.

D (LONDON UK)

...as a woman who doesn't have a naturally quiet, gentle, submissive and dependent personality, I've had to grow in two areas. One is the conviction for me to grow, and allow the Holy Spirit to work in me those feminine traits that are not natural for me, which are biblical, like nurturing, submission and gentleness. The second is how I, as a woman, maturely show and act out of the gifts that God has given me, like leadership, teaching and preaching in a restorative way to still be feminine, and not come across as a usurper. I think that there are traits, mannerisms and attributes which are more common to, or associated with, women that when portrayed by someone makes them more feminine (maybe more dependent on the eye of the beholder). Some feminine traits are different in cultures, social groups, generations, etc.

Healthy masculinity: strength that is humble, activity and drive that are not self-seeking, provision that is honest, protection that is releasing, taking ownership and responsibility, laying your life down.

L (MIDDLE EAST)

———————————

To me, what it is: strength in who we are as women, knowing our abilities and reaching out to strengthen others in their walk. Being humble but not a pushover. Having confidence, as a woman, and passing this on to others so they find their feet too. Caring, nurturing, building but also pioneering, risk-taking and walking tall as a child of God. I could go on and on...oh I forgot - enjoy a good perfume!

Healthy masculinity for me is humble confidence and strength, caring for the needs of others, dying to self and expecting to give rather than receive, loving God and being able to cry about it, being able to say 'I don't know', asking for help, respecting women and being willing to mentor them without fear of temptation because they see wisdom, brain power, abilities, creativity and anointing in women. Not feeling threatened but being open-handed when dealing with others, able to give their position away without a 'Yes, but'. Not needing a position to make them feel secure but able to feel comfortable in their own skin because of being secure in who they are. Able to share their right to discuss/decision making with women knowing that a more healthy 'whole' will come out of it...oh yes, smells like a good aftershave when one walks past them.

A (CAMBRIDGE UK)

———————————

Femininity is freedom; it's assurance of self, it's resilience, it's joy. Femininity looks through a lens of opportunity before limits, of empathy before ego, of yes before no. Femininity is the journey of working out my womanhood. Alone, or with other expressions of itself, femininity is powerful – but – it feels *complete* when I'm moving in step with masculinity. It feels painful, and almost risky, to confess this because I so often witness violation within gender partnerships but ultimately, I know that femininity needs to be championed by its masculine counterparts to deeply thrive. Women need the protection, and advocacy, and understanding of men (fathers, brothers, sons, friends and lovers) to truly flourish.

As a social construct, femininity is aggressively reduced to my appearance, my sexuality, my clothes and my independence – this has exhausted me, instead of empowering me, for my whole life. I feel most beautiful, most feminine, when I am being filled with the Holy Spirit. I look at Him, He reflects onto me, and in that moment I know who I am again – I am feminine.

(Healthy) Masculinity is advocacy; it's integrity, it's strength beyond the physical, it's absolute security. Masculinity steps out in boldness, welcomes challenge and swims against the tempting tides of stagnancy. Masculinity beckons femininity into an adventure with a raised voice that champions, yet does not patronise, includes yet does not oppress, leads yet does not dominate. In our society, the identity of masculinity has been grossly subverted, and now requires the prefix – healthy. Stereotypes reign supreme in ways that pressure men to lack emotion, lead with harshness and perpetuate misogyny. In the home, my experience of masculinity has been consistent and freeing, but outside of the home, it stands on my chest with a suffocating weight of disrespect, supremacy and objectification.

In partnership with toxic masculinity, I am small, exploited and angry. In partnership with healthy masculinity, I am safe, celebrated and invincible. I long for the standards of masculinity to be universally raised, prioritising steadiness and empathy for the good of both men and women everywhere.

J (LONDON UK)

———————

Without wanting to ignore all of our differences, I'd say that very often women have more nuanced responses to people, situations, etc. There's more empathy, discernment and compassion, yet without this being a soft option. Women have the steel behind the velvet glove. My mum always said that women were more adaptable than men because they had to be. In her day at least, it was the woman who had to move and cope with where the men were (that may not be the same today, but to be honest I think it often is). And I'd say we often have greater strength than men especially in a crisis. And we're also drop dead gorgeous, especially compared to men!

You know how the ancient Hebrew men used to thank God every day that he hadn't made them a woman, well, in principle at least, I thank God every day that he has made me a woman!

C (LONDON UK)

———————

In an age where many would like to make "gender" as a concept redundant in meaning, it almost feels controversial just describing my thoughts on femininity. To be honest I felt an initial hesitation to answer this question. Growing up I had strong females and males around me who really helped me develop a healthy sense of embracing femininity. What this looked like was an emphasis on being kind, communicative, gentle, whilst also being strong, resilient and vocal. It has been a journey in personal discovery of a healthy sense of what it means to be a woman. I've also keenly felt at times that I go against the stereotype of what it means to be feminine. For instance, I always felt called to have a career, and if I ever had a husband I knew that I wanted our marriage and home-life to be a partnership rather than allocated traditional roles. After being married, and now with children, the idea would sometimes creep in about whether I am fitting the mould of being a godly woman and demonstrating the unique gifting of femininity that women have.

As well as not necessarily fitting the mould in the home environment, I work in a male-dominated environment, where I have at times been mistaken for the assistant rather than the manager. This treatment from others would leave me questioning again what my role is as a woman, and what I could do to be taken "seriously" at work. This led to a few changes in the way I dressed for a few years. I would dress quite androgynously - a shirt, plain trousers and jumpers. I felt that if I hid my femininity my ideas would be heard and perhaps I wouldn't be a distraction. After a while, as my confidence grew in who God was calling me to be I realised I could embrace the way God has made me. I started to buy dresses and wear jewellery again, as this is what I enjoyed wearing. I realised I could bring my unique quality as a woman in the workplace - this was a strength and it added a richness to what I was doing because I started being authentic. I found my voice was still quiet but I started being heard because I was confident in the skills that I had to bring and in the experiences that I had. I really felt God tell me to stop hiding, that I had a place, a voice, a seat at the table and that I didn't need to de-feminise myself to progress. How would I sum up femininity? For me, it is that sensitivity, softness and gentleness, it's that perception, wisdom and discernment that women often have. It's being strong, vocal and resilient. Femininity is a strength, undergirded by a lot of grace and gentleness, it should not be underestimated or devalued or misunderstood as being weak. Sometimes the quietest voice in the room can be the most powerful. I am VERY BLESSED to have been surrounded by good and godly men throughout my life. I didn't realise how blessed I was until meeting others with absent or bad fathers and seeing the brokenness that ensues from that. Good fathers provide for their families, and I don't just mean financially. Actually my dad never had a lot of money, but what he did have was consistency. He was home every day after work at the same time and he would play with us, talk to us about our day. He would cook for us and make sure we were fed. He was a lot of fun. He taught us how to ride bikes. He played football with my brothers. I think the key here is that he spent time with us. He was present. Very simple, but it made all the difference to the family. I have a good husband, again I am beyond blessed. Very similar qualities to my dad, he is consistent, he doesn't break his promises, he is committed and I feel so safe with him.

He leads, he will initiate, which didn't always come naturally. Even as a strong independent woman, I feel loved when my husband leads well, it gives me the sense that he has vision for us and the family and he's anticipating what we need. Pivotal to being a good man is being someone who provides in every sense - physical, emotional and spiritual. My dad would give us hugs and play fight with us. My husband is able to listen really well and provide emotional support. And as a Christian woman it is so encouraging when our brothers are engaged and help sharpen our faith, by leading by example and creating safe spaces for their sisters. Men have such an important role, often as leaders, to ensure they are creating safe spaces where women are flourishing in their gifting - the church is so much fuller and richer when we can bring our 'whole' selves to serve.

T (LONDON UK)

———————————

I was intrigued to find that my first knee-jerk response was to think of a gentle-sounding woman, with delicate features, long blond hair & clothed in floaty, floral, pink clothes, smelling sweet! And then I quickly realised that I actually know no-one like that! Femininity has to be something far deeper than appearances, as across the world appearance differs so greatly. And so I define it as what I see females bringing to situations, decisions, events all around me. I see what they do as a bit like a bath sponge. A beautiful dichotomy of strength & vulnerability. Under pressure, its strength & malleability is shown. It's absorbent, responsive to what's around it & able to hold onto much, whilst always ready to pour out & give. Its uniqueness is its gentleness, which soothes, brings healing, refreshing & cleaning. Like a sponge, femininity is usually welcomed, enjoyed because it's unobtrusive. I couldn't think of femininity without thinking of masculinity. For that I see a pumice stone. Firm, unyielding, abrasive, but if used rightly, it will also bring healing as well as shape and cleansing. How interesting that in order to stay healthy & pure, the body needs both the sponge & the pumice.

S (KENT UK)

Annotated Bibliography

If you've got this far, you'll realise that I've attempted to draw together and present the different views of various scholars, pastors, theologians and thinkers.

This is an opportunity to give credit where it's due. Some of the names mentioned at the beginning deserve a bit more attention; where the book isn't full of quotations, here is an opportunity to sum up where I got certain perspectives from. There have, of course, been numerous conversations and interactions over the years that have added to the content of this book, so what follows below is by no means comprehensive.

ADAMS KATIA, EQUAL. This was the first book that I read from an egalitarian perspective that really made me stop and think. It's well written, persuasive and theologically serious. I first read about the way ancient Greek was used 'androcentrically' in Katia's book, and this has proven to be a key point to keep my eyes on. She has also helped me particularly when thinking about the 1 Timothy 2 passage. I would like to thank her for stepping up to the plate and writing with vigour and clout on the matter. She opened the door that led to the realisation that this subject is not as simple as many make out.

BARTLETT ANDREW, MEN AND WOMEN IN CHRIST. I thought this book was excellent and particularly appreciated the author's objectivity and level-headedness. His determination to let the text speak plainly and thoroughly was very commendable. While the author attempts to show that he is somewhere between the two positions, for all intents and purposes I would say that he is essentially egalitarian. He has been helpful when thinking about 1 Corinthians 7 and the mutuality of marriage, as well as 1 Corinthians 11 and the mystery of head coverings! His chapters on these two matters were both very lucid and informative.

BIRD MICHAEL, BOURGEOIS BABES, BOSSY WIVES, AND BOBBY HAIRCUTS. Michael, an Australian theologian, has moved from complementarian to (mostly) egalitarian. The style of his book is very readable and humorous, even though he is a heavyweight thinker. I sense that his tone reflects a humility around the subject that enabled me to think more freely and peacefully without fear. I was also helped by his example of happily occupying a zone that lacks 100% clarity. Here is an example: *"The apostle Paul would roll over in his grave if he knew that Christians were treating his commandments like rabbinic case law and were compiling huge lists of things women can and cannot do... I do not know what the middle ground is called, who holds it, or where it even is, but I have reached the point where I do not want to be pigeon-holed into either camp. I do not profess to have complete clarity on every exegetical issue, but personally I would rather listen to a sermon by a gifted woman than a sermon by an ungifted man"* (loc 662, Kindle version).

BECK JAMES (EDITOR), TWO VIEWS ON WOMEN IN MINISTRY. Contributors Linda Belleville, Craig Blomberg, Craig Keener and Thomas Schreiner do a great job of critiquing one another's presentations in a spirit of unity and with obvious affection and respect for one another. This book is so helpful, as you are drawn into the closest you'll get to a conversation in written form. I commend this book to anyone who wants to feel like they are joining in the conversation; it's a great introduction to the subject.

BENTON JOHN, GENDER QUESTIONS. The author, a local pastor in the UK, does a very good job of humbly presenting the complementarian position in light of the challenges of 'the contemporary world'. His tone is gentle and winsome and he gets it right when he says that 'all women should feel like VIPs in the company of mature Christian men' (page 74). I also commend the author for 'going there' on masculinity and femininity and writing two whole chapters on the subject in his book.

DAVIDSON RICHARD M, FLAME OF YAHWEH - SEXUALITY IN THE OLD TESTAMENT. The author has written a very thorough book on a fascinating subject and, while clearly an expert in the field, he writes with accessibility. Davidson does a great job of celebrating the holy gift of marital intimacy in this tome, and is not afraid to ask difficult questions. While his book is not expressly about gender per se, he faces the matter head on repeatedly, and as such has been a great help. I was also encouraged to reconsider 'patriarchy' by his work, a word and concept that is, for the most part, despised in the West; it's always helpful to be around authors and speakers who willingly face inevitable flak but in doing so, help us think a little clearer.

DEYOUNG KEVIN, MEN AND WOMEN IN THE CHURCH. Clear, confident and unyielding. This is a small book, but it sets out the complementarian position with weighty resolve. While none of the arguments were new, I was impressed by the author's desire to both 'hold the line' and 'paint a picture'.

LEE-BARNWELL MICHELLE, NEITHER COMPLEMENTARIAN NOR EGALITARIAN. The author's work is excellently written and is therefore a joy to read. She also brings a maturity and objectivity to her work that made me immediately trust her motives. I was particularly helped by her historical overview at the beginning, and also the way she helpfully contrasted the 'equality and rights' agenda with the Kingdom agenda of inclusion and unity among the sexes. She was also very helpful when it came to reframing leadership and authority in light of true gospel service.

MCLEAN CLAY, MCLEAN MINISTRIES. This is a podcast series on God's design for women (rather than a book). I found his approach very refreshing as a clear advocate for the dignifying and releasing of women, coupled with a passionate devotion to the word of God. I think this series was first taught in the 1990s and given that, it feels surprisingly current. His content on how women have been seen as either goddesses or prostitutes in many of the ancient pagan cultures, and how the true revelation of woman cuts right across both, was sobering and eye-opening.

PAYNE LEANNE, THE BROKEN IMAGE/CRISIS IN MASCULINITY. The author's clarity around masculinity and femininity, both in light of God's own attributes as well as in humanity, was incredibly helpful. The author has, of her own admission, been shaped by the views of C S Lewis, some of whose views on gender are controversial. I do believe, however, that the kernel of what both Lewis and Payne reach for has within it vital truth that we will be the poorer for ignoring. Payne was a prayer counsellor who ministered healing to many broken people through prayer and the truth of God's word.

PIERCE RONALD W & MERRILL GROOTHUIS REBECCA, DISCOVERING BIBLICAL EQUALITY. This book is essentially a response to 'Recovering Biblical Manhood and Womanhood' and is - in a sense - the main textbook for the egalitarian perspective. With over 500 pages from 20+ contributors (Gordon Fee, Linda Belleville, Craig Keener to name a few) it packs a punch. All of the key texts are explored, as well as a section on cultural/hermeneutical matters and a 'living it out' section at the end. Gordon Fee's chapters on 'male and female in the new creation' and 'the priority of Spirit gifting for church ministry', Walter I Liefeld's chapter on 'the nature of authority in the New Testament' and Rebecca Merrill Groothuis' chapter on 'Equal in being, unequal in role' were particularly helpful and stimulating.

PIPER JOHN & GRUDEM WAYNE, RECOVERING BIBLICAL MANHOOD AND WOMANHOOD. First printed in 1991, this almost 500 page textbook from 20+ contributors was a landmark piece of work, where the Danvers Statement, first published in 1988, can be found on pages 469-471. This book is full of heavyweight contributors (Piper, Grudem, Schreiner and Moo, to name a few), and it covers all the key texts (except 1 Corinthians 7, which is given only very brief attention in the Q&A of pages 87-89). It is the most far-reaching book for understanding the complementarian position, and while somewhat dated now, and also perhaps somewhat questionable in terms of application, the main principles of what complementarians stand for are faithfully presented here. I found Elisabeth Elliot's contribution, 'The Essence of Femininity: A personal perspective' particularly penetrating and moving.

STACKHOUSE JR JOHN G, FINALLY FEMINIST. As is clear from the title, the author has come to the point of being an 'evangelical feminist' in his conviction. His style is clear and gentle and he is obviously a very thoughtful and godly man. This book was my introduction to what is sometimes known as 'trajectory theology' or a 'redemptive movement hermeneutic', whereby that which is seemingly clearly put forth in scripture is freshly considered in light of the culture in which it was written and then critiqued in light of the culture we find ourselves in today. He asks the question, "Does our application of what is written need to be freshly and even radically adapted in light of overall perceived general truths of God's nature and wider cultural developments?"[1]

WILLIAMS TERRAN, HOW GOD SEES WOMEN. This was personally very provocative to read as Terran - now an egalitarian - has spent many years as a leader in a complementarian movement, and as such completely gets my world. At times in the book it felt like he was reading my mind as he seemed to answer each question just as I thought of it! While I felt that his book was at times unhelpfully weighted towards the anecdotal and was also somewhat caricaturing of the complementarian position, it was nevertheless brilliantly written and, as far as I'm concerned, theologically sharp. His vision to see women dignified and standing tall alongside men was magnificent and inspiring, and we all owe him a debt in this regard.

WINGER MIKE, BIBLETHINKER.ORG. This is a YouTube channel/podcast. This series on the role of women is, at the time of writing, still in process. Mike is clear, thorough and, for my money, pretty objective in the way he deals with his content and conducts his research. Mike repeatedly states that he wanted to become egalitarian as he began his study, but that his research led him to move increasingly towards complementarianism. His episodes on creation, the use of the word 'head' *(kephale)* in the New Testament and on the matter of submission, were particularly helpful.

---

1   Here is an example: "Readers who have gotten this far may wonder if there is a kind of sleight of hand or even a sort of theological judo going on here. I am defending egalitarianism by granting complementarians almost everything they claim and then replying that gender distinctions are a result of sin in fallen human society, not divinely ordered human relations. Thus, such distinctions are practised in the church only as a kind of desperate expedient, an accommodation to our hard hearts that is to be done away with when the time is ripe. I then argue that this time has come, not because I somehow discern that we are in the end times, as some enthusiastic egalitarians argue, but because I observe that modern society has become ready to accept homes, churches, secular institutions that welcome women into all roles, including leadership" (Chapter 2, page 57, The Paradigm).

Lightning Source UK Ltd.
Milton Keynes UK
UKHW050734040123
414803UK00006B/52

9 781916 278172